DOCTOR WHO
THE HANDBOOK
The Fourth Doctor

DOCTOR WHO
THE HANDBOOK
The Fourth Doctor

David J. Howe
Mark Stammers
Stephen James Walker

First published in Great Britain in 1992 by
Dr Who Books
an imprint of Virgin Publishing Ltd
332 Ladbroke Grove
London W10 5AH

Reprinted 1993

A catalogue record for this book is available from the British Library

ISBN 0 426 20369 0

Typeset by D&S Design
1 Edith Grove, London SW10 0JY

Printed and bound in Great Britain by
Cox & Wyman Ltd, Reading, Berks

For Ted, Sheila, Alan, Robert and Caroline. - DJH

For Alison. - MS

For Anita Cotis. -SJW

Acknowledgements

Sincere thanks to Justin Richards and Peter Anghelides, editors of the *Doctor Who* reference work *In-Vision*, for their help and for permission to quote from their releases. Also to Andrew Pixley for assistance above and beyond . . ., Guy Daniels and Richard Bignell of *Private Who*, John Freeman and Gary Russell of *Doctor Who Magazine*, Gary Leigh of *Dream Watch Bulletin*, Christopher Barry, Barry Newbery, Terrance Dicks, Jack Weller, David Gibbes-Auger and Rosemary Howe. Thanks also to all those unsung *Doctor Who* fanzine editors and writers for providing many happy hours of entertainment and education.

Contents

Foreword

'We'll never see him again,' said Sarah Jane Smith with finality as she and Brigadier Lethbridge-Stewart stood in the UNIT lab once occupied by the now missing Doctor, who was foremost in both their minds.

As Sarah's thoughts turned to memories of the friend she had known as the Doctor, she felt that she could almost hear the familiar stentorian tones of his timeship, the TARDIS. The next moment she realised that she really could hear them and, looking round in astonishment, watched as the reassuring shape of a blue police telephone box slowly materialised in its usual place in the corner of the laboratory, its familiar blue lamp flashing mournfully. The sound stopped and the box was there. Real. Solid.

As Sarah and the Brigadier watched, the door slowly opened to reveal the pale and weak figure of the Doctor.

'Doctor!' Sarah blurted, running to help as he wearily supported himself against the door frame.

'Hello Sarah,' he whispered hoarsely. 'I got lost in the time vortex. TARDIS brought me home.' The Doctor managed to push himself out of the TARDIS and, clutching his head, fell heavily to the floor of the laboratory.

As Sarah dropped to help him, turning him carefully over onto his back, the Brigadier retrieved a cushion off one of the nearby chairs and placed it under his head.

Sarah sat back on her haunches. 'Oh Doctor, why did you have to go back?' she asked hopelessly, sorrow welling within her.

11

'I had to face my . . . my fear, Sarah,' said the Doctor haltingly. 'I had to face my fear,' he repeated in a whisper. He closed his eyes. 'That was more important than going on living.'

Sarah looked at the tired and drawn face of her friend. He seemed to be growing weaker by the second. A tear formed in the corner of her eye and ran down her cheek. 'Please . . . don't die.'

The Doctor opened his eyes slightly and gazed up at her. 'A tear Sarah Jane?' he murmured, letting go of her hand and raising his hand to her damp cheek. 'No . . . don't cry,' he whispered kindly. 'While there's life there's . . .'

Sarah gazed down at him and realised that the light was rapidly fading from his eyes. His hand dropped lifelessly from her cheek to his chest.

The Doctor was dead.

Sarah gently reached up and closed his eyes. She looked tearfully up at the Brigadier who was crouching beside her. He returned her gaze, keeping his own emotions tightly in check as befitted an officer of his rank.

A humming noise distracted them from their grief and Sarah tracked its source across the room until her eyes lighted on a bureau by the window. As she looked, a cross-legged figure suddenly appeared hovering above the ground, surrounded by a pale white aura.

The newcomer smiled. 'It's all right,' he said gently. 'He is not dead.'

'I don't think I can take much more,' muttered Sarah, rising to her feet.

'I'm sorry to have startled you my dear,' apologised the robed figure.

'Won't you introduce me to your friend, Miss Smith?' asked the Brigadier, placing the man's sudden appearance to the back of his mind for the moment. After all, he had seen far stranger things in the company of the Doctor.

Sarah tried to pull herself together. 'Yes, this is the Abbot of . . . no, it's Cho-Je . . . I mean it looks like Cho-Je but it is really K'anpo Rinpoche . . . I think.' The explanation seemed to make things worse and Sarah sniffed to try and stop herself from bursting into tears.

The Brigadier looked from Sarah to the figure floating in front of him. 'Thank you,' he said briskly. 'That makes everything quite clear.'

'The Doctor is alive,' insisted Cho-Je.

'No, you're wrong. He's dead,' contradicted Sarah through the lump in her throat.

'All the cells of his body have been devastated by the Metebelis crystals,' explained the little man, 'but you forget . . . he is a Time Lord. I will give the process a little push and the cells will regenerate. He will become a new man.'

At this the Brigadier looked up, recalling the last time the Doctor had changed his appearance. 'Literally?' he asked.

Cho-Je inclined his head. 'Of course he will look quite different.'

The Brigadier realised what was about to take place and muttered 'Not again'.

'. . . And it will shake up the brain cells a little,' continued Cho-Je. 'You might find his behaviour . . . somewhat erratic?'

Sarah clutched at the straw which was being offered and stepped eagerly towards the monk. 'When will all this happen?' she asked.

Cho-Je smiled again. 'Well, there's no time like the present is there?' He raised his hands momentarily in the direction of the Doctor and then faded from their sight as abruptly as he had arrived.

'Goodbye.' Cho-Je's voice echoed from nowhere. 'Look after him.'

The Brigadier, sensing that events were moving too fast for comfort, sprang into action. 'Now wait a minute!' he demanded to thin air, but Sarah had glanced at the prone figure of the Doctor.

'Look, Brigadier, look!' she gasped, grabbing his arm. 'I think it's starting.'

The Brigadier looked at the Doctor with some resignation. 'Well. Here we go again,' he commented dryly.

On the floor, in front of their eyes, the face of the Doctor changed, shifting rapidly from that of the Doctor they knew to that of someone else. A new era was beginning.

From *Planet of the Spiders* part six by Robert Sloman

On Saturday, 8 June 1974, at two minutes and sixteen seconds past six o'clock, the familiar features of the third Doctor melted away to be replaced by those of a stranger: the fourth Doctor. As the credits came up signifying the end of the eleventh season of *Doctor Who*, fans were left with a gap of six months to ponder what lay ahead.

If *Doctor Who* had been cancelled with the departure of Jon Pertwee it would no doubt have been remembered as a very successful series of its type which had been fronted by three excellent actors, spawned a number of memorable concepts and characters (most notably the dreaded Daleks) and given years of pleasure to a generation of Saturday tea-time viewers. As it was, of course, the series did not end there – it was doing far too well for that even to have been a consideration in the minds of BBC executives. Instead, Tom Baker embarked on what was to become an epic stint as the Doctor, lasting from 28 December 1974 to 21 March 1981, a period of six years, two months and 25 days; and during that period *Doctor Who* would rise to a higher plane of popularity than ever before.

When asked about his reasons for leaving the series, Jon Pertwee has often cited the slow break-up of 'his team'. His long-serving co-star Katy Manning had left at the end of season ten to be replaced by Elisabeth Sladen, and script editor Terrance Dicks and producer Barry Letts had also decided to move on. The tragic death in a car accident in 1973 of Pertwee's friend Roger Delgado, who had played the Doctor's arch enemy the Master throughout the era of the third Doctor, had meant that the programme lost one of its most popular villains. But the decision to leave or stay was ultimately taken out of Pertwee's hands when his request for an increase in his fee was rejected by the BBC's Head of Drama, Shaun Sutton, and he was informed that he would not be required for the twelfth season. The BBC clearly felt it was time for a new Doctor, and the production office wasted little time in setting about the task of finding a replacement. After a lengthy period of searching, Tom Baker was introduced to the press as the fourth Doctor on 16 February 1974.

This new Doctor was born into a Britain emerging from the nightmare of oil shortages which had led to the rationing of fuel for cars, sent huge numbers of the population's homes into the dark during frequent power cuts, and left more than a few irate young *Doctor Who* fans staring by candlelight at a blank TV screen which should have been filled with the latest adventures of their hero. Where the Daleks and the Cybermen had failed, the group of Arab countries that comprised OPEC had succeeded in temporarily defeating the Doctor – a dastardly plan of the Master's perhaps? 1974 also saw the departure of Edward Heath as Prime Minister and the return of Harold Wilson's Labour Government. West Germany won the World Cup, and ABBA took the Eurovision Song Contest, and then the pop charts, by storm.

Joining the Swedish supergroup in the charts were artists such as Mud, Slade, Gary Glitter and The Bay City Rollers.

With the exit of Jon Pertwee some TV pundits, and indeed some fans of the series, could have been forgiven for thinking that *Doctor Who* had run its course and that there was little new ground left for it to cover. After all, the series was already eleven years old, an almost unheard-of age for any drama production other than a soap opera. Yet the next seven seasons would see *Doctor Who* establishing itself as a true British institution and a worldwide hit, with a reported 110 million viewers in some 43 countries, making it BBC Enterprises' biggest money-spinner. Its ratings attained their highest-ever level and, for perhaps the only time in its history, it came to be accepted as a truly mainstream TV success – no longer could it be dismissed as simply a kids' show or a cult favourite. Tom Baker himself became not so much a star as a national hero.

In particular, this period saw *Doctor Who* break into the American TV market. By the end of the fourth Doctor's era, it had gained an enormous cult following estimated at around 56,000 American fans, who could turn on their TVs at virtually any time and expect to find *Doctor Who* episodes playing on one or more of the Public Broadcasting Service (PBS) stations scattered across the United States.

One of the main reasons for the success of the fourth Doctor was the enormously exciting and eccentric personality of Tom Baker. How this virtually unknown actor managed to make the role his own is just one of the things examined in this Handbook. Also covered are his seven seasons of adventures which varied greatly in style and content; seasons which added many new facts to *Doctor Who*'s mythology, as well as being representative of changes which took place in the way television drama was produced from the mid-seventies to the early eighties.

As in all previous eras, the style of the programme was very much influenced by its incumbent producer. There were four producers during the Tom Baker years, and all their respective contributions are described within these pages, as are the external factors which influenced their decisions, especially the growing criticism from and influence of pressure groups such as the National Viewers and Listeners Association, headed by Mrs Mary Whitehouse, and the newly formed fan group, the *Doctor Who* Appreciation Society.

Also in this book, the season thirteen story *The Brain of Morbius* is taken as a case study to illustrate the production of *Doctor Who* in the mid-seventies. It reveals the behind-the-scenes work required to produce four twenty-five-minute episodes of a television drama.

If the seventies were the years of your childhood, this book will jog your memories of the thrill of travelling with the fourth Doctor. If you are too young to have been there at the time, and have recently met up with this Doctor through the many BBC Video releases, then maybe it will give you a taste of what it was like to watch unfold before you possibly the most exciting era of *Doctor Who*.

PART ONE – THE DOCTOR

1: Tom Baker – In His Own Words

ON HIS EARLY LIFE:

'I was brought up in the Scotland Road area of Liverpool among Irish pubs and Irish priests, and brainwashed with a preoccupation with death. Which is perhaps why I still wander round graveyards collecting strange epitaphs.'

Quoted in 1979 in Marvel Comics' *Starburst* No. 10.

'One of my earliest memories is of my Auntie Chrissie. She was a street bookmaker before they legalised betting shops. She and my Uncle Willy and Uncle Terry took the betting slips on the street corner. My mother would pick up some of the bets standing in a graveyard while I was with her. It was the most discreet place she could think of.

'In those days people used to die of things like 'flu and TB so, as an altar boy, I went to about four or five funerals a week, especially in the winter. The relatives used to give you a sixpenny bit. Once I was standing at a graveside and on this particular day the wind was biting and I was crying with the cold. This feller looked at my tears, squeezed my little arm and patted my little head, and gave me a two-shilling piece. Two shillings! I mean, that was twenty-four ice creams. So after that I began to cry all over the place and I became a highly paid professional mourner, almost.'

Interviewed by William Marshall in 1979 for the *Daily Mirror*.

'I was always looking for a way out, but how was I to manage it? I was from a poor background: from a house with no books, and parents with no experience of how to form one's life. Here was a young man desperate to make his mark, fantasising and dreaming. Not clever at school. Rather overgrown and therefore odd to look at. "Good heavens! Is he only eleven? But he's six foot one!" people said. In addition I was skinny and had a curved back because I could hardly ever stand up straight.

'When people came to the school to talk about careers I was always intensely interested. Then one day a man came and talked about monasticism. I was interested because having been brought up by a very devout Roman Catholic mother – my father was away at sea all the time – I was very preoccupied with religion. The man warned us that we would have to take a vow of chastity, poverty and obedience, but that didn't matter to me. The chastity was enforced by my age, the poverty was understood and as far as obedience went – well, everybody kicked my backside. And it appeared that they fed you as well, and you had sheets on your bed. So at 15 I went into a monastery in Jersey, and later Shropshire, as a noviciate. But I must admit that I did it only to get away from my background.

'After six years I left and six weeks later I was called up to do my National Service. It was in the Army that I gained the conviction that I could act and enjoy it. I had acted at school and had been offered a job at the Abbey Theatre in Dublin when I was 15, but my mother wouldn't let me go. But now I decided, "This is what I want to do." I've had some terrible moments of depression and sometimes I've felt really isolated and lost, but I've never wavered from that feeling.

'I was appearing in a late-night revue in York, playing a dog, when I was spotted by a talent scout from the National Theatre. Lord Olivier interviewed me and gave me a job. My first part was playing a horse. Sir Laurence encouraged me and helped me a lot. He was responsible for my getting the part of Rasputin in *Nicholas and Alexandra*. The film was made in Spain at a time when I was in two plays at the National and rehearsing a third. I was shuttled back and forth to Spain to film my bits. I was whisked about in limousines and first-class plane seats. It was heady stuff. I was asked, "How does a working-class boy like you adjust to an air-conditioned Cadillac?" I replied, "Terribly easily."'

Interviewed by Peter Dacre in 1978 for the *Sunday Express*, 12 March.

'Those years with the Brothers of Ploermel were terribly exciting and demanding. I enjoyed the suffering and deprivation and silence, although I haven't stopped talking since. I enjoyed the hysterical self-indulgence of feeling unworthy.

'I am absolutely certain that when men are together and deprived of women, they become homosexual. I wanted to embrace a young brother called Olivier-Jean so much that my bones used to *crack*. When you're young, it's very difficult to think about anything but lust. By the end of the six years, I was absolutely worn out by my sexual urges, and a priest advised me to get out.

'Once I was doing my National Service and encountering girls, I discovered sex, started practising it in a frenzy and rejected the Church very swiftly. It left me with a huge residue of guilt. Sometimes God knocks on the side of my head now and says, "Let's get back together." But I prefer guilt, lust, anxiety, lies and confusion. I prefer the uncertainties of life.'

Interviewed by Corinna Honan in 1992 for the *Daily Mail*, 28 March.

'I simply feigned idiocy right through my National Service and got away with murder. In my second year I was able to turn up on muster parade in red leather slippers. Harmless dementia is considered something sacred as long as there's no violence in the unhingement. I went around saying preposterous things. I'd say, "I won't be shouted at by a bunch of professional murderers," and of course they'd shout at me, so I'd proceed to cry. And that simply unhinged them. Finally, they just left me alone because I was too much trouble.

'I was a terribly withdrawn, pained, skinny man and the Army released me. I loathed Queen's Regulations. It was the enforced contact with people of disparate backgrounds that did it. I was coerced into a Unit show. When I discovered I could make people laugh, it gave me a new strength.'

Quoted in 1979 in Marvel Comics' *Starburst* No. 10.

ON BEING AN ACTOR:

'When I was starting out in the fifties, I was anxious to get started and *so* nervous about trying to make my way. Most people will tell you they want to achieve something, learn something, build a pattern; to find a partner, have somewhere to live that's nice and where they can feel a bit safe; to have a couple of children and a car, collect a few books and go on holiday. That's what most people want, I think. And then there are actors.

'Concomitant with being an actor is that dreadful, exhausting state of being self-aware all the time, because you're marketing your appearance, you're marketing what you sound like. You're worried about whether you're ugly or going bald or getting fat. You're worried about dental bills or worried that no-one wants you. In other words you are *ill*. To want to be an actor, especially these days, is to be ill. It's a kind of illness – this terrible pernicious itch to want what threatens you most, which is insecurity. Performers, like other people, are mesmerised by what threatens them most. They have to learn to love it and live with it and create out of it.

'Performers create out of anxiety, they don't create out of jolliness or a happy song. They have to exorcise the most terrible memories of the last effort, to forget past failures and hope all the time that they're going to please someone. Actors are just professional pleasers, like waiters!'

Interviewed by John Freeman in 1991 for *Doctor Who Magazine* Nos. 179–181.

'I'm feeling much jollier and philosophical about most things now. You see the other thing was that it [*Doctor Who*] weighed on me because no-one would employ me. I'd like to think that was because I was a huge success and therefore had no credibility as anything else. That's the way actors always justify it. And then the last two years, thanks to the BBC, again, with *The Law Lords* and *The Silver Chair*, and then *Medics* and *Cluedo*, suddenly things have looked up again.'

Speaking at a press conference to publicise the release on video of *Shada*, 11 May 1992.

ON FANTASTICAL CHARACTER ACTING:

'Everyone wants to do something amazing and have the funniest lines or the greatest costume or the best exit or entrance. I mean, we adore what's fantastic, don't we? People are obsessed with fantasy, whether they know it or not. Middle-aged paunchy men – I'm well past that! – dream of being the footballer Maradona or the cricketer Viv Richards. I mean, Richards is just forty, and how many forty-year-old men look at him and wish they were him, and wouldn't dare tell their friends?

Everyone has a heroic impulse, a desire towards being amazing, towards achieving, towards being heroic.'

Interviewed by John Freeman in 1991 for *Doctor Who Magazine* Nos. 179–181.

ON THE ATTRACTION OF PLAYING THE DOCTOR:

'To be honest it was nothing about the character that influenced me at all, it was sheer necessity! I was desperately out of work and was terribly depressed by this. Suddenly, along came the possibility of playing Doctor Who. It was just relief to play a major part!

'Because I didn't watch *Doctor Who* much, I had no notion of what this would do. It just so happened that with the new scripts that Barry Letts (and later Philip Hinchcliffe) had commissioned, the directors, costume and set designers who moved in . . . well, it all came together. I didn't know what was happening. I just responded to that, which I suppose is the great secret, isn't it?

'I was working very hard on a building site in Ebury Street, next door but one to where Mozart wrote his first symphony, when I got the job. The builders were actually very good to me and I have a happy memory of that, but of course I didn't *want* to be on a building site, because I hadn't much skill. I wanted to be an actor.

'When I got the part I had this feeling of just *huge* relief, and also one of great pride. I didn't tell my workmates I'd got the job. I had the day off and went to the BBC and then it was in the first edition of the *Evening Standard*. I knew they all took that paper – and bang, all was revealed! So there they were, looking over the tops of their papers at me. It was a great moment of pleasure. They were very proud of me – and I was very proud of them.'

Interviewed by John Freeman in 1991 for *Doctor Who Magazine* Nos. 179–181.

ON HIS DOCTOR'S COSTUME:

'I think that the style of the costume represented my personal style of dress, which is rather casual. I was inspired by a designer called Jim Acheson, who was young and conscientious and very witty I thought. I met several lovely designers at the BBC. June Hudson, latterly, was a designer I saw a lot of. But Jim Acheson and I went out to play for a few weeks and we gradually got this tatty costume together which was a mixture of sort of scruffiness and elegance. Scruffiness in the way it was worn but elegance in the cut of the coat – and madness in the size of the scarf. The hat was Herbert Johnson. Yeah, I had some influence in it but it was mostly Jim's inspiration really.'

Interviewed by Dave Dean in 1982. Published in *Private Who* No. 3.

'Jim Acheson designed the scarf, bought the wool and gave it to someone's relation at the BBC called Begonia Pope, who was thrilled to be working for the Corporation. She didn't ask any questions; Jim gave her the design and she knitted up all the wool. Jim of course had no knowledge about knitting, except for colour. He bought ten times the amount of wool that was needed, and she knitted the lot! He omitted to say it was just a scarf, like the sort you'd see on the Left Bank in Paris. When I put it on it was hilarious and Jim instantly said, "Keep it, it's funny."'

Interviewed by John Freeman in 1991 for *Doctor Who Magazine* Nos. 179–181.

ON HIS DEBUT AS THE DOCTOR:

'I didn't know how I was going to do *Doctor Who*. I had no idea at all – not until the very first rehearsal, and even then I didn't know . . . I just did it. I just played the script and something evolved and the audience liked the way I did it, obviously, so we kept it like that. But sometimes it was funny and sometimes not so funny and sometimes it was thrilling. It was just an accident really.'

Interviewed by Dave Dean in 1982. Published in *Private Who* No. 3.

ON BREAKING HIS COLLAR-BONE DURING RECORDING OF *THE SONTARAN EXPERIMENT*:

'When I fell, I banged my head as well, and I wasn't sure when I fell . . . how badly I was hurt, because the pain was very bad and it was quite deep. In fact it was just a shock of the collar bone which is the swiftest bone to mend but when it breaks it made you feel very sick. I thought, am I hurt badly? And it wasn't that I was afraid of dying. I mean I thought, how am I going to get on with the show? I was taken away for investigation and when I came back, Barry Letts and Philip Hinchcliffe were looking all grey-faced in the pub and I swanned in and had several large gins.'

Speaking at a press conference to publicise the release on video of *Shada*, 11 May 1992.

ON *DOCTOR WHO*'S UNIQUE FORMAT:

'I think if I bothered about the plots, I wouldn't get much done. The plots won't stand up to severe examination. The mass of our audience is children and they're only interested in the high spots of the Doctor's adventures anyway.'

Speaking on *Woman's Hour*, 12 January 1977.

'Given fundamental expertise from the producer downwards, the real gold of the thing is the formula. Given that you haven't got a bonehead at the top or a powerful subversive somewhere down the line, you couldn't really fail with it. The first reason we are so successful – the very first reason – is that we are incomparable. Nothing admits to comparison with *Doctor Who*. When people try to plagiarise our situations or our attitudes they fall down, because it's obvious plagiarism. They don't really start with this marvellous thing that the character's an alien, and the wonderful heroic comedy-thriller notion that he can travel in this daft box. That's why I think the formula, which is so wonderful, engages such a huge audience.'

Interviewed by John Fleming in 1980 for Marvel Comics' *Starburst* No. 19.

'I think the formula lent itself to Gothic areas, not because science fantasy should do that but simply because we have that long film background of Gothic horror, tension and fantasy, the tragi-comedy if you like. Do you remember the old Hammer films, especially the late-night ones when one had been drinking? You'd get gales of laughter from one particular section of the audience and the rest would be sat po-faced. It's rather like going to a theatre with a lot of actors or musicians and they're picking up one thing and someone else is seeing it on another level.

'*Doctor Who* was like that. I was always constantly trying to translate whatever was happening to me and add it to the role, drawing on other experiences. One of the reasons I spent so much time on the road promoting the programme was that I was drawing on the children from the audience. What they told me they liked, I did more of, or else adapted it and did variations. I used to get hints of what they liked. So it might have appeared I was being very nice to them, but actually what I was doing was "vampiring" them for ideas. It was quite shameless!'

Interviewed by John Freeman in 1991 for *Doctor Who Magazine* Nos. 179–181.

ON NOT WATCHING *DOCTOR WHO*:

'I didn't watch it before I was in it and I certainly didn't watch it while I was in it, because that would only make me unhappy. My reasoning was, "What is the point in watching it?", because we worked under such pressure; I always wished I could do it better, you see, and there was never any time, with a maximum of maybe two or three takes per scene. If there was any doubt, I sometimes deliberately used to blow it out on such a scale that they had to do a retake. Directors know about this!

'Occasionally I might have watched a sequence over which we'd had an argument, but I didn't watch it as a rule because I would never have been pleased with it. I might watch it now out of curiosity after so long, but generally if it's marvellous someone will tell me about it and if it isn't so marvellous I'll just be unhappy.'

Interviewed by John Freeman in 1991 for *Doctor Who Magazine* Nos. 179–181.

ON THE PLEASURES OF REHEARSALS:

'Most of the time it was a pleasure to get to work, to get off the street and out of the ghastly world of reality, away from the bloody TV news and into Rehearsal Room 603. It was just bliss.

'During rehearsals we used to mime a lot and pretend the monsters were there. You'd get actors from other shows peeping in through the bullseye windows and laughing at us – not in a derisive way but with pleasure at all this over-acting. They were still enjoying it, and lots of people – lots of very distinguished actors – wanted to be in it and used to tell me so in the BBC canteen, which moved me very much. I remember polished actors like John Woodnutt being killingly funny about it, and there were others, like Bill Fraser, Freddy Trieves and George Baker.'

Interviewed by John Freeman in 1991 for *Doctor Who Magazine* Nos. 179–181.

ON AUDIENCE REACTION:

'One of the surprising things about *Doctor Who* is the range of the audience. Although I have always thought of it as a children's pro-gramme – not a childish programme, mind you – we have a big adult audience. And over the past two years we have discovered that there are a lot of *Doctor Who* fan clubs at the universities. I was astonished to be invited to St John's and Somerville Colleges at Oxford, and I spoke to absolutely packed halls. If I accepted all the invitations I could be going to the universities three or four times a week.

'Some actors get a bit neurotic when they are approached by people and called by the name of the character they play. I don't mind being called Doctor Who – which I am all the time. I can't tell you just how dull life was when I was just Tom Baker. Simply nobody recognised me.

'I must always remember that I do not have an existence as Tom Baker. Apart from my close friends and colleagues, everybody calls me Doctor Who. Even children in push-chairs point at me in the street. But I am very aware that they are looking not at Tom Baker but at this image they have of this character. It is important to me, therefore, that I never disappoint people, especially children. I would never be seen being raucous in the streets, or plastered, or smoking cigars. When I want to go out to play I do it discreetly in selected actors' bars or clubs. Even then there is sometimes no escape. A friend once took me to a select West End club. "We won't be bothered here," he said. We had not been there more than a few minutes when a chap raised his glass and said, "My dear Doctor, how nice to see you here." My friend was astonished, because the man was a judge.'

Interviewed by Peter Dacre in 1978 for the *Sunday Express*, 12 March.

'The programming of *Doctor Who*, in my view, is absolutely brilliant, because it follows the sports round-up, the brief news, sometimes a programme like *Basil Brush*, and it's then followed by *The Generation Game* or *The Duchess of Duke Street* or whatever it is; but that time on a Saturday vitally influences the attitude of the audience. I mean, if you pushed it on, rolling back the frontier to half past ten at night, the audience would be drunk! How are they going to follow our script? They can't possibly follow our script when they're stone cold sober, but if they go out and drink Red Barrel or some inflammatory drink like that, it scrambles people's heads!'

Speaking on stage in August 1979 at the *Doctor Who* Appreciation Society convention PanoptiCon III.

'Sometimes I enjoy being recognised. Especially by children. It gets very debilitating when you're accosted by adults all the time. But *children* – I love it, especially if I'm on the move. Going home from work on the train last night, I made three tube changes and all the kids were coming back from Hyde Park with their mothers. They were so densely packed and I was threading my way through and, quite often, a child is actually being led towards me and he recognises me and he smiles and then he wonders why he smiled. And then it clicks, but by the time it's clicked I've gone. It's terrific fun, that kind of contact. Great fun. I love it with the *small* children – it's amazing, that.

'You see, to use a very overworked word, it's a participatory programme. In your average family of a man and his wife and three children, with the children going in age from say nine to three, when it comes to Saturday night viewing it becomes a bit of a charade. Children are very quick to cotton on to some kind of regular routine. So, when they watch *Doctor Who*, several things happen. It's not passive in a two- or three-child family. The older child of nine or ten might be actually following the narrative very carefully and quite critically. His six year old brother, when the monsters come up, is wincing a bit. And the little fellow, getting in on the act, is behind the sofa or he's in the kitchen looking through the crack in the door. Now, the parents notice this and enjoy it. I've talked to hundreds of parents: they enjoy this. The moment you actually give children that attention – just like, indeed, adults – you get this marvellous response. When our music comes up – and the opening music to *Doctor Who* is absolutely *wonderful* – that's the signal for the weekly sit-down and the sharing.'

Interviewed by John Fleming in 1980 for Marvel Comics' *Starburst* No. 19.

'I love small children. By an accident of temperament I get on very well with them. I am perfectly happy to spend a lot of time with them. Wherever I go now I get enormous attention – from children and adults. Their response is so warm and generous that my life is different from most other people's. I would be lying if I didn't say that it gave me a huge amount of pleasure. I am one of the few men in England to whom "Don't talk to strange men" doesn't apply. When I bump into small children in the park I can pick them up or embrace them and no policeman will come and move me on. Sometimes I see parents looking a bit anxious, but when they come over and see it is Doctor Who they are as thrilled as their children. Nothing appeals to me more than *Doctor Who*.

'If I am in a bar alone everybody feels they can talk to me. Sometimes it gets irritating. I am quite happy to stand alone with my gin and tonic trying to finish a crossword or reading.'

Interviewed by Dan Slater in 1979 for the *Sun*.

'People are quite kind to me; children are always wonderful. But I've had my share of rudeness. The trouble with becoming a "name" on TV is that you are licensed in the public's mind to play just one role. I have to behave like the Doctor. I'll put up with any pathetic, troublesome old drunk, simply because I could not bear the thought of him going home and telling his kids, "I saw Doctor Who today and he told me to sod off." As a viewer, I wouldn't like to see someone from a children's programme behaving badly. It would be like seeing Robin Day dancing on the table in a restaurant.'

Interviewed by Charles Catchpole in 1981 for unknown newspaper, 21 March.

ON COMPANION LEELA'S VIOLENT STREAK:

'I've forgotten the details of the character, but I do remember being *appalled* at her aggression, without me having the ammunition to put forward my side of the argument. There was a moral dimension, an ethical dilemma, because she *killed* things. It wasn't just my character, *I* was furious at the beginning. There was some facetious dialogue about it, some claptrap like "I don't really think you should do that." The point is that these gentle ironies are quite inappropriate when life and death are at stake. What I tried to give it was outrage and burning indignation – that if it didn't change, if *she* didn't change, the character would have to go. I don't mean Louise Jameson, but I would have to threaten Leela with this because I could not coexist with someone whose solution to problems was to kill. So they modified that and Louise was very good and hugely successful. But I was very rattled by it.'

Interviewed by John Freeman in 1991 for *Doctor Who Magazine* Nos. 179–181.

ON THE TARDIS:

'I often felt, myself, that they didn't really pursue the wonderful, cosmically funny aspect of the TARDIS being bigger on the inside than on the outside. I couldn't understand why on the inside of the TARDIS there shouldn't be a whole market town with a cathedral which we could keep the wellingtons in! Instead it was always just a control room – we occasionally went into other areas – but, in my view, no-one ever wrote a story which suggested the logic of dimensional transcendentalism; that inside the TARDIS is not just a console room but a whole *world*.

'It would be amazing, to go into the TARDIS and have the assistant say "My god Doctor, look – there are thousands of sheep there!" And the Doctor would say "Good grief, so there are. I remember now . . ." And of course he can't remember the exact details but the sheep would have come in at some difficult time and he'd saved them, intending to transport them somewhere. Why *isn't* a world shown, instead of waving it away with some facetious, smart-assed remark? I mean, who cleans for the Doctor? Why isn't there someone suddenly bellowing "Where have you been? I've been waiting. Don't you remember you took me on to clean for you?" To which the Doctor would say, "Did I? I really must get a hold of myself . . ."'

Interviewed by John Freeman in 1991 for *Doctor Who Magazine* Nos. 179–181.

ON THE DOCTOR'S ROBOT DOG K-9:

'I don't really have opinions about bits of metal . . . I suppose it was a good idea to have K-9. It's an insufferable pun, but it did work. It worked very well because of what John Leeson, who was the voice of K-9, did in rehearsals, which was much more interesting than K-9 itself. For instance, despite all the money we spent on him, K-9 couldn't run over a matchbox. He could be moved of course from a distance, by remote control, but what John Leeson did was much more interesting than K-9 ever was. So I had strong feelings for what John Leeson did, but not for that dreary metal dog.'

Interviewed by Dave Dean in 1982. Published in *Private Who* No. 3.

'K-9 was a blasted hard thing to act with! Off-set there'd be John Leeson doing the voice, and because the thing is so small all the dialogue shots had to be done at its level. We had tremendous technical problems with it as well. It was always breaking down, especially on location when we'd get annoyed because we were always running behind schedule, so that was just another hold-up.'

Interviewed by Richard Marson in 1984 for *Doctor Who Magazine* No. 92.

ON HIS FOUR *DOCTOR WHO* PRODUCERS:

'Barry Letts only produced my first one – although it was he who got me the job. Then Philip Hinchcliffe was with us for quite a while – he was a good, hard-working producer. Graham Williams came on and worked like a dog at a rather trying time for all of us when money was getting scarce and we were behind schedule. John Nathan-Turner did my last year and was very kind to me, very accommodating. I saw a lot of him socially – we were both bachelors at the time. He's good company and he cares so much for the programme. In their own ways, and as far as the series would allow, they were all trying to ring the changes, I suppose. They had their job and I had mine, and we worked quite closely together; the only conflict we ever had was professional and that kind of conflict is essential.'

Interviewed by Richard Marson in 1984 for *Doctor Who Magazine* No. 92.

ON THE HORROR CONTENT OF *DOCTOR WHO*:

'We often discuss the horror content, and they take it very seriously at our office because they're experts at it. They're willing to listen to me of course – after all I go out and meet the children. On the other hand, there is often a scene when we're shooting it that looks unbearably horrifying – but that won't be how it's edited. I don't do the editing, that's not my job. That's the director's brief. Then finally the producer and the head of the department decide how far to go. But it is very often an arbitrary thing. Only two people can decide. We've come under a lot of stick from Mrs Whitehouse especially. I understand that she won't even have lunch with me!

'I sometimes think that the stories are very frightening, but the consideration always is that television takes place in a domestic context. And one can go further in terror. Children like to be terrorised. At home they'll be watching the television and seeing something happening to me, and then they move their eyes through a very small arc and they see their fish fingers, or their mum, or their dad. It's a family event. You have the little ones behind the sofa. I know about this, I've spoken to hundreds of children. Little ones behind the sofa, or looking through fingers, or looking through cracks in doors. And the whole thing in many ways is rather diffused by that, because it is so obviously fictional.'

Speaking on *Woman's Hour*, 12 January 1977.

ON THE DOCTOR'S MORE HUMOROUS STYLE UNDER GRAHAM WILLIAMS:

'I don't know what Graham was told, but although he and I worked together and there were some successes in his time, he and I weren't really all that close. I was just responding to whatever was going there.

'I don't want to try to define what my style was; I just responded to the scripts and finally filtered them through me. As you know – I've been quoted many times – Doctor Who was not an acting part any more than James Bond is an acting part. By acting I mean an actor's definition of an acting job, which is when a character actually develops and discovers something so amazing that there is actually a transformation. Either that or there is a realisation that he has been entirely wrong. This isn't so with heroes. There's an utter predictability about playing heroic parts. Heroes, you *know* what side they'll come down on. Doctor Who isn't suddenly going to become obsessed with sex or money or gratuitous violence – he's predictably good, like an innocent child. Within that predictability, within all that certainty, the fun of doing it was, "How do you surprise the audience and hold them and make them want to watch again and again?"'

Interviewed by John Freeman in 1991 for *Doctor Who Magazine* Nos. 179–181.

ON TENSIONS DURING PRODUCTION:

'One grew to know what the difficulties were for the technical crew who had to realise the story, and one co-operated the best one could. I mean, I was often, I'm afraid, impatient and difficult. Not out of malice or intention, but I'm an anxious sort of actor and I'm easily thrown. I think sometimes I was impatient and difficult and I regret that but, I mean, it was with the best will.'

Interviewed by Dave Dean in 1982. Published in *Private Who* No. 3.

'I found the schedule very hard, but then I find all acting difficult – it requires a huge amount of work before I'm really happy with my own performance, and on television you never have the time. I used to long for just a few extra days to get it exactly right, but we always had a punishing deadline to work to. As soon as one story was completed I'd find another wad of scripts to learn for the next week, and so on. I did get tired but I couldn't stop concentrating because if I did it wouldn't have worked at all. By the time I left I was seven years older and consequently I didn't have the same resources of energy I'd had when I joined.'

Interviewed by Richard Marson in 1984 for *Doctor Who Magazine* No. 92.

'Sometimes things just didn't gel during recording because I was very possessive and irrational about it. Sometimes I felt that this was *my* show, although when new actors came on it I wanted to love them, albeit only for the duration of the production. I wanted them to be really *amazed* at this world they came into, so that when we started rolling the cameras there would be this realistic element of people being constantly amazed by me and by what was going on around them.

'There was tension all the time, which I wanted, but sometimes when it didn't go as well as other times I became very irascible. I read an article the other day which said how moody I was, and I said to my wife, "Moody? They say I'm moody! Am I moody?" And she said, "Well . . ." I cut in with "Well it's ridiculous, isn't it? *Me*? *Moody*? It's like saying I've got no manners!" So she said, "Well sometimes you're very moody and often you've got the manners of a pig!" '

Interviewed by John Freeman in 1991 for *Doctor Who Magazine* Nos. 179–181.

ON CONTRIBUTING IDEAS:

'The scripts were often dull. I didn't get a buzz of excitement after reading them. I always felt that the series gave you such free rein, such scope for imaginative plots, and that our writers were throwing the chance away with dramatic stereotypes. So I was shamefully badly behaved with the scripts – I maltreated our writers' reputations in rehearsal more than anything else, I found it so frustrating. It's not that they were really terrible scripts, but they weren't great either. We did so many as well; I'd get a huge pile of them to wade through every so often, and it was always the same – a bit of a let down.

'I was always suggesting this or that – maybe an extra line or a different situation – and the director would say yes or no. Generally they were very kind to me. They humoured some of my extravagances but took me seriously as well. That was nice – it gave us all a working respect for each other. And some of my ideas they kept in!'

Interviewed by Richard Marson in 1984 for *Doctor Who Magazine* No. 92.

'Over the years I came to understand what the Doctor could and could not do better than any writer or director who has only one story to worry about. I used to spend a long time checking the scripts and dialogue to make sure they conformed to how the Doctor should be played. If I found any scenes that depicted him as being over-emotional or gratuitously violent then I would argue very strongly for their removal.'

Quoted by Peter Haining in W. H. Allen's *The Doctor Who File*.

'I don't want to give the impression that I claim too much authority. Obviously the writers did try to write for me and the producers did indulge me a great deal, because most of the time I was the one making the contact with the audience. Because I had been doing the thing so long it became more and more impossible for me to accept any kind of guidance. I felt I knew it all. I was there week after week. I knew the shots, the set-ups; I knew how to do the corridor sequences; I was swift on the words (such as they were) and I knew I had to give the audience a bit of variety.

'So sometimes a director might say, "Tom, I think in this sequence . . ." and I'd cut in and say, "No, let's not do that because we did that last week in an identical situation." Sometimes they'd realise I was only trying to be helpful and we'd reverse it, just to get the variation. So because I was the constant factor I became more and more proprietorial, and in the end it became obvious I had to go.

'I got more and more irascible and people seemed to think the programme was me, we became so *utterly* intertwined. This was very bad, and a sign that I had to go. Also I didn't find rehearsals as funny as I had done.'

Interviewed by John Freeman in 1991 for *Doctor Who Magazine* **Nos. 179–181.**

ON THE SERIES' VILLAINS AND MONSTERS:

'I quite liked the Wirrn, as they were grotesque. But the Daleks and the Cybermen I found, from the point of view of playing the Doctor and beating them, insufferably tedious, because they were utterly predictable and witless and not really ingenious. But never mind – it doesn't matter what I feel about them. Undoubtedly the Daleks seized the imagination of the first generation of *Doctor Who* watchers, and of subsequent generations. I never much cared for them really, but I can see it's what the viewers like.'

Interviewed by Dave Dean in 1982. Published in *Private Who* **No. 3.**

'I loved some of our monsters because they were so funny. We used to have a regular set of actors who'd play them so we were all very chummy. I adored the Krynoid – the giant walking vegetable – and I also liked the Wirrn. They were both fun. Then there was the giant rat in *The Talons of Weng-Chiang* – I thought that looked rather good. We also had some superb villains. Michael Wisher was brilliant as the creator of the Daleks. I remember once he was playing a scene and he was also doing the Dalek voices, and I said "Can we all go home now?", because he was in total control. Some of our villains were quite chilling – I used to try to believe in them so as to communicate their threat to the audience, and often I didn't have to try very hard, they were so good.'

Interviewed by Richard Marson in 1984 for *Doctor Who Magazine* No. 92.

'I must say I did enjoy Davros in *Genesis of the Daleks*, because Michael Wisher did work so seriously and was unbendingly passionate about the character. He used to make us howl with laughter! He's a very accomplished actor and he had us gripped from the first rehearsal, he was so unselfconscious. When he used to rehearse with a paper bag over his head, that used to crucify me! I used to yelp. He never relaxed, which is very important for an actor. You must *never* patronise your own character – this is what happens if people stay too long or are recalled into cameo parts. Always play a character from his point of view and never be hard on him, because if you do that it instantly betrays a lack of commitment. You've got to believe absolutely; never give him or her a hard time. You must play it the way you believe it should be played.'

Interviewed by John Freeman in 1991 for *Doctor Who Magazine* Nos. 179–181.

ON LEAVING *DOCTOR WHO*:

'It was in the works for months before. I struggled with all the arguments for and against staying, but seven years is a long time. I'd given the show all I felt I could give it, but I loved it so much that in other ways I didn't want ever to go. I didn't want anybody to start feeling awkward about me being there, so I had to take the initiative and say "It's time I did something else and let somebody else come in." I had the happiest years of my life with *Doctor Who* – it was such a thrill to be the Doctor.'

Interviewed by Richard Marson in 1984 for *Doctor Who Magazine* No. 92.

'There was a kind of slight fatigue. And also I was becoming neurotically proprietorial about it . . . the signs were that it was entirely mine, so in other words it was really time to go because that meant that I couldn't be influenced. And when you can't be influenced, then it's time to go to another village isn't it really, another pub from wherever you are. Because once you're cut off from the influences, there'll be no growth in any direction, however slight it may be. You're not going to have a jolly time.'

Speaking at a press conference to publicise the release on video of *Shada*, 11 May 1992.

ON HIS FAVOURITE STORY:

'I do get asked that question a lot, and I don't really know the answer. I didn't watch them all, but sometimes I do remember them. What I enjoyed about *Doctor Who* was the day-to-day work, the grinding routine of rehearsals and trimming and trying to make it witty televisually. I think I did enjoy one called *The Ark in Space*, because I particularly liked the designs on that. I admired the designer, Roger Murray-Leach, very much and I think that it was very well realised.'

Interviewed by Dave Dean in 1982. Published in *Private Who* No. 3.

'I can never remember story titles, and I never watched the series so all I can remember are the sequences I filmed – which were all out of order anyway – and of course rehearsals, which used to go so quickly. My favourite kind of stories were the "different" ones – and the ones I was happy with for personal reasons, like the Renaissance one. That was a good one; I felt quite happy with that. The one set on the giant Ark was another I liked – it had some beautiful, clever sets and quite a good script. Then there was the one with the giant man-eating plants, which had Tony Beckley, who was such a fine actor, in it.

'I wouldn't want to give the impression that I didn't enjoy making *Doctor Who*, but sometimes it was very, very exhausting, and occasionally I'd be ill as I was on my last few stories. But usually I used to have so much fun – I'd never have stayed so long otherwise. I was amazed recently when I saw how many episodes I'd made – I thought, "Goodness, was it really that many?" – and the days when I felt I needed to get out were, happily, few and far between.'

Interviewed by Richard Marson in 1984 for *Doctor Who Magazine* No. 92.

ON HIS LEAST FAVOURITE STORY:

'Looking back on it, it would have to be my last one, *Logopolis*. I remember not liking the final shot because I was leaving by then. I remember I wanted to be gone. I remember thinking the shot wasn't particularly heroic or witty, and they recorded it straight from above with me lying flat. It was very difficult to be heroic in that situation because, to do that, I should have at least been able to get up on one elbow. But it had to be that way, because they wanted to do that dreary old reverse shot of me looking into a circle of faces. They were stealing the shot anyway, from a film.

'It was all right for them, but not for me, and I went away with that slight niggling disappointment. I can still remember the shot after all these years – I didn't like the images, it wasn't heroic enough.'

Interviewed by John Freeman in 1991 for *Doctor Who Magazine* Nos. 179–181.

ON NOT APPEARING IN *THE FIVE DOCTORS*:

'That was a decision I had to think long and hard about. The original plan was to have me with Lis and have us all come together at the end. I finally decided I wouldn't do it because I simply couldn't face the prospect of going back. I was lucky also to have other offers, but when I say I couldn't face the happiness again I mean it. I went to see John Nathan-Turner and explained all my reasons, and in spite of the difficulties it caused he was very understanding. The programme is my past now – it would, I think, have been a mistake to try to turn the clock back even for that one story.'

Interviewed by Richard Marson in 1984 for *Doctor Who Magazine* No. 92.

'Well, it was too close to my leaving really, and I was very impatient. I didn't want to be seen with either new Doctors or old Doctors. In my own mind, I was the most recent. Thinking about it, perhaps that was another good reason for my leaving. I began to lose that sense of fun and silliness I had. I began to take the Doctor very seriously and I thought, "Who are these guys?" I didn't know them and I didn't care about them. At first I said I would, and then I read the script and John Nathan-Turner tried to be very accommodating – he always was for me – and he was very disappointed that I couldn't bring myself to do it.

'It was simply that I felt there was a danger that it could be very competitive. I felt it would just be a novelty scheme and I wasn't interested in novelty at the time. I was looking for good drama.'

Interviewed by John Freeman in 1991 for *Doctor Who Magazine* Nos. 179–181.

ON LOVE AND MARRIAGE:

'I have no intimate friends. Not one. Fifty or sixty people are acquainted with me but nobody knows Tom Baker. I am a secretive soul.

'The price of being an unmarried, middle-aged man tearing around the world is that I am so often alone. I consider myself a bachelor and have been now for many, many years. I enjoy the freedom that being unmarried gives me. I can do whatever I'm offered as an actor and go anywhere – which you can't do with the same ease if you are married. I have only myself to think of.

'I envy people with a happy domestic life, wife and children, a house and dogs, but it is a big weight. I choose to be alone and free to go to Brazil or Egypt or wherever I want. I pay the price – you can't have it every way. I don't think of myself as a confirmed bachelor. I am simply an unmarried man. I am not any kind of woman hater. The marvellous thing about falling in love, or getting married, is that reason plays no part in the process at all.

'When I was married to Anna Wheatcroft I realised that we were two innocent people who got married and who weren't very good together. It wasn't all that difficult to become unmarried. I think it is rare that it is ended by mutual consent, but that is how we ended our marriage. I see my ex-wife from time to time. Being divorced is always a matter for regret when you've got children because, however you look at it, it is a defeat. But I pay my dues, and I am in touch with them in an official way. My sons are grown up now. One is 20, and about to go to university. The other is 17 and not far behind. I was with them when they were very small and I enjoyed them a great deal.

'I don't think I would like to start all over again having children, although I really adore them. Some men start new families well into their middle age, but that is not for me. *Doctor Who* allows me to have all the pleasure of intimacy with lots of children without any of the anxieties of starting all over again.'

Interviewed by Dan Slater in 1979 for the *Sun*.

'We were incredibly aware of each other from the very first moment when Lalla joined the show. She was in one episode with me, then I went away during a break in the series. We came back to work together again and it happened. We fell in love. I realised that after she left the programme I couldn't envisage living without her.'

Interviewed by Jack Bell in 1980 for an unknown newspaper.

'I know a good thing when I see it. It's a great pleasure to go home now! Lalla's a super cook. She laughs a lot at me – she finds it amusing that I'm so chatty at all hours, even in the morning. Well, I'm not *raucous* exactly, but I'm pretty perky first thing. We're always having meals with her parents. We all get along very well. I'm very confident and happy.'

Interviewed by Maureen Patton in 1981 for the *Daily Express*, 21 March .

'I do find co-existence very difficult. Marriage is full of mutual irritations, but the only alternative seems to be this punishing loneliness of being on your own.

'I'm not an accomplished bachelor. I'm quite good at the linen and making beds, but I don't like vacuuming and I can't master ironing boards – vicious things that always collapse on you. One of the prices you pay for being on your own is that very swiftly you can become old womanish and over fussy. I've seen it so often in loners and confirmed bachelors. Luckily I'm very gregarious. I still have my old haunts in Soho: the Coach and Horses, the French, the Swiss and the Colony Room.

'I am still optimistic that Lalla and I might get back together again. This separation is just a period to test out attitudes. Lalla wants my happiness and what is good for both of us. Anyway, actors are prone to making gestures. I still believe in marriage and there are masses of advantages to being with Lalla. She is extraordinarily well-read, witty, and wonderful good company. The trouble is that it's easier to see all that from a distance rather than as one of the participants in our relationship, in much the same way that agony aunts can be very rational and philosophical about other people's problems because they're not involved.

'Any marriage is difficult, but two jumpy, insecure, freelance actors, flogging themselves at work and desperately seeking approval all the time, have got less chance of making it than most. I ring Lalla up nearly every day to see how she is and what's happening. I don't do it from emotional dependency, but just as a friendly, civilised, polite thing to do. When you are separated you can't just excise all the nice things about the other person. When you have been very generous to each other emotionally you must still remember that. The trouble, when you separate, is that although you may be united in times of happiness, it's rare to be united in times of anxiety. So that just as one person says,

"I think it would be a good idea to sever things now," the other is thinking, "I'm sure it's starting to get better." So it's not logical and it's very hard to be reasonable. But I ring Lalla anyway to see how her play is going and to see how the cats are. I do miss the cats . . .

'I often wish that Lalla was with me, when I'm alone in the flat. Thoughts of her float about in my head all the time. But even if we don't get back together again, I would never think of our marriage as a failure. We have been very happy together and that's what matters, not how long it lasted. I always remember Germaine Greer, when asked if she regretted her short-lived marriage, saying "No, it was a huge success – for three days!"'

Interviewed by Jenny Nisbet in 1982 for the *Daily Express*, 8 June.

'I wouldn't say I'm close to my children. I wouldn't say I'm close to anyone, except my wife, Sue Jerrard. I don't have much capacity for friendship because of my self-centredness. I'm not generous enough to give to individuals. These things are heightened in actors when you are thinking about yourself all the time and worrying about where the next round of applause is coming from.

'I've lost my religion and sometimes I think I've lost everything in life because I'm a great betrayer. The title of my autobiography is going to be *All Friends Betrayed*. That's made me more anxious to hold onto my dear wife. I used to be very fragmented, and I do need to be adored. I feel this overriding security in her affection; she reassures me constantly. Now that I've located admiration, I'm hanging onto it for grim death.'

Interviewed by Corrina Honan in 1992 for the *Daily Mail*, 28 March.

'I do adore my wife. I think about her and phone her every day while I'm away filming, and I couldn't exist very well without her. She guards and protects me, because, as you know, I'm not very good at reality.'

Interviewed by Julia Beasley in 1992 for *Woman's Weekly*, 24 March.

ON SPARE-TIME PURSUITS:

'I adore being in pubs – it is my idea of bliss. I spend a lot of time philosophising in ale houses. I go to a pub and if there are some chums there who are interesting I stay. If they are not I just move on.

'I am a joyous drinker. The idea of deliberately going out to get plastered horrifies me. What is the point of doing something that interferes with fundamental functions? I can't bear doing anything that would make me sexually impotent or stop me working or concentrating. I am not saying that from time to time I don't get stinko, but that is an accident – and I love those accidents. You meet a couple of chums, then you meet someone else and the next thing you know you are as high as a kite. That's lovely.

'I am sometimes unreliable and my acquaintances know that. People will say, "Come to dinner," and I'll say, "Yes, all right, I'll come if I feel I can contribute, and if you don't like that arrangement don't invite me." I don't turn up if I suddenly feel on the night that I am not going to make a contribution. Perhaps it is just me licensing myself to be unreliable.

'I like to be in the middle of things. I like to live near enough to the centre of London so that I can walk home from the theatre or a late night jazz concert. I go out to dinner three or four times a week. Recently I had a week off and I went to the theatre every night, saw three movies and read two books.

'Nearly everything I do is related to acting. We are professional pleasers, and that works against deep relationships. To spend a lot of time with an actor like me must be boring for people who want to take the relationship seriously. I am not a good proposition when it comes to deep, private relationships because I am totally preoccupied with work. I live a profoundly shallow life – or a deeply superficial one.'

Interviewed by Dan Slater in 1979 for the *Sun*.

'I love reading – I simply couldn't survive without books. I appreciate art, music, poetry – I love beauty of any kind. I like people too – there's so much in life to be enjoyed, I can at least say I'm never bored.'

Interviewed by Richard Marson in 1984 for *Doctor Who Magazine* No. 92.

'I read a lot of escapism. I watch very little television: mainly the news or news comment. I sometimes watch Brian Walden at the weekend and have a glass of wine. I read a lot of newspapers every day; I take four so-called serious newspapers and often two tabloids, which I scour. I read some Dickens every day and Shaw.

'I also have a self-appointed job as a churchyard keeper in which I look after the dead near my house. There are two cemeteries and I feel very proprietorial about them. I keep them mown and tidy and I know lots of the dead people there, and I know the names of lots of them. I had a pruning session recently. They're full of sinister-looking yew trees. This time of year is the growing season so I'm kept busy. Yesterday I was in that cemetery for four hours!

'So if I'm home I go in and do various odd jobs, a bit of mowing or a bit of weeding or just a bit of looking, keeping things in check. It's nice to think about the dead and wonder what they were like and to speculate on so little evidence. The speculation fires one's imagination because, as you know, on gravestones it doesn't really say what they were like. You don't know whether they were happy or what their last words were, and some of what's written, well it's downright lies! When they say "Not dead, only sleeping," well! I had my Honda mower near a fellow's head yesterday and he *definitely* wasn't sleeping, let me tell you!'

Interviewed by John Freeman in 1991 for *Doctor Who Magazine* Nos. 179-181.

ON DEATH:

'Must go out and get the papers. Check the obituaries. If mine's in I can stop worrying. I've always felt at home with the dead. Dear old things.'

From *Just Who on Earth Is . . . Tom Baker* video (1991) by Reeltime Pictures.

'There is a kind of implacable logic in my life. My early memories are of graveyards, I live by a graveyard and I want a good gravestone as a sign that I existed. I might be frightened to die. But if there were two cameras there, I might make an effort. One for close-ups and one for wide angles!'

Interviewed by Corrina Honan in 1992 for the *Daily Mail*, 28 March.

'I've always admired the dead. I find them so uncritical. Where I live in the country, on two sides of my house there are churchyards and when I wake up in the morning I look out at the gravestones and no matter how sorry for myself I feel, I think, well, it could be worse. And so I bought myself a second-hand gravestone, in order to give some money to the parish really. Unfortunately, the man who'd had it before me, well, his name wasn't Baker, but I've had it smoothed down a bit and just on the top of it, being modest, there's a star and underneath it it says "Tom Baker 1934–". I didn't have the courage to put in a second date. As for the epitaph – I'll leave that to someone else.'

From *Myth Makers 17: Tom Baker* video (1989) by Reeltime Pictures.

ON FANS:

'I can't imagine life without fans. So when the fans run out, and the fans of the Doctor run out, and the fans of Tom Baker run out, then what we're talking about is when there's no more love left. And when there's no more love left, there's nothing left. And I'd be nothing then.'

From *Just Who on Earth Is . . . Tom Baker* video (1991) by Reeltime Pictures.

'. . . and I could try, perhaps more convincingly, to demonstrate that I am grateful, and that it all was such fun. And that by and large, if you'll pardon that amazing expression, it goes on being fun. And maybe the fans won't go away, as one of my interrogators suggested so frighteningly a little while ago they would. Perhaps you won't and if you won't then I won't. We'll both stay.

'Good health.

'Thank you.'

From *Just Who on Earth Is . . . Tom Baker* video (1991) by Reeltime Pictures.

2: The Fourth Doctor

The character of each of *Doctor Who*'s seven Doctors has been vitally influenced by the personality of the actor playing the part. As Barry Letts, producer of the series from 1969 to 1974, once put it, 'No actor playing the Doctor should be acting *all* the time. There has to be enough of his own personality showing on the screen. It makes life easier for him, for the script writers, in fact for everybody.' Graham Williams, producer from 1977 to 1980, shared this view, maintaining 'We are utterly dependent on the individual actor's portrayal of that part.' The casting of a new Doctor is therefore one of the most crucial factors determining how the character will come across on screen.

When the third Doctor, Jon Pertwee, reached the end of his time in the series, it was Barry Letts who had the principal responsibility for choosing the next lead actor. One name he considered was that of 39-year-old comedian and former pop singer Jim Dale, well known for his appearances in the *Carry On...* films; but on the whole he favoured casting someone rather older. Amongst those he approached were Richard Hearne, whom he eventually discounted as the actor was set on the idea of playing the part in the style of the popular Mister Pastry character he had created in the forties; Michael Bentine, who was quite keen to take the role but decided against it because he would not be happy working on a series without being able to contribute to the scripting; and Graham Crowden, who was also quite enthusiastic but ultimately decided that he would not want to make such a long-term commitment to one particular series.

Many ideas were considered for the image of the new Doctor, including having him look like Albert Einstein and play a violin in the manner of Sherlock Holmes to emphasise his eccentricity. As Letts told *Doctor Who Magazine* in 1981, 'All of us who were involved in the casting wanted a Doctor who would be radically different from Jon Pertwee's style of portrayal. It was no good just turning out a carbon copy as that would have given the audience the impression that the new Doctor was a watered down version of the previous one, and that would have been unfair to Jon's successor.'

While Letts was still unable to find a suitable candidate for the role, time was marching on and writers had to be briefed to start work on scripts for the fourth Doctor's initial run of stories. In view of the likelihood that the part would eventually go to an actor of advanced years who would be unable to cope with strenuous physical action, the production team decided to introduce a new young male companion to undertake any 'rough stuff' which might be called for. So was born the character of UNIT medic Harry Sullivan.

With time running short to decide on a new Doctor, Barry Letts received inspiration from another source, as he later explained:

'Eventually it was my head of department, Bill Slater, who suggested Tom Baker. Now, I'd heard of Tom from such productions as *Nicholas and Alexandra,* in which he had taken on the role of Rasputin, so I invited him along to the production office for discussions. I asked him if he had any video tapes of past things he'd worked on and he said no, but added that just around the corner was a cinema showing his latest film *The Golden Voyage of Sinbad.* I duly went along to see it and was impressed. Shortly afterwards, we asked him if he would like to accept the part.'

Speaking on stage at a US *Doctor Who* convention in 1985, Tom Baker recounted his own, rather colourful version of these events:

'I once wrote a letter to the BBC demanding that I be employed. I said that somewhere there, there was a job for me, and it was disgraceful that I hadn't been given it . . . The man I wrote to, Bill Slater, had been to a *Doctor Who* casting session that afternoon – the part just happened to be free, that's the way it happens sometimes – and he'd had no ideas. My letter demanding employment was the last letter he read as he was getting into bed. Now, here is a coincidence. I actually knew his wife quite well. No, I don't mean in the Biblical sense; I was acquainted with his wife. I mean, we had sometimes held hands in various canteens – you know, actors are rather extravagant about those sort of things . . . Anyway, he was getting into bed and he conscientiously read his last letter, with a terrifying sigh, and said, "Bloody Tom Baker, demanding employment." And she said, "Oh really, I thought he was doing rather grand things?" He replied, "No, no, he says here I've got to give him a . . ." Then he said, "Do you know, I've just come from a casting session this afternoon, for *Doctor Who*." To which Mary Webster – which was his wife's name – said, "Ring him up now, Bill."

'So at eleven o'clock I was lying on my mattress on the floor, being rather self-consciously bohemian and feeling tragically sorry for myself, which sometimes can be rather a pleasant sensation, and the phone went. He said, "Bill Slater here, BBC. Come and see me tomorrow." And then my life took another change. That's how it happened. I can scarcely believe it myself. And that's the truth – just imagine if I wanted to elaborate on it!'

With Baker cast as the Doctor, the next step was to decide exactly how he would approach the part. He initially had few ideas of his own, and was happy to be guided by Barry Letts and the series' script editor, Robert Holmes. Letts later told *In-Vision* about the preliminary discussions they had:

'Basically, with Tom Baker, we decided to go away from Jon Pertwee. People came up with all sorts of ideas which would have looked like an attempt to duplicate Jon – a poor man's Jon Pertwee. So what we looked for was a strong personality in its own right. We had a meeting in the Balzac restaurant – there was Tom, Philip Hinchcliffe, Bob Holmes and me. This was before Philip took over from me as producer. We discussed the way Tom was going to play the Doctor. The floppy hat and so on was Tom's idea stemming from me saying that the one thing he mustn't be was a dandy, as Jon had played him that way. And what came out of that conference was fed back to costume designer Jim Acheson.'

Philip Hinchcliffe, *Doctor Who*'s producer from 1974 to 1977, also talked to *In-Vision* about these early discussions:

'I had no hand in casting Tom. He was a *fait accompli*. But I did have a hand in developing the character. Barry was very good about that. I formed a relationship with Tom, and discussed with Barry what the character would be.

'I had quite firm ideas about the Doctor's character. I discussed with Tom what we thought he could do with it. We discussed what he ought to look like. I also did a sort of crash course on the programme – I hadn't really seen that much of it, although luckily I'd seen quite a lot of the Jon Pertwee stuff. That was the first thing I did, in fact. Then I formulated a view of the character, which I suppose was partly from that tradition, and the Sydney Newman "cosmic hobo" phrase stuck in my mind. I'd read a fair bit of science fiction, not a lot, so I spent my preparation time reading further from writers and authors whom perhaps I knew about but had never really read. I read voraciously throughout the whole genre.

'I got really interested in all sorts of concepts. It was like suddenly discovering a really fascinating area which I had only vaguely known before. Bob Holmes already had a very good background and was very well read. He also had the drop on me because he could remember all these old movies which I've never seen! So out of all that we formulated the character. I liked the idea of him being sort of bohemian.

'At the time, heroes were really going out of fashion. Your hero could be a little bit more vulnerable, a little bit more complex. So our Doctor wasn't quite the same moral authority. He was getting a little bit back to the first Doctor – he was irascible, unreliable, and humans were not quite sure whether they should trust him or not. But basically he was an heroic character. He was less powerfully heroic, though. He had to work a bit harder to get out of problems; and we gave him some pretty tough opposition, I think, so he couldn't just "with one bound" be free all the time!

'Tom kept going round saying "I'm not really human – how do I portray a 500-year-old Time Lord?" And I said "Olympian detachment, Tom. You're very good at Olympian detachment." So he used to quote this back at me. But basically, the Doctor is a human hero – we all identify with him so easily. He is the ultimate essence of human virtue. But at the same time, biographically as it were, he's got to sort of be non-human. So Tom was quite keen to get some of his "non-humanness" into it. Bob was as well, which is probably why, at times, we showed him being a bit detached.'

Barry Letts's desire to avoid the fourth Doctor being perceived as 'a poor man's Jon Pertwee' was clearly reflected in Tom Baker's debut adventure, *Robot*. Here the appearance and behaviour of the new incarnation presented a stark contrast to those of the old. Whereas the third Doctor had been the epitome of seventies elegance in his velvet smoking jacket, bow tie and frilly shirt, the fourth took on the look of a slightly scruffy bohemian eccentric with his baggy jacket, broad-brimmed hat and long, winding scarf. And whereas the popular image of Pertwee's portrayal had been that of a dashing man of action, often using Venusian Aikido – his own brand of unarmed combat – to tackle his enemies, Baker's Doctor was introduced as someone whose preferred approach to problems was one of contemplation rather than action. On the rare occasions in *Robot* when the new Doctor did become involved in a violent confrontation, he seemed to win almost without trying to, his opponents falling over him or tripping over his scarf. Even the scenes immediately following the Doctor's regeneration, as he wanders around in a nightshirt and finds the TARDIS key hidden in his shoe, can be seen as a light-hearted reworking of similar sequences in Jon Pertwee's debut story, *Spearhead from Space* – again emphasising the contrast between the two Doctors.

Comments made by Jon Pertwee and Tom Baker in the numerous interviews each gave while playing the Doctor show just how important each actor's own personality was in shaping these contrasting interpretations of the role. Pertwee invariably came across as a very active man, often speaking of his love of strenuous sports such as water-skiing, and his interest in high-powered vehicles and state-of-the-art gadgetry. Tom Baker, on the other hand, was always reflective and thoughtful, telling of his years as a monk and offering insights and self-analysis.

The script for *Robot* was written by Terrance Dicks, the man from whom Robert Holmes had just taken over as script editor. Talking to *In-Vision*, Dicks confirmed that in his description of the fourth Doctor he had been greatly influenced by Baker's own personality:

'There was very little to go on, except that I had met Tom by then and talked to him, so I had some idea what he was like. And I'd been in on the casting of Tom before I wrote the script. Tom in the flesh does have this type of loony scatter brain, so I played on that very much. I also used the device, which you can always use in the first episode, that the new regeneration is unstable. So he starts off being rather crazy and gradually quietens down and becomes more reasonable by the end of it. So I thought, if they don't like that interpretation, or if Tom doesn't like that interpretation, they could always say "Well, he was a bit weird then, but he's different now, he's stable." In fact I think they always kept quite a lot of the arbitrary erraticness that I started him off with.

'In any case, the changes are superficial. It's always the same man; his surface mannerisms may change. So the dramatic thing of writing the serious Doctor stuff actually changes very little indeed. The flourishes are different, and the kind of jokes and witticisms.'

The 'flourishes' which Dicks gave the new Doctor included having him, in the words of the script, 'seemingly ignorant of people's conversation, preoccupied with child-like pursuits – although actually deep in concentration.' Another description read: 'He has a general tendency to adopt gawky, sprawling stances. It is characteristic of his new incarnation that he always tends to lie, lean, perch or hang in some unlikely position rather than sitting conventionally.' These characteristics were picked up by Christopher Barry, the director of *Robot*, and faithfully reflected on screen; and, as noted by Terrance Dicks, traces of them were to remain throughout the fourth Doctor's era.

The 'alien detachment' of which Philip Hinchcliffe spoke was also apparent from an early stage. It was highlighted in a speech which Robert Holmes wrote for the Doctor to deliver in his second story, *The Ark in Space*, when contemplating his discovery of a group of humans lying in suspended animation in an orbiting space-station after the apparent destruction of all life on Earth:

'Homo sapiens – what an inventive, invincible species. It's only a few million years since they crawled up out of the mud and learned to walk, puny defenceless bipeds. They've survived flood, famine and plague. They've survived cosmic wars and holocausts. And now here they are, out among the stars, waiting to begin a new life, ready to outsit eternity. They're indomitable . . . indomitable.'

It was Holmes again who, in his script for the following season's *Pyramids of Mars*, had the Doctor making specific comment on his alien nature. When his companion, Sarah Jane Smith, chides him on his pensive mood, reasoning that he should be happy to be returning to Earth, he tells her:

'The Earth isn't my home, Sarah. I'm a Time Lord . . . You don't understand the implications. I'm not a human being. I walk in eternity . . . It means I've lived for something like 750 years.'

In *The Seeds of Doom*, the Doctor refuses to help a group of scientists at an Antarctic base to amputate the arm of a colleague who has been infected by an alien Krynoid. 'You must help yourselves,' he explains, and one gets the impression that he is referring not just to the scientists but to the human race as a whole.

It was to this otherworldly aspect of the Doctor that Tom Baker drew particular attention in interviews he gave shortly after winning the role. 'I want to play him in an individual way,' he told *The Times* in February 1974, 'with the suggestion that although he has a human body he comes from somewhere else.'

Baker did not, however, want the Doctor to seem omniscient or invulnerable. As Peter Haining's 1986 book *The Doctor Who File* quoted him as explaining:

'I came to believe that the Doctor should have an air of naive innocence about him to counter his enormous wealth of knowledge and past experience. He had to seem vulnerable and therefore more interesting to an audience I felt would quickly tire of the Doctor as Superman!

'My basic approach to new situations was to walk boldly into them and say with a broad grin, "Hello, I am the Doctor." Now the audience may be aware, from previous scenes, that the Doctor is going into a situation of dire peril, but their attention is held, subconsciously knowing that, any second now, he is going to get knocked to the floor!'

Giving the Doctor this air of constant optimism and naive trustfulness – unwilling to think ill of any person or creature until presented with hard and often painful evidence of their villainy – was just one of the ways in which Baker sought to keep his portrayal fresh and interesting.

Before long, the fourth Doctor had become, as Barry Letts had hoped, a very popular character in his own right, and a highly identifiable one with his imposing stature, his extraordinary hat and scarf, his rich booming voice, his broad toothy grin, his bag of jelly babies and his yo-yo. This eccentric image was quickly seized upon by journalists in the popular press, whose standard description of the fourth Doctor was along the lines of 'the gangling, 6ft 3in figure in the floppy hat and the long scarf'.

There were however a number of respects in which the character changed and developed as time went by. While his thoughtful side continued to be apparent – one particularly celebrated instance of this being a scene in *Genesis of the Daleks* in which he questions his right to destroy the Dalek race at birth – he also became more physical in his approach to problems, making the Harry Sullivan character partly redundant. He was at perhaps his most aggressive in *The Seeds of*

Doom, the story which closed his second season of adventures. In this story he was seen violently assaulting several of his adversaries, breaking a chair over the head of one of them, and even wielding a gun. None of the previous Doctors had ever been quite so unrestrained as this in the use of force to combat evil.

Although the degree of violence in *The Seeds of Doom* was exceptional, this was by no means the only story in which the Doctor was seen to get heavily involved in forceful action. At one point in *The Masque of Mandragora*, for instance, he lashes out with his feet to try to avoid capture and also takes part in a swordfight, as he does again in *The Androids of Tara*. *The Deadly Assassin* and *The Talons of Weng-Chiang* provided further examples of him tackling his enemies physically. On the other hand, where he did employ such tactics it was almost always because he or one of his friends was under threat or in imminent danger. For the most part he showed a clear disposition towards reaching peaceful solutions; and he was certainly committed to preserving life wherever possible. He castigated his companion Leela for her tendency to rely on her hunting knife to get her out of difficult situations, and showed a similar disapproval of violent behaviour by others – for example, private eye Duggan's propensity for throwing punches in *City of Death* (although ironically it is with one such punch that Duggan saves the day at the end of the story).

An equally if not more significant development in the Doctor's character was a growing inclination for him to resort to tomfoolery to confuse and outmanoeuvre his enemies, accompanied by his adoption of a generally more outrageous and amusing disposition. His brooding, contemplative moods came to be offset by bursts of manic activity; he began to assail his opponents with flippant retorts and cheeky wisecracks; and it became increasingly common for him to be seen staring goggle-eyed into camera. All these things helped to give the fourth Doctor a uniquely zany, off-the-wall persona.

This shift of emphasis was born out of Tom Baker's keen determination to keep the character constantly surprising and engaging – an aim which came increasingly to preoccupy the actor, as he told *Doctor Who Magazine* in 1984:

'The Doctor is a moral being – you know exactly what he's going to do and why. There's very little that's unexpected about him. Character development – well, there's no such thing because the Doctor is a heroic stereotype who conforms to the patterns of behaviour you expect him to conform to. His character basically stays the same. The challenge is to make that character as diverting and as interesting as possible within the given framework. I'd think, "How can this be made different?" or, "There's something new to be exploited here," but it got harder and harder to keep the character fresh. The scripts often didn't help, either.'

Although the fourth Doctor could never have been considered an entirely conventional hero, being – as Philip Hinchcliffe observed – more 'complex' and 'vulnerable' than that, Baker was frequently frustrated by what he perceived to be a lack of imagination and ingenuity on the writers' part in representing the character. While the actor's own natural inventiveness had been held in check to a degree during Hinchcliffe's time as producer, under Graham Williams he came to demand more and more input into the scripting process, using rehearsals as an opportunity to rewrite, sometimes with the assistance of his co-stars, any action or dialogue with which he was unhappy. This gave him the freedom to make the stories, and especially the character of the Doctor himself, much more tongue-in-cheek and exuberant; a philosophy which he carried through into his performance.

This method of working was taken to perhaps its furthest extent after Lalla Ward joined the series as the second incarnation of the Doctor's companion Romana. In Ward, Baker found a kindred spirit – they later married – and together they frequently made radical amendments to the scripts with which they were provided. 'We used to have the most awful problems with our writers,' Ward told *Doctor Who Magazine* in 1984. 'Tom and I used to have to rewrite most of our dialogue with the director, usually because it wasn't right for the parts we were playing. And it happened from the start. Our actual rehearsal time, which was incredibly tight, was reduced still further as a result. So the programme was always a heavy workload – we had this responsibility for the show and we were doing so many a year against the problems of a small budget and scripts that we wouldn't have done without at least an element of rewriting.'

On screen, there was an obvious rapport between Baker and Ward, and the dialogue in the scenes they shared together was often highly witty and sophisticated. There was even at times a hint of playful surrealism about it, such as in the following conversation as they prepare to descend from the top of the Eiffel Tower in the opening episode of *City of Death*:

ROMANA: Shall we take the lift, or fly?

DOCTOR: Let's not be ostentatious.

ROMANA: All right, let's fly then.

DOCTOR: That would be silly. We'll take the lift.

This exchange is given added significance by a scene at the end of the story in which the pair, having returned to the top of the Eiffel Tower, are then shown back on the ground again only moments later, so that it appears the only way they could have got down so quickly is indeed to have flown!

Speaking to *Doctor Who Magazine* in 1991, Baker said: 'Naturalism isn't my strong point – I'm not even good at coming through doors convincingly! But never mind, even if you can't come through a door convincingly, perhaps you can come through a door interestingly or, dare one say, amusingly . . .'

Baker meant this comment quite literally. Such had been his anxiety not to let his portrayal of the Doctor become stale or repetitive that he had indeed tried to find interesting ways of doing such normally mundane things as coming through a doorway or sitting in a chair. At one point in *The Invasion of Time*, for instance, he had insisted on having the Doctor trip whilst walking along a corridor, for no other reason than that it made the scene more unusual and entertaining. And as was so often the case, it also raised a laugh.

At the time, some critics felt that Baker's performance had gone too far in the direction of humour, making the Doctor appear almost a buffoon – just as, during Philip Hinchcliffe's time, some had felt that too much violence had entered into his portrayal. In his 1984 interview with *Doctor Who Magazine*, Baker explained his attitude both to violence and to comedy in the series:

'I didn't like real violence – the mindless type of thug violence you always get in American police series. I can't say how much that bores me. I always preferred to outwit the baddies – I don't think it's necessary to blow them from here to kingdom come. I mean, it's dull, isn't it? What's new about that? I don't feel we really went too far with the violence in the show. I think if it had been over-the-top somebody would have said so. The problem in a show where good always wins over bad is how to do it in a new way. Usually our scripts would blow them up.

'As for the comedy, I think a lot of the criticism we got was from people who were used to the old way. The audience expected the old cliché scripts – the comedy element was only part of it, but I felt it was a wonderful way of winning the children's imagination. I always felt *Doctor Who* was a children's programme, watched by children of all ages. With a comic approach it was more diverting to laugh our villains into destruction. You can't tell me we lost all our tension – in the comedy there were very serious bits; that contrast is extraordinarily effective. I don't think we overdid either violence or comedy – in fact I think we could have gone further with both elements.'

While the Tom Baker era went furthest in the direction of violence in his third season of stories, without doubt it went furthest towards comedy in his sixth and penultimate season. Baker's final year as the Doctor saw him returning to a predominantly serious characterisation more in line with his original interpretation of the role.

The main reason for this late change of style was the appointment of a new producer, John Nathan-Turner. Nathan-Turner disliked the type of humour which had become a standard feature of *Doctor Who* during his predecessor's tenure and was determined to stamp his own mark on the series – something which initially caused clashes between him and Baker. However, although more serious, Baker's performance in this last season remained as charismatic as ever. It was also, at times, more sombre and brooding than ever before – an impression enhanced by the darker, more subdued costume he was given at this time. This led to the fourth Doctor's final adventure, *Logopolis*, in which the manifestation of the mysterious figure of the Watcher portended his imminent regeneration. Eventually, in foiling the latest scheme of his archenemy the Master, he sacrificed his own life to achieve one last, all-important victory – saving the universe itself from destruction.

PART TWO – FICTION

3: The Stories

'Look Brigadier, look! I think it's starting.'

Sarah Jane Smith's words, as she and Brigadier Lethbridge-Stewart of the United Nations Intelligence Taskforce (UNIT) watched their companion change his appearance, ushered in a new era for the Doctor.

The new Doctor was bohemian in manner and dress, preferring to enrich his knowledge with new experiences through travel rather than to remain in one place and time. Indeed, on recovering from his regeneration and as soon as he was able to walk, he headed straight for the TARDIS and paid a brief visit to a distant planet where he helped (or so he thought) a survey team repair their damaged computer. (The timing of this visit was suggested by Terrance Dicks in his novelisation of *The Face of Evil*, but not confirmed in the televised adventures.) Back at UNIT, he helped the Brigadier investigate the theft of computer components and the plans for a new disintegrator gun . . .

Note: In the following listings, the technical details are as follows: 'Time' refers to the starting time, rounded to the nearest minute, of the original transmission of an episode in England; 'Durn' indicates the exact duration of the episode on the master tape; 'Viewers' gives the official viewing figure in millions; 'Chart Pos' is the position of the episode in the top 200 programmes for that week. Where a dash appears in the 'Viewers' or 'Chart Pos' column, this signifies that no information was collected by the BBC for the transmission in question. 'OB' stands for Outside Broadcast recording.

SEASON TWELVE

Robot (4A)

EP	DATE	TIME	DURN	VIEWERS	CHART POS
1	28.12.74	17.35	24'11"	10.8	25
2	04.01.75	17.33	25'00"	10.7	17
3	11.01.75	17.30	24'29"	10.1	22
4	18.01.75	17.32	24'29"	9.0	30

PRODUCTION DETAILS

OB: 28.04.74–01.05.74

Studio: 21.05.74, 02.06.74, 06.06.74 and 07.06.74 – all in TC3

Electronic components and secret plans have been stolen both at night and in broad daylight and with the Doctor confined to sick bay there is little the Brigadier can do. When the Doctor recovers, he inspects the site of the most recent theft and realises that he and his friends are up against something distinctly non-human as heavy vehicle tracks have been found in the vicinity of the supposedly secure buildings which housed the components. Later, the perpetrator actually drills through the ground to gain access to a heavily armed vault at Emmett's Electronics.

It is Sarah who first meets the culprit, a massive robot invented by one Professor J. P. Kettlewell while working for the Think Tank, a government installation involved in developing emerging technologies. The robot has been reprogrammed under the direction of the director of Think Tank, Miss Hilda Winters, and used to obtain the means for constructing a disintegrator gun. With this the Scientific Reform Society, of which she is a leading member, can obtain the computer codes controlling the nuclear weapons of the world's leading powers. In this way, the SRS hope to hold the world to ransom until their demands for a purer way of life are met.

Kettlewell, although claiming no knowledge of Miss Winters's activities, is actually a party to them, and is ultimately killed by his creation when he realises his error and tries to stop the robot from wiping out a group of UNIT troops.

The robot suffers an electronic/mental breakdown on killing its creator, and this coincides with the Brigadier's attempt to destroy the behemoth with the disintegrator gun. Unfortunately this causes the robot to grow and the now gigantic creature goes on the rampage among the UNIT troops, protecting only Sarah Jane with whom it feels an affinity. The Doctor manages to save the day by brewing up a virulent metal virus described in Kettlewell's notes and using it to eat away the towering titan until there is nothing left but a small heap of decaying rust, which itself is soon destroyed by the virus.

With this problem sorted out, the Doctor, now fully recovered following his change of appearance, decides that the time has come to travel once more. He persuades Sarah Jane and UNIT medic, Surgeon-Lieutenant Harry Sullivan, to join him. The Brigadier is less than pleased to see the TARDIS dematerialise, as the Doctor has been invited to an audience at the Palace.

WHO FAX

● Novelised as *Doctor Who and the Giant Robot* by Terrance Dicks in 1975. Novel renamed *Doctor Who: Robot* in 1992.

● Story released on BBC Home Video in 1992.
Robot was inspired in part by the 1933 film *King Kong*.

● The regeneration of the Doctor was re-used from its recording at the conclusion of *Planet of the Spiders*; however, the shots of Sarah Jane Smith and the Brigadier were rerecorded.

● A new title sequence featuring Tom Baker as the Doctor was created by graphic designer Bernard Lodge for this story.

● *Robot* was the first *Doctor Who* story completely recorded on video tape using colour video cameras.

● Director Christopher Barry considered, amongst other people, Colin Baker, better known as the actor who played the sixth Doctor, to play the part of Miss Winters's number two, Arnold Jellicoe. The part eventually went to Alec Linstead.

● This story saw the debut of Surgeon-Lieutenant Harry Sullivan, played by Ian Marter. Marter had previously appeared in *Doctor Who* in the Jon Pertwee story *Carnival of Monsters*, playing Lt John Andrews, an officer on board a kidnapped cargo ship, and before that had auditioned for the part of Pertwee-era regular Mike Yates.

Marter later successfully novelised several *Doctor Who* stories, and wrote the spin-off novel *Harry Sullivan's War*. He died in 1986.

COMMENT

Robot is an enjoyable opener for the fourth Doctor. It has a strong plot, and the Brigadier, Harry and Sarah are in pivotal roles, thus taking some of the focus away from the new Doctor. The title creature is a masterpiece of design and the towering metal costume worn by Michael Kilgarriff is one of the most effective robots ever to appear on Doctor Who. *What lets the story down is some of the Colour Separation Overlay (CSO) work which, although generally very well achieved, tends to fail on shots of the robot, as the silver metal reflects the blue backcloth, and these blue areas then pick up the CSO backgrounds. Another much-maligned effect is the use of a toy tank in a model shot for one of the battle sequences, something that director Christopher Barry now says he would not have used had he known how it would look.*

The Ark In Space (4C)

EP	DATE	TIME	DURN	VIEWERS	CHART POS
1	25.01.75	17.36	24'58"	9.4	27
2	01.02.75	17.31	24'49"	13.6	5
3	08.02.75	17.32	24'05"	11.2	17
4	15.02.75	17.32	24'37"	10.2	24
Repeat Compilation					
	20.08.75	18.35	69'47"	8.2	29

PRODUCTION DETAILS

Studio: 28.10.74, 29.10.74 in TC3, 11.11.74, 12.11.74 in TC1

The TARDIS's first port of call is a seemingly deserted space-wheel orbiting Earth sometime around the 131st century. On board, the Doctor, Sarah and Harry discover that the wheel is an Ark containing the last surviving remnants of the human race in suspended animation. The Earth was evacuated thousands of years before as solar flare activity threatened to destroy all life, and the cream of humanity was selected to board Space Station Nerva, now nicknamed the Ark.

The Doctor discovers that the Ark has been visited in the past by a single Wirrn Queen. The Wirrn are an insect species first encountered by humankind in Andromeda. They lay their eggs close to or within a food source so that their larvae have nourishment, both physical and mental, available once they hatch. The Wirrn larvae also secrete a slime which can invade other creatures and transform them into Wirrn, retaining the knowledge and intelligence of the host.

On the Ark, the Wirrn Queen had already taken the body of Technician Dune, and with his knowledge of the ship, had laid her eggs close to the solar stacks – the Ark's power source – intending to use the remaining sleeping humans as food stock for her young. This task completed, the Queen, having been shot by the Ark's automatic defence system, had hidden herself away in a storage locker and died.

The Doctor reactivates the controls of the Ark, and accidentally revives a small complement of the crew. The leader, Lasar (nicknamed Noah), becomes infected by a Wirrn grub when he checks the solar stacks and is slowly taken over. Vira, Libri, Lycett and Rogin, however, gradually grow to trust the Doctor and help in his plan to lure the hatched Wirrn insects into a transport ship before ejecting it into space.

With one final act of human sacrifice the Noah/Wirrn neglects to set the rocket stabilisers, resulting in the shuttle exploding in space and destroying the invading Wirrn.

The Doctor offers to pop down to Earth using the Ark's transmat system to ensure that the diode receptor beacons are correctly tuned. Sarah and Harry elect to accompany him and the three leave.

WHO FAX
- Novelised as *Doctor Who and the Ark in Space* by Ian Marter in 1977.
- Story released in edited form on BBC Home Video in 1989.
- *The Ark in Space* started life as a story by John Lucarotti which turned out to be unsuited to the series's current style. As there was no time for Lucarotti to work on it further, this task fell to script editor Robert Holmes. As Holmes had to change so much, the story was transmitted under his name.
- The Wirrn grubs were constructed by designer John Friedlander out of plastic bubble-wrap packaging, painted with latex and sprayed green.
- This is the first story to feature the Doctor's yo-yo, which he uses to

take a gravity reading.

● Sets from this story were reused in *Revenge of the Cybermen* as a cost-cutting exercise.

● The music played to Sarah in part one is Handel's *Largo*.

● A scene in which Noah, infected by the Wirrn, pleads with Vira to kill him, was cut by producer Philip Hinchcliffe as he thought it too disturbing.

COMMENT

The Ark in Space is one of the most effective stories presented by the programme. By setting the three time-travellers, together with four revived humans on the Ark, against an insidious menace that can attack the group from within as well as from without, it proves that you do not need vast sets or large casts to achieve good drama.

The sets, in particular the cathedral-like cryogenic storage room and the gently curving corridors around the outside of the Ark, are superb. The story is both claustrophobic and dramatic and all the cast perform admirably. Of particular note is the first episode which features only the three leads investigating the deactivated Ark, and in which Tom Baker's portrayal of the Doctor was truly established.

The Ark in Space is a pointer to how the programme was to develop under the assured guidance of Philip Hinchcliffe and Robert Holmes.

The Sontaran Experiment (4B)

EP	DATE	TIME	DURN	VIEWERS	CHART POS
1	22.02.75	17.30	24'27"	11.0	18
2	01.03.75	17.30	25'00"	10.5	17
Repeat Compilation					
	09.07.75	18.25	47'42"	8.2	29

PRODUCTION DETAILS

OB: 26.09.74–01.10.74

Arriving on a desolate and windswept Earth the Doctor starts realigning the transmat refractors while Sarah and Harry go off to explore. Harry slips and falls into a pit and Sarah runs back to the Doctor to get help. The Doctor, however, has been captured by a trio of Galsec space travellers who were lured to Earth by a phoney distress call and stranded there when their ship was destroyed. Sarah, unable to find the Doctor, makes friends with a fourth space traveller, Roth, who tells her of the alien in the rocks who is experimenting on them. Before long, Sarah and Roth are captured by a robot and dragged off to the rocks.

Harry finds his own way out of the pit via a series of underground tunnels and emerges close to an outcrop of rock. He watches as Sarah and Roth are presented to the alien who turns out to be a Sontaran.

Field-Major Styre is part of the Sontaran G3 Military Assessment Survey, experimenting on the humans to try to determine their resistance to battle, as Earth has now taken on a strategic importance in the Sontarans' ongoing war with the Rutans. The Doctor interrupts Styre's experiments and challenges him to unarmed combat. The Sontaran readily agrees but has not realised that Earth's unfamiliar gravity will give the agile Doctor the advantage. While the Doctor is keeping Styre occupied, Harry enters the alien's spacecraft and removes the terrulium diode bypass transformer, so that when Styre, exhausted by the fight, returns to revitalise himself, he is instead drained of all his energy and destroyed.

As a final warning to the main Sontaran fleet, the Doctor sends a message to them, telling of their emissary's destruction and warning that without Styre's report they cannot know the strength of human resistance and so had better look elsewhere – brinkmanship at its most effective.

The Doctor and his friends use the transmat with the intention of returning to the beacon – they have good news for Vira.

WHO FAX

● Novelised as *Doctor Who and the Sontaran Experiment* by Ian Marter in 1978.

● Story released on BBC Home Video in 1991.

● The working title for this story was *The Destructors*.

● Kevin Lindsay, who had previously played the Sontaran Linx in *The Time Warrior*, returned to play Styre. As the actor suffered from a heart condition (resulting in him collapsing at one point during the recording of *The Time Warrior*) Styre's latex mask and helmet were redesigned to be less bulky and to give better ventilation for breathing. Lindsay also played the Sontaran Marshal, seen only on a monitor screen when Styre, and later the Doctor, reported progress.

● One of the Galsec humans, Krans, was played by Glyn Jones, who had previously written *The Space Museum* back in 1965.
● During the recording on Sunday, 29 October 1976, Tom Baker slipped and broke his collar bone. Following this accident, Baker had to do his scenes with his scarf and coat concealing a neck-brace.
● Field-Major Styre had five fingers on each hand, rather than three as sported by Linx in *The Time Warrior*.

COMMENT

The Sontaran Experiment *is a welcome diversion from the other stories in the twelfth season. Because the location work is very effective, the viewer is left with a feeling of believability which is often missing from studio-based stories.*

Kevin Lindsay again turns in an excellent performance as the lone Sontaran officer, and the rest of the cast go through their paces with a high degree of conviction. The only less than satisfactory aspect is Styre's robot, which somehow lacks any true menace, being rather too ungainly to constitute a believable threat.

Genesis of the Daleks (4E)

EP	DATE	TIME	DURN	VIEWERS	CHART POS
1	08.03.75	17.30	24'30"	10.7	23
2	15.03.75	17.30	24'51"	10.5	15
3	22.03.75	17.30	22'38"	8.5	42
4	29.03.75	17.31	23'38"	8.8	36
5	05.04.75	17.30	23'27"	9.8	30
6	12.04.75	17.55	23'30"	9.1	26
Repeat Compilation					
	27.12.75	14.59	85'53"	7.6	56
Repeat (Episodes edited into two omnibus editions)					
1	26.07.82	19.24	45'05"	4.9	76
2	02.08.82	19.24	44'54"	5.0	69

PRODUCTION DETAILS

Location and Ealing filming: January 1975

Studio: 27.01.75, 28.01.75 in TC1, 10.02.75, 11.02.75 in TC8, 24.02.75, 25.02.75 in TC6

The Time Lords intercept the transmat beam and unceremoniously dump the Doctor, Sarah and Harry in what appears to be a quarry in a battle zone. A lone Time Lord emissary explains to the Doctor that they have decided the time has come to do something about the Daleks. They would like him to prevent their development or change it so that they become less aggressive and less of a threat to the future of the universe. The Doctor reluctantly agrees — what choice does he have? — and learns that the battlefield on which they have arrived is on Skaro, just before the Daleks are due to be created.

The Doctor and Harry are captured by the Kaleds, a humanoid race engaged in a thousand-year war with the Thals, by whom Sarah is taken prisoner. The Doctor meets the Kaleds' chief scientist, Davros, who has been crippled and confined to a wheelchair and mobile life support system which looks suspiciously like the base of a Dalek.

Davros has been experimenting with genetic mutations to try and discover what the final mutated outcome will be of all the chemical and radiation weapons which have devastated the planet. Knowing this form, he devises a protective casing in which the last survivors of the Kaled race will live, thus ensuring his race's continuation. What he designs is a mark three travel machine, recognised instantly by the Doctor and Sarah as a Dalek.

Unfortunately Davros is not only a genius, he is also insane and plots with the leaders of the Thals to ensure that his work is not discontinued. The result is that the Dalek machines are activated with Davros's mutants inside them and the killing begins. Davros has ensured that his mutants have an overriding instinct to survive, resulting in a totally ruthless life form which sees all other creatures as a potential threat to itself. The Daleks intend to survive by systematically destroying all life which is not Dalek. This begins with the destruction of most of the Thals but soon moves to include the Kaled Elite Scientific Corps and ultimately Davros himself.

Against this show of power and ruthlessness the Doctor is impotent. He gets the opportunity to destroy the creatures but finds himself unable to take the ultimate step. What gives him the right to wipe out a race of intelligent creatures? Ultimately the decision is taken from him, and although he later changes his mind and tries to destroy the incubator room (a task ultimately and inadvertently performed by a Dalek), his intervention means only that the Dalek menace is contained underground for longer than it otherwise would have been.

With the Doctor having achieved as much as he can, the travellers grasp hold of a Time Ring given to them by the Time Lord at the start of the adventure. The ring whisks them off through time and space.

WHO FAX

● Novelised as *Doctor Who and the Genesis of the Daleks* by Terrance Dicks in 1976.

● Story released on BBC Home Video in 1991.

● Michael Wisher rehearsed for his role as Davros with a paper bag over his head.

● *Genesis of the Daleks* was the first time viewers saw the origins of the Daleks on screen. Previously Terry Nation had told a completely different version in the *TV Century 21* Dalek comic strip of the sixties, and the *Radio Times* had also presented an alternative account of their origins in a text story *We are the Daleks!*, again by Nation, in its special publication marking *Doctor Who*'s tenth anniversary.

● This was the last time viewers were to see the Time Lords as powerful and mysterious beings, aloof from other races and able to travel through time and space seemingly at will.

● One of the Nazi-like Kaled officers, Ravon, was played by Guy Siner, now better known as Lieutenant Gruber in *'Allo, 'Allo*. Hilary Minster, who played one of the Thal soldiers, also appears in that series.

● This story had the working title *Genesis of Terror*.

COMMENT

Genesis of the Daleks *is perhaps Terry Nation's greatest contribution to* Doctor Who *after the Daleks themselves. The story is a masterpiece of television drama, drawing on the imagery of the Second World War in its depiction of death, violence, and individuals obsessed with gaining power for themselves. Davros is the ultimate fascist, played to perfection by Michael Wisher and complemented by Peter Miles's studied portrayal of Davros's confidant Nyder. The story is populated with good, well-acted characters, from Ronson and Ravon on the Kaled side, to Sevrin the Muto and Bettan the Thal freedom fighter amongst their opponents. The Daleks take a back seat to the evil, manipulative plans of Davros, and the story races to a climax which decries the effectiveness of war, and which does its best to avoid glamorising the horrors of death*. Genesis of the Daleks *won the* Doctor Who *Appreciation Society's (DWAS) award for best story of the season in a poll taken during 1981*.

Revenge of the Cybermen (4D)

EP	DATE	TIME	DURN	VIEWERS	CHART POS
1	19.04.75	17.36	24'19"	9.5	24
2	26.04.75	17.31	24'24"	8.3	28
3	03.05.75	17.51	24'32"	8.9	25
4	10.05.75	17.31	23'21"	9.4	22

PRODUCTION DETAILS

Location filming: c. 20.11.74

Studio: 02.12.74, 03.12.74 (studio unknown), 16.12.74, 17.12.74 in TC3

Instead of returning them to the TARDIS, the Time Ring takes the travellers back to the Ark, but to the 29th century, many thousands of years earlier: a time when as Nerva Beacon, it was warning space traffic of the existence of a new moon, Neo Phobos, circling Jupiter. This is actually the remains of Voga, nicknamed the Planet of Gold, as that metal can be found there in abundance.

Rather than sit and wait for the TARDIS to turn up – it is travelling back in time to meet them – the Doctor decides to explore, and finds that the beacon has fallen victim to a space plague, spread by Cybermats, which has killed all but a handful of the humans on board.

One of the humans, Kellman, is a traitor working with a small band of Cybermen to invade and destroy Voga, ensuring the removal of a major supply of gold – lethal to the Cybermen as in the form of dust it coats their chest units and suffocates them.

The Cybermen invade the beacon and force the Doctor and the remaining humans – Commander Stevenson and Lester – to carry down into the heart of Voga Cyberbombs which will then be detonated to destroy the planet. What the Cybermen don't know is that Kellman is a double agent, secretly working with one faction of the Vogans on the planet below, the Guardians led by Vorus. Their plan is to lure the Cybermen to the beacon so that the Vogans can launch a missile at it.

The Doctor manages to rid himself of the bomb he has been forced to carry, and prevents the missile from hitting the beacon, which has by now been abandoned by the Cybermen. He then destroys the fleeing Cybermen by giving instructions to aim the missile at their ship instead.

The TARDIS conveniently arrives as the panic subsides and the Doctor, Sarah and Harry slip away to meet the Brigadier who has sent an urgent space/time telegraph message to the Doctor requesting his assistance with a problem on Earth.

WHO FAX

● Novelised as *Doctor Who and the Revenge of the Cybermen* by Terrance Dicks in 1976.

● Story released in edited form on BBC Home Video in 1983. This was the very first *Doctor Who* video release.

● *Revenge of the Cybermen* saw the Cybermen return to the screen in their own story for the first time since *The Invasion* (1968). They had appeared fleetingly in *The War Games* (1969), *The Mind of Evil* (1971) and *Carnival of Monsters* (1973).

● This story used some of the sets from *The Ark In Space*.

● Gerry Davis wrote the script *Return of the Cybermen*, which Holmes then rewrote extensively, adding a new subplot involving the Vogans, as *Revenge of the Cybermen*.

● Stock footage of a Saturn V rocket launch can be seen in part four. This footage was also used in *Genesis of the Daleks*.

COMMENT

In dramatic terms Revenge of the Cybermen *is not bad, but the story is let down on a number of counts. Firstly, the Cybermen had been slowly reduced in menace since* The Tomb of the Cybermen *in 1967, with only two appearing in most of* The Wheel in Space, *and playing second fiddle to Tobias Vaughn and the Cyber-Planner in* The Invasion. *What should have been a return to grace for the creatures ended up as something of a damp squib, as both their appearance and voices lack any of their earlier menace. Secondly, despite a high-quality cast, including Ronald Leigh-Hunt and Kevin Stoney, somehow the characters fail to come alive and there is none of the sense of dramatic urgency which made* The Ark in Space *so effective.*

The location work in Wookey Hole is very well done, and the Vogans work well as an alien race. The other problem with the story, however, is that there is just a little too much running about and not enough solid plot to follow. One of the weaker Tom Baker adventures.

SEASON THIRTEEN

Terror of the Zygons (4F)

EP	DATE	TIME	DURN	VIEWERS	CHART POS
1	30.08.75	17.46	21'41"	8.4	29
2	06.09.75	17.45	25'08"	6.1	61
3	13.09.75	17.47	24'09"	8.2	32
4	20.09.75	17.22	25'22"	7.2	45

PRODUCTION DETAILS

Location filming: c. 20.03.75
Studio: 07.04.75, 08.04.75 in TC3, 22.04.75, 23.04.75 in TC4

The Brigadier has summoned the Doctor as there have been several mysterious attacks on oil rigs in the North Sea off the Scottish coast. The Doctor, somewhat dismissive of the urgency, reluctantly agrees to help. In the meantime, Harry finds a body washed up on the beach, but when he tries to help he is shot by the Caber, a highland gamekeeper employed by the Duke of Forgill.

Harry is taken to the sick bay of the Hibernian Oil Company, where Sarah is attacked by a hideous orange humanoid monster and knocked unconscious. When she comes to she finds herself locked in a pressure chamber.

Investigating all these happenings, the Doctor realises that the oil rigs have been attacked by something huge and monstrous – it later turns out to have been a cyborg called the Skarasen, drawn to the rigs by a homing device, the target reciprocator – and that the attacks are being controlled from Loch Ness. He rescues Sarah but Harry has been abducted and duplicated by the humanoid creatures. The Doctor realises that the Duke of Forgill himself is involved, and in Forgill Castle Sarah discovers an entrance to an underwater spacecraft.

The craft belongs to the Zygons, who centuries ago arrived on Earth, and with their ship crippled, awaited rescue. Their home planet has since been destroyed in a stellar explosion and now they want to take control of the Earth. To this end the Zygon leader Broton has taken on the form of the Duke to infiltrate a World Energy Conference in London which they plan to destroy with the Skarasen.

The Zygons on Earth are destroyed when the Doctor engineers an explosion in their space craft, and Broton is shot by UNIT troops at the Conference. The Skarasen, now without the controlling influence of the target reciprocator, makes its way back to the only home it knows, Loch Ness, there to be occasionally mistaken for the fabled Loch Ness Monster.

The Doctor and Sarah decide to travel back to London by TARDIS, but Harry, feeling that his time with the Doctor has all got a little too much for him, elects for the safer and more reliable method of British Rail.

WHO FAX

● Novelised as *Doctor Who and the Loch Ness Monster* by Terrance Dicks in 1976. Novel renamed *Doctor Who: Terror of the Zygons* in 1993.

● Story released in edited form on BBC Home Video in 1988.

● Working titles for this story were *The Loch Ness Monster*, *The Loch Ness Terror* and *The Zygons*.

● This story was originally planned as a six-parter to end season twelve, but was cut down to four parts at the scripting stage when it was held back to launch season thirteen.

● The design of the Zygons was based partly on the human embryo.

● The effects featuring the Skarasen were achieved using two puppets. The first was three feet long and designed for stop-motion work of the creature moving about on land. The other was a large version of the head and neck section, used mainly for scenes of the monster emerging from the River Thames at the end of part four.

● The Zygons were designed to glow internally by the provision of a series of lights inside the rib cage and the head, all powered from a concealed battery pack. This idea was not used much during recording.

● This was the last story to feature the full UNIT team of the Brigadier, RSM Benton and Harry Sullivan.

● A scene of the TARDIS arriving invisibly at the start of part one was dropped after filming because of technical difficulties discovered during editing.

COMMENT

Terror of the Zygons *is an excellent story let down by just one element – the Skarasen. Douglas Camfield's direction is magnificent, not revealing the Zygons in all their alien glory until the very end of part one, and drawing the viewer into the unfolding narrative. John Woodnutt is superb as both the Duke and as Broton, and Angus Lennie's superstitious Scottish landlord, Angus Ferguson McRanald, comes across as a very memorable character.*

The Skarasen, however, simply does not work. Some of the scenes of it crossing the moors are effective, showing just part of the creature rather than the whole thing, but the story's climax, with the monster popping its head up out of the Thames, is risible and unbelievable. This is a great shame as the rest of the production is flawless.

Planet of Evil (4H)

EP	DATE	TIME	DURN	VIEWERS	CHART POS
1	27.09.75	17.45	24'02"	10.4	19
2	04.10.75	17.46	22'30"	9.9	24
3	11.10.75	18.07	23'50"	9.1	29
4	18.10.75	17.46	23'43"	10.1	26
Repeat					
1	05.07.76	18.37	24'02"	5.0	61
2	06.07.76	18.28	22'30"	5.0	63
3	07.07.76	18.21	23'50"	4.3	87
4	08.07.76	18.26	23'43"	3.9	99

PRODUCTION DETAILS

Ealing filming: June 1975

Studio: 30.06.75, 01.07.75 in TC6, 14.07.75, 15.07.75 in TC3

En route to London, the TARDIS picks up a faint distress call from the edge of the known universe and the Doctor promptly dashes to the rescue.

The TARDIS arrives on the planet Zeta Minor in the Morestran year 37,166, where a Morestran scientific expedition has been slowly killed off by forces unknown. Now only Professor Sorenson is left, and he is not all that he seems to be.

The TARDIS's arrival coincides with that of a military probe ship from Morestra, sent to find out exactly what has happened to their expedition. Sorenson is confused and unable to supply the answer, but when members of the military crew start dying, the logical suspects are the Doctor and Sarah, strangers who just happened to arrive as the killings started.

The real cause is in fact a creature comprised of antimatter, which emerges on to the planet to try to retrieve the antimatter that Sorenson has taken from the crossing point of the two universes, a bottomless black pool deep in the forest.

The creature will not allow the Morestrans to leave with antimatter on board their ship and when they try, the forces that hold it intensify until they are held stationary in space, struggling against the increasing pull back to the planet.

The Doctor realises that Sorenson himself is infected with antimatter and is becoming antiman, a bestial creature capable of draining the life from other beings. The ship's commander, Controller Salamar, who has become increasingly unstable under the great pressures of command, cracks, and goes after Sorenson with a neutron accelerator. Instead of killing him, the radiation from this causes the creature which Sorenson has become to multiply. The ship is soon overrun with snarling deadly creatures, able to walk through doors and intent on sucking the life from the crew.

The Doctor finds the original Sorenson antiman and takes him back to the planet in the TARDIS, pushing him into the pit. This fulfils an earlier bargain the Doctor had made when he too fell into the pit. Sorenson is returned intact, and the Morestran ship is released.

The Doctor takes Sorenson back to the Morestran ship and then he and Sarah leave to try to keep their appointment with the Brigadier in London.

WHO FAX
● Novelised as *Doctor Who and the Planet of Evil* by Terrance Dicks in 1977.
● The appearance of the antimatter creature was inspired by the creature from the Id in the 1956 film *Forbidden Planet*; and Robert Louis Stevenson's classic 1886 story *The Strange Case of Doctor Jekyll and Mister Hyde* was an influence on the story's plot.

- This was the first time viewers saw the TARDIS interior in a Fourth Doctor story. The set was, however, constructed for the following serial in transmission order, *Pyramids of Mars*, which was recorded first.
- Salamar was played by Prentis Hancock, fresh from playing Paul Morrow in the first season of *Space: 1999*.

COMMENT

Planet of Evil *is an effective shocker. It starts out as one thing and then turns into another along the way. Initially viewers believe that the menace is coming from the planet, with first the Morestran survey team and then the military force succumbing to its life-draining powers, but then the threat transfers to Professor Sorenson himself, whose fine portrayal by Frederick Jaeger steals the show.*

The rest of the cast are competent, and even Prentis Hancock's unstable Controller Salamar works within the confines of the story – even if this is the same type of character he always seems to play. The effects are very good indeed, and the jungle of Zeta Minor is one of the most convincingly realised alien environments ever seen on television.

Pyramids of Mars (4G)

EP	DATE	TIME	DURN	VIEWERS	CHART POS
1	25.10.75	17.47	25'22"	10.5	28
2	01.11.75	17.48	23'53"	11.3	15
3	08.11.75	17.46	24'32"	9.4	37
4	15.11.75	17.45	24'52"	11.7	22
Repeat Compilation					
	27.11.76	17.51	62'25"	13.7	7

PRODUCTION DETAILS

Location filming: 29.04.75-02.05.75

Studio: 19.05.75, 20.05.75 in TC3, 02.06.75, 03.06.75 in TC6

Sarah, investigating the TARDIS's wardrobe, has found a dress previously worn by the second Doctor's companion Victoria. She is showing it off to the Doctor when the TARDIS is buffeted by an external force and a hideous jackal-like face appears in the console room, terrifying Sarah.

The TARDIS arrives on Earth, but the alien contact has pushed the ship off course slightly, and instead of arriving at UNIT HQ in the present day, the Doctor and Sarah find themselves in an old priory in the year 1911. The priory stands on the same site that UNIT HQ will occupy in the future.

The priory belongs to Professor Marcus Scarman, an archaeologist and Egyptologist. Scarman is in Egypt and a mysterious Egyptian, Ibrahim Namin, is looking after his affairs until he returns. Dr Warlock, a friend of Marcus's, grows suspicious when he finds that he is unable to contact him. He confronts Namin in the priory but can get no information from him. When he has left to see Laurence Scarman, Marcus's brother, Namin activates his servants – walking mummies – and prepares to speak to his true master through an upright sarcophagus, actually the portal to a space/time tunnel through which Sutekh the Destroyer, an Osiran worshipped as a god by the ancient Egyptians, plans again to walk the Earth. Sutekh took over the mind and body of Marcus Scarman when the latter excavated the pyramid in which he was trapped, and he sends this walking cadaver back to Namin via the space/time tunnel. Namin is killed and Sutekh, through Scarman, sets about making arrangements to free himself from the pyramid where his brother Horus trapped him aeons ago.

Sutekh seals off the priory from the outside world and instructs his servicer robot servants (the mummies) to construct a rocket which will destroy a pyramid on Mars which is sending a signal holding him trapped on Earth. The Doctor tries to stop the rocket by detonating a box of explosive in it, but Sutekh prevents the explosion by force of will and the Doctor has no choice but to travel to Sutekh's pyramid via the space/time tunnel and distract the Osiran so that the rocket will be destroyed. This places the Doctor under Sutekh's control and he is returned to the priory in order that he may transport Scarman to Mars. There, Scarman can ensure that the bonds which hold Sutekh are finally broken.

Scarman, with Sutekh's help, navigates the puzzles which guard the way into the pyramid on Mars and switches off the power. The Doctor, now free of Sutekh's influence, realises that there is a time delay between Mars and Earth. He rushes back to Earth and connects equipment from the TARDIS to the space/time tunnel, extending its end point into the far future. Sutekh, travelling down the tunnel, is unable to reach the end in his lifetime, and dies. The energy from the tunnel sets fire to the priory which burns down as the Doctor and Sarah leave.

WHO FAX

● Novelised as *Doctor Who and the Pyramids of Mars* by Terrance Dicks in 1976.

● Story released in edited form on BBC Home Video in 1985.

● Although the script states that Sarah Jane is wearing an old dress of Victoria Waterfield's, it is not a costume which had previously been used in the series.

● The Doctor's age is given as 750 years old.

● *Pyramids of Mars* was voted best story of the season by the *Doctor Who* Appreciation Society in their first-ever season poll.

● The story was originally commissioned from writer Lewis Griefer, but Robert Holmes completely rewrote the scripts; the pseudonym Stephen Harris was used on transmission. Griefer's original story involved alien seeds hidden in the British Museum and mummies chasing around the exhibits.

COMMENT

Mysterious Egyptians, walking mummies, animated cadavers and an all-powerful super-villain add up to a very enjoyable adventure for the Doctor and Sarah. Again the quality of the cast is superb, with Bernard Archard chilling as the possessed Marcus Scarman and Michael Sheard excellent as his brother Laurence. Although Gabriel Woolf has little to do except sit, never revealing his face, his creation of Sutekh through voice alone is evocatively powerful, and well conveys the amorality of the being.

It is the incidental touches which make this adventure so good. There is the Marconiscope which picks up the beamed warning from Mars; the character of Ernie Clements, the luckless poacher; and the interplay between the Doctor and Sarah, particularly when she believes him to be dead.

The Android Invasion (4J)

EP	DATE	TIME	DURN	VIEWERS	CHART POS
1	22.11.75	17.47	24'21"	11.9	17
2	29.11.75	17.46	24'30"	11.3	24

| 3 | 06.12.75 | 17.47 | 24'50" | 12.1 | 14 |
| 4 | 13.12.75 | 17.56 | 24'30" | 11.4 | 15 |

PRODUCTION DETAILS

Location filming: 22.07.75–25.07.75
Studio: 11.08.75, 12.08.75 in TC3, 25.08.75, 26.08.75 in TC8

The Doctor and Sarah arrive on what appears to be Earth, at what they hope is the correct time, and try to make contact with UNIT. The local English village of Devesham seems deserted until all the villagers arrive in a lorry, driven by silent white-suited and space-helmeted men. The villagers act strangely, remaining silent and immobile until the clock chimes, when they all instantly start to behave normally.

The Doctor is immediately suspicious and his suspicions are confirmed when he is attacked and chased by the white-suited men, who are in fact androids with guns in their index fingers.

The TARDIS dematerialises of its own accord after Sarah inserts the key in the lock, and the Doctor realises that this is not Earth. It is in fact the planet Oseidon, home of the Kraals, who have created an exact replica of Devesham and its nearby Space Defence Station in order to test their android villagers prior to a full invasion of Earth.

The Kraals are being helped by a human astronaut, Guy Crayford, who is resentful at his fellow humans who he believes abandoned him in space. The Kraals have convinced Crayford that they rescued him and rebuilt him after a crash, and he discovers too late that this is a lie to gain his trust.

Styggron, the Kraal leader, intends to infect the humans on Earth with a virulent virus and to replace prominent figures with his androids causing as much disruption as possible and thus weakening resistance to the planned invasion. The TARDIS has travelled on to Earth alone, and the Doctor and Sarah are forced to travel in Crayford's rocket, the XK5 space freighter, which is also being used to carry the spearhead of the Kraal invasion. Arriving on Earth, they try to persuade UNIT troops at the Space Defence Station that there is an invasion imminent, but the Brigadier is away in Geneva, and Guy Crayford is being hailed by all as a hero. The Doctor manages to jam the control frequency of the now active android duplicates (including copies of himself, Harry Sullivan and RSM Benton), and prevents Styggron from releasing his virus.

Styggron accidentally infects himself during a fight with the android Doctor and is killed.

The Doctor and Sarah leave UNIT to clear up and to deal with the explanations, while they slip back to the TARDIS.

WHO FAX

● Novelised as *Doctor Who and the Android Invasion* by Terrance Dicks in 1978.

● This story saw John Levene making his final appearance as RSM Benton and Ian Marter as Harry.

● Nicholas Courtney was not available to play the part of the Brigadier, and his lines were instead given to Colonel Faraday, played by the late Patrick Newell.

● This was the first non-Dalek story written for *Doctor Who* by Terry Nation since *The Keys of Marinus* (1964).

● The shots of Crayford's rocket taking off in part three were actually stock footage from NASA of a Saturn V blasting off.

● This story came bottom in the first DWAS season poll.

● Working title: *The Kraals*.

COMMENT

The Android Invasion *suffers because it follows an exceptional run of very strong stories. However, Terry Nation's script is entertaining and well thought out. All the characters work well, in particular Milton Johns' Guy Crayford who comes across very sympathetically. The Kraals look good but somehow fail to impress. The androids are, however, well realised, in particular when the android Sarah is unmasked, and in the sequences at the end when the Doctor battles the android Doctor.*

The opening is particularly memorable, with a UNIT soldier running jerkily through the woods straight towards and over a sheer drop.

The Brain of Morbius (4K)

EP	DATE	TIME	DURN	VIEWERS	CHART POS
1	03.01.76	17.56	25'25"	9.5	30
2	10.01.76	17.47	24'46"	9.3	32
3	17.01.76	17.46	25'07"	10.1	23

4	24.01.76	17.55	24'18"	10.2	28
Repeat Compilation					
	04.12.76	17.51	60'31"	10.9	17

PRODUCTION DETAILS

Studio: 06.10.75, 07.10.75 in TC1, 20.10.75, 21.10.75 in TC3, 24.10.75 (studio unknown)

The Time Lords again divert the Doctor from his intended destination, and bring the TARDIS to the planet Karn, where Doctor Menhedri Solon is engaged in creating a new, patchwork body for his master Morbius, an evil dictator whose brain he rescued after Morbius was destroyed by the Time Lords for his crimes.

The Doctor joins forces with the ancient Sisterhood of Karn to defeat Morbius, and to ensure that his brain is finally destroyed.

WHO FAX

● Novelised as *Doctor Who and the Brain of Morbius* by Terrance Dicks in 1977.

● Story released as a one-hour compilation on BBC Home Video in 1984 and in an episodic version in 1990.

● See chapter 6 on the making of this story for a full synopsis and details of how a *Doctor Who* adventure was brought to the screen during Tom Baker's era.

COMMENT

The Brain of Morbius *works both as a piece of good drama and as an entertaining piece of* Doctor Who. *This is due in part to very strong performances from Philip Madoc as Solon and Cynthia Grenville as Maren. The sets are also noteworthy, especially as the story has no location work and no filming at Ealing Studios. Particularly impressive is Morbius's citadel; and the ultimate appearance of the Morbius Monster and the ensuing mind-battle are generally regarded as classic scenes from the programme.*

Working against the story are the studio-bound setting and the obvious limitations in budget compared with the classic Frankenstein *films of the thirties. However, the production manages to rise above these limitations and director Christopher Barry makes the most of his cast and the space available to present a marvellous example of the Gothic and macabre mixed in with* Doctor Who's *own unique formula.*

The Seeds of Doom (4L)

EP	DATE	TIME	DURN	VIEWERS	CHART POS
1	31.01.76	18.01	24'10"	11.4	16
2	07.02.76	17.31	24'09"	11.4	30
3	14.02.76	17.57	24'51"	10.3	32
4	21.02.76	17.47	24'26"	11.1	23
5	28.02.76	17.48	25'06"	9.9	26
6	06.03.76	17.47	21'51"	11.5	15

PRODUCTION DETAILS

Location filming/OB: 27.10.75–31.10.75

Studio: 17.11.75, 18.11.75, 01.12.75, 02.12.75 in TC4, 15.12.75, 16.12.75 in TC8

Following the adventure on Karn, the Doctor and Sarah return to Earth. Some time later news reaches them that a strange, unidentified vegetable pod has been discovered in the Antarctic by John Stevenson's research team at Camp Five. The Doctor's suspicions are aroused and he and Sarah hurry to the scene.

The pod is from a Krynoid, an alien vegetable which feeds on a host planet's animal life until the planet is dead. In the course of investigating the pod, the scientists at the Antarctic had fed it, causing it to germinate, taking over the body of Charles Winlett, one of their team. As Winlett slowly mutates into a plant creature, so its lust for blood grows and it escapes, running wild on the base.

News of the pod is leaked by an unscrupulous politician working for the World Ecology Bureau and reaches botanist and plant collector Harrison Chase, who decides that he has to add this unique specimen to his collection. He despatches his henchman Scorby and botanist Arnold Keeler to bring the pod back. They take possession of a second pod which had been discovered and set explosives to destroy the base before returning to England, leaving Sarah tied up beside the bomb. The Doctor manages to rescue Sarah and traps the Krynoid with the bomb just before it detonates.

The Doctor and Sarah return to London on the trail of the second pod and trace it to Chase's mansion. They gain access to the grounds with the help of Amelia Ducat, an ageing painter of flora, but are caught by the patrolling guards. Chase realises that he has to investigate what Keeler and Scorby have told him about the infected human at the Antarctic base, and arranges for the pod to be germinated under controlled conditions while a human host is forcibly held nearby. Unfortunately the host turns out to be Sarah.

The Doctor rescues his companion in the nick of time, but Keeler is less lucky and is infected by the plant. His transformation into a Krynoid is accelerated by Chase who arranges for him to be fed. Growing in strength, the Keeler-creature escapes from captivity and goes on the rampage through Chase's estate, growing stronger and larger by the hour.

Eventually the Krynoid grows to giant proportions, dwarfing Chase's house. Chase, by now totally insane, decides to turn the Doctor into compost for his garden by feeding him into a pulverising machine. The Doctor escapes this grisly fate, but Chase is not so lucky and falls into the grinder following a struggle.

Meanwhile UNIT, led by Major Beresford, have been called in and they arrange to bomb the Krynoid before it can pollenate and spread its pods across the Earth.

After all the excitement, the Doctor and Sarah decide that they need a holiday on Cassiopeia, but much to Sarah's dismay the ever-unpredictable TARDIS takes them back to the Antarctic.

WHO FAX

● Novelised as *Doctor Who and the Seeds of Doom* by Philip Hinchcliffe in 1977.

● An Axon costume from *The Claws of Axos* (1972) was painted green and reused as the humanoid Krynoid.

● A scene of Keeler strapped to a bed, struggling to resist eating a plate of raw meat as the Krynoid within him slowly takes control, was cut by producer Philip Hinchcliffe as being too terrifying.

● In this story the Doctor gives his age as 749.

● This was the last story to feature UNIT as an ongoing organisation until *Battlefield* (1989).

● The first two episodes bore plot similarities to the 1951 Christian Nyby film *The Thing from Another World*. The story was also reminiscent of numerous hostile-plants-attack-mankind tales like John Wyndham's *The Day of the Triffids* and, on TV, *The Quatermass Experiment* (1953) and the *Out of the Unknown* episode 'Come Buttercup, Come Daisy, Come . . .?' (1965).

● This was the final serial directed by Douglas Camfield before his death in 1984.

● Production of the serial was plagued with problems including a flu epidemic hitting the cast, an actor being injured in a car crash and replaced, and part one's edited tape going temporarily missing shortly before transmission.

COMMENT

This story, although written as a six-parter by Robert Banks Stewart, can easily be viewed as a two-parter followed by a four-parter. In the former the main setting is an isolated one – an Antarctic base where something very nasty is growing. The Doctor and Sarah arrive in time to save the day, and viewers are introduced to the link to the remainder of the story in the person of Harrison Chase. Tony Beckley's obsessive collector of flora is another in a long line of well-characterised and chillingly memorable villains, and here he is well matched against Sylvia Coleridge's magnificent Amelia Ducat. These two characters seem to have all the best lines as the Doctor and Sarah muddle through a tangled plot of desires and intrigues before the military arrive to blow everything up.

The Seeds of Doom is fast paced and enjoyable, and the Krynoid is also effective, although it works better as a tragic half-man than as a mobile blob of greenery.

SEASON FOURTEEN

The Masque of Mandragora (4M)

EP	DATE	TIME	DURN	VIEWERS	CHART POS
1	04.09.76	18.12	24'31"	8.3	40
2	11.09.76	18.07	24'44"	9.8	22
3	18.09.76	18.12	24'34"	9.2	29
4	25.09.76	18.13	24'45"	10.6	23

PRODUCTION DETAILS

Location filming: April 1976
Studio: 03.05.76–07.05.76, 08.06.76 in TC3

The Doctor and Sarah are investigating some unfamiliar areas of the TARDIS and come across the secondary control room, wood panelled and with a smaller central control console. Switching on the scanner, the Doctor realises that they are coming close to the Mandragora Helix, a spiral of energy radiating outwards with a controlling influence at the centre.

The TARDIS is captured by the Helix and drawn to a still point at its centre. After a brief look outside, the Doctor dematerialises the ship, but a sparkling piece of Mandragora energy has entered the TARDIS and emerges at the next point of call, Earth towards the end of the 15th century. The Doctor and Sarah find that they are in Italy in the Dukedom of San Martino, and realise that the Mandragora energy is loose and up to no good.

The energy enters an underground temple where the outlawed star-worshipping Brotherhood of Demnos gathers, and reveals itself to them during one of their ceremonies. The worshippers, led by the court astrologer Hieronymous, are awed and Hieronymous receives instructions to make ready for Mandragora's full appearance.

Hieronymous is one of the pawns in the evil Count Federico's plans to take control of the Dukedom for himself. He has already arranged for the old Duke to die under 'mysterious circumstances' as predicted by the stars, and is planning for the same to happen to the new Duke, Giuliano. Hieronymous, increasingly under the influence of Mandragora, realises that the Doctor is a threat and hypnotises Sarah with instructions to kill him.

The Doctor becomes aware of the trap when Sarah innocently asks how she can speak and understand the local language – something that had not previously bothered her in all the times and places she had visited. He de-hypnotises her and makes arrangements to remove Mandragora's influence from Earth. At the height of a masked ball, the Brethren of Demnos attack the court, and Hieronymous, who has now been completely taken over by Mandragora, confronts the Doctor in the underground temple. The Doctor has earthed himself and the altar so that as the Helix energy blasts him it is carried safely away. In this way he drains all the Mandragora energy on Earth, leaving the planet safe, at least until the constellations are again in the correct configuration for the Helix to re-establish contact.

WHO FAX
- Novelised as *Doctor Who and the Masque of Mandragora* by Philip Hinchcliffe in 1977.
- Story released on BBC Home Video in 1991.
- Provisional titles for this story were *The Catacombs of Death* and *The Curse of Mandragora*.
- As well as a new TARDIS interior, this adventure also saw a new TARDIS exterior prop being used. This was both lighter than the original and easier to transport.
- It is revealed that the reason Sarah can understand Italian (and other alien tongues) is that this is a Time Lord gift which the Doctor allows her to share.

COMMENT
This is one of the most impressive historical adventures presented by Doctor Who. *The attention to period detail is evident in all aspects, from the elegant costumes to the lavish sets, and a top-rate cast, including a young Tim Piggott-Smith, turn in faultless performances.*

Norman Jones's Hieronymous tends to steal the show but then that is only to be expected as he is the lead 'baddie', and even Sarah Jane has a little more to do than usual, allowing Elisabeth Sladen room further to develop her character.

The location filming in the village of Portmeirion adds an authentic Italian ambience to the story and the special effects, while simply achieved, look impressive on the screen.

The Hand of Fear (4N)

EP	DATE	TIME	DURN	VIEWERS	CHART POS
1	02.10.76	18.11	24'50"	10.5	24
2	29.10.76	17.51	24'48"	10.2	29
3	16.10.76	18.07	24'22"	11.1	20
4	23.10.76	18.03	25'00"	12.0	19

PRODUCTION DETAILS

Location filming: c. 15.06.76

Studio: 05.07.76–07.07.76, 19.07.76, 20.07.76 in TC8

The Doctor and Sarah return to present-day Earth when the TARDIS arrives in a deserted quarry, silent except for the howl of a warning klaxon. Too late they realise that the quarry has been set with explosives. Sarah is buried under rubble from a massive explosion.

As the quarry men and the Doctor frantically search for her she regains consciousness to find herself entombed. Seeing a hand reaching for her she grasps it only to find that it is a fossil. Some sort of energy moves from the hand into her mind, knocking her unconscious once more.

Sarah is found and taken to hospital where nothing appears to be wrong with her. She comes round and takes a blue-stoned ring from the fossil hand and places it on her own. Light from the ring stuns Doctor Carter, and Sarah leaves the hospital in a trance, taking the fossil hand with her and heading for the nearby Nunton Complex for Research and Development, where she enters the fission room.

The stone hand soaks up all the deadly radiation, comes alive and grows into an alien creature from the planet Kastria. Eldrad was a criminal who plotted to destroy Kastria when he was denied power. He disabled the spatial barriers which held back the solar winds, so that life on the surface became impossible. Caught and sentenced to death, he was placed in an Obliteration Module – a space capsule – which was sent out into deep space. Before the last surviving Kastrians lost contact, the capsule was blown up. However, Eldrad's hand was not totally destroyed and this part of the silicone-based body drifted to Earth where it lay for centuries.

Eldrad, who appears to all intents and purposes female – he patterned his regenerated body on Sarah's – persuades the Doctor to take him back to Kastria where he might reclaim his heritage. There he discovers that his heritage is a dead planet: the Kastrian race is long gone and the race banks of his people were destroyed by the last King, Rokon, and the Kastrian people in a final act of defiance in case Eldrad should ever return. He has his wish: he is King . . . of nothing.

Furious, Eldrad, whose body has now been reconfigured into its proper form, tries to get the Doctor to return him to Earth so that he might rule there instead. The Doctor and Sarah run, and when Eldrad storms after them, they trip him into a deep crevasse using the Doctor's scarf.

The Doctor and Sarah return to the TARDIS where without warning the Doctor receives a summons to return to Gallifrey. He tells Sarah that she must leave him as humans are not permitted on his home world. Sarah is let off the TARDIS supposedly in her home town of Croydon, but does not recognise the street – the Doctor has done it again!

WHO FAX

● Novelised as *Doctor Who and the Hand of Fear* by Terrance Dicks in 1979.

● The provisional title for this story was *The Hand of Time*.

● *The Hand of Fear* marked the last regular appearance of Elisabeth Sladen as Sarah Jane Smith. The character returned in the twentieth-anniversary special, *The Five Doctors* and also in a fifty-minute special, *K-9 and Company*.

● During the explosion in the quarry, one of the cameras recording material from ground level was destroyed. Luckily the film in the case was salvaged and footage was used in the completed programme.

● The Obliteration Module was based on the design of the Martian War Machines in George Pal's 1952 film *The War of the Worlds*.

COMMENT

Not one of the best-remembered Tom Baker adventures, The Hand of Fear *nevertheless has much going for it. The alien Kastrians are well developed as a tragic race, and Eldrad's emergence as their ultimate exterminator is as much a surprise to the viewer as it is to Eldrad himself. Judith Paris's female Eldrad is very well acted; she imbues the character with a sense of tragedy and suppressed power which leaves the viewer unsure whether to trust her or not. When his body is transformed into the male form, Stephen Thorne, who had previously played Azal in* The Dæmons *and Omega in* The Three Doctors, *again uses his voice to great effect.*

As with all Doctor Who *of this period, the location filming is magnificent, adding much to the overall feel and look of the adventure. The scenes set in the power station are very well done, as is the studio sequence when the fossilised hand slowly comes to life.*

The story ends with the Doctor saying an abrupt goodbye to Sarah

Jane. This is certainly not what viewers had been expecting since, as with Jo Grant before her, the Doctor had showed rare affection for Sarah Jane. To have the Doctor show no emotion whatsoever at their parting comes as something of a surprise.

The Deadly Assassin (4P)

EP	DATE	TIME	DURN	VIEWERS	CHART POS
1	30.10.76	18.09	21'13"	11.8	15
2	06.11.76	18.05	24'44"	12.1	11
3	13.11.76	18.07	24'20"	13.0	12
4	20.11.76	18.07	24'30"	11.8	12
Repeat					
1	04.08.77	18.21	21'13"	4.4	72
2	11.08.77	18.21	24'44"	2.6	139
3	18.08.77	18.21	24'14"	3.8	99
4	25.08.77	18.22	24'20"	3.5	104

PRODUCTION DETAILS

Location filming: 26.07.76-30.07.76

Studio: 15.08.76–17.08.76 in TC3, 01.09.76, 02.09.76 in TC8

Experiencing premonitions of the death of the Time Lord President, the Doctor materialises the TARDIS in the cloisters area outside the Capitol on Gallifrey. There it is impounded by the Chancellory guards, led by Commander Hilred, but the Doctor manages to elude them, his escape aided by a mysterious figure in black. He returns to his ship before it is moved into a museum inside the Capitol by order of Chancellor Goth as an example of an antiquated Type 40 TT capsule.

The Doctor discovers that it is Presidential Resignation Day, an important occasion in Time Lord life when the retiring President must name his successor. Speculation is rife as to who his choice might be. Favourite is Chancellor Goth but only the President knows for sure.

Donning the robes of one of the Time Lords, the Doctor arrives in the Panopticon, the centre of the time-honoured ritual. He sees a staser weapon on the balcony aimed at where the President will appear and rushes to prevent the murder. When he arrives, there is no one there, just the staser. Seeing a gun in the crowd as the President appears, he aims the staser and fires ... and the President falls down dead, apparently shot by the Doctor.

The Doctor is arrested for murder and put on trial. At the last moment he invokes Article 17 of the constitution and nominates himself as a presidential candidate. This gives him immunity until after the election, and as it is traditional for the incoming president to pardon all political prisoners, the Doctor seems to have secured his continued existence for the time being.

Further investigation reveals that behind all the machinations is the Master, now past his twelfth and final regeneration. He is a wizened husk, seeking to control the Presidency to obtain the symbols of office, the Sash and the Great Key of Rassilon, which in reality have a far more practical purpose than believed. They are the key to the Eye of Harmony, the legendary source of all Time Lord power.

The Doctor, with the help of Coordinator Engin and Castellan Spandrell, links his mind to the Amplified Panatropic Computer (APC) Net, a giant computer containing the accumulated wisdom of the Time Lords, to try to find out what is going on. In the surreal world of the Matrix he finds himself in a life-or-death struggle with a mysterious hooded opponent. They battle each other through a forest-like virtual reality and the Doctor proves the stronger. His opponent is revealed as Goth, whom the Master has been using as a puppet. Following his defeat in the mind battle, Goth dies.

The Master absconds with the Sash and the Great Key of Rassilon and reveals the Eye of Harmony beneath the Panopticon floor. He starts to disconnect the device so that, using the Sash, he can draw off enough power to enable him to regenerate, but the Doctor manages to stop him before Gallifrey is destroyed. The Master falls down one of the fissures which have opened up in the floor.

Believing his old adversary dead, the Doctor takes his leave of Gallifrey, not seeing that the Master has in fact survived, having absorbed sufficient energy through the Sash. The Master leaves Gallifrey in his own TARDIS, somewhat incongruously disguised as a grand-father clock.

WHO FAX
● Novelised as *Doctor Who and the Deadly Assassin* by Terrance Dicks in 1977.

● Story released on BBC Home Video in 1991.
● Working title: *The Dangerous Assassin.*
● *The Deadly Assassin* saw the Master return to *Doctor Who* for the first time since Roger Delgado's death in Turkey in 1973.
● The Doctor appears without a companion for the only time in the series' history.
● When the story was repeated, the freeze-frame cliffhanger ending to part three was edited out of the original master tape following complaints on the original transmission about the Doctor's face being held underwater. Part four was also slightly edited. This explains the difference in duration of the repeat episodes.
● The story opened with a roller-caption superimposed over the Cloister set with a voice over by Tom Baker: 'Through the millennia, the Time Lords of Gallifrey led a life of peace and ordered calm, protected against all threats from lesser civilisations by their great power. But this was to change. Suddenly, and terribly, the Time Lords faced the most dangerous crisis in their long history . . .'

COMMENT

The Deadly Assassin *was panned by the President of the DWAS when first transmitted and came bottom in the Society's season poll. The main criticism was that it presented a view of the Time Lords completely at odds with what had previously been revealed about them. Despite this, it is an immensely enjoyable and multilayered story, rich in both visuals and action. Peter Pratt's masked and cowled Master is superb and seems to ooze evil, while the Time Lords and their society act as an effective backdrop to the main plot concerning the Doctor, the Chancellor and the Master.*

Part three consists mainly of a nightmare sequence set inside the world of the Matrix, and contains many horrific images and concepts. Many phobic elements are present – spiders; drowning; injection needles – together with other memorable threats to life and limb: being run down by a train; falling off a cliff; being split in two by a sword; being riddled with bullets from an attacking airplane. There is no wonder that this story was selected for special comment by Mary Whitehouse and that overseas the story was either banned or heavily edited. None of this detracts from the fact that The Deadly Assassin *is one of the boldest dramas the programme has yet presented.*

The Face of Evil (4Q)

EP	DATE	TIME	DURN	VIEWERS	CHART POS
1	01.01.77	18.22	24'58"	10.7	23
2	08.01.77	18.30	24'58"	11.1	19
3	15.01.77	18.22	24'40"	11.3	20
4	22.01.77	18.27	24'46"	11.7	19

PRODUCTION DETAILS

Ealing filming: c. 20.09.76
Studio: 11.10.76, 12.10.76, 25.10.76, 26.10.76 in TC3

The TARDIS arrives on an unnamed planet where a tribe of savages, the Sevateem, worship a god called Xoanon. Xoanon speaks to them through their holy man, or shaman, Neeva, and he exhorts them to find a way through a deadly energy barrier which separates them from the forbidden land beyond, which is controlled and enjoyed by the Tesh.

The Doctor finds that his face is also the face of the Evil One – indeed there is a massive carving of it on a cliff near the Sevateem's village. Only one tribe member feels that the Doctor is good. This is Leela, cast out from the tribe for daring to question the wisdom of Xoanon.

Leela helps the Doctor to investigate further, and he discovers that he can get through to the other side of the time barrier by way of passages carved out of the cliff, behind the stone image of his own face.

Xoanon is a super-computer, which arrived on the planet when a space craft from the Mordee Expedition crashed there many years ago. Some of the ship's crew were originally to have surveyed the world for possible colonisation, but then the Doctor arrived on an earlier visit and helped the technicians to repair the computer. Unfortunately he neglected to erase his own personality print which subsequently made it schizophrenic.

The computer then arranged for the crew to be split up: the technicians (Tesh) on the one side and Survey Team 6 (Sevateem) on the other. It began an experiment, raising the Tesh as ascetic telepaths who would tend with religious fervour to its every need, while allowing the Sevateem to descend into savagery.

The Doctor realises his original mistake, and manages to use the reverse memory transfer system to wipe the additional personalities from the computer, leaving it sane and in proper control once more.

Leela, deciding that she no longer wants to stay on her own planet, pushes her way into the TARDIS, much to the Doctor's chagrin. It seems he has gained another companion.

WHO FAX

● Novelised as *Doctor Who and the Face of Evil* by Terrance Dicks in 1978.

● Leela, played by Louise Jameson, is introduced.

● One of the voices of Xoanon was played by six-year-old Anthony Frieze, who had won a competition to visit the *Doctor Who* set. He was permitted to say one line – 'Who am I?' – which was ultimately used as the climax of part three.

● The timing of the Doctor's first encounter with Xoanon was said in Terrance Dicks's novelisation of this story to have been immediately after his regeneration in *Robot*. This was not derived from any information given in the televised version.

● Working title: *The Day God Went Mad*.

● The mad computer was inspired by Harry Harrison's *Captive Universe*.

● Leela was based on a cross between Mrs Emma Peel from *The Avengers* and the terrorist Leila Khalid.

COMMENT

The Face of Evil *contains much that is good, but overall the production is unmemorable. On the good side there are strong performances from David Garfield as the Sevateem's high priest Neeva and from Brendan Price as Leela's friend Tomas, but the remainder of the Sevateem and the Tesh are faceless, lacking any true character and existing merely to provide the required number of bodies for the fight scenes. The sets are unimaginative, the Sevateem's forest is unremarkable and the clinical corridors of the Tesh are . . . corridors.*

The plot strains credulity by suggesting that the Doctor's tampering brought the whole thing about, and that a computer could develop god-like powers of its own volition.

The Robots of Death (4R)

EP	DATE	TIME	DURN	VIEWERS	CHART POS
1	29.01.77	18.20	24'06"	12.8	14
2	05.02.77	18.22	24'15"	12.4	17
3	12.02.77	18.23	23'51"	13.1	15
4	19.02.77	18.26	23'42"	12.6	18
Repeat (episodes 1 & 2 and 3 & 4 edited together)					
1	31.12.77	18.28	46'01"	10.0	29
2	01.01.78	16.45	45'24"	7.0	80

PRODUCTION DETAILS

Ealing filming: 02.11.76–05.11.76

Studio: 22.11.76, 23.11.76, 05.12.76–07.12.76 (studio unknown)

Leela and the Doctor arrive in the scoop of a massive sandminer, Storm Mine 4, which is combing an alien world for precious ores (lucanol and zelanite amongst others) for the controlling company.

The miner is run by Commander Uvanov and his small human crew aided by numerous robots which are split into three classes: in overall control is a single Super Voc, under him come the Voc class robots, and at the bottom of the hierarchy are the mute Dum robots. Almost as soon as the Doctor and Leela escape from the scoop and into the main part of the ship, just prior to a sandstorm, mysterious deaths start to occur, beginning with the strangulation of mineralogist Chub.

The humans are picked off one by one by an unknown and unseen killer. The remaining crew immediately suspect the Doctor and Leela, but the time travellers are able to convince Chief Mover Poul, a government agent working with D84, another Super Voc posing as a Dum, that they are not the killers.

The culprit is revealed to be one of the human crew, Chief Fixer Dask, who is in reality the scientist Taren Capel. Capel was raised by robots and regards them as superior to humans. He has been reprogramming the robots on the mine to kill the humans leaving a totally robot community.

The Doctor manages to trick Capel into outlining his plans for conquest while a helium canister discharges itself into the room.

Capel's voice is altered by the gas, and a rogue SV7 kills him as it cannot recognise its master's voice and has been ordered to kill all other humans.

WHO FAX

- ● Novelised as *Doctor Who and the Robots of Death* by Terrance Dicks in 1979.
- ● Story released in edited form on BBC Home Video in 1986.
- ● The designer, Ken Sharp, based his concept for the look of the sandminer and the robots on an art deco style. This idea was carried forward into the make-up and the costumes for the human crew.
- ● This story saw the final appearance of the TARDIS's secondary control room, introduced in *The Masque of Mandragora*.
- ● Commander Uvanov was played by Russell Hunter, better known as Lonely in *Callan*.
- ● The music played to the crew in part one is 'None but the Weary Heart' by Tchaikovsky and 'Girl with the Flaxen Hair' by Debussy.
- ● The sandminer was inspired by a similar ship in Frank Herbert's *Dune*.

COMMENT

Doctor Who *generally works well when it is borrowing from another source, and* The Robots of Death'*s reworking of Agatha Christie's* Ten Little Niggers *is a case in point.*

This story is simply gorgeous to look at, with the scenic design complementing perfectly the costumes and the make-up. Star of the show is Miles Fothergill's unemotional SV7, with Gregory de Polnay's D84 coming a close second. The human cast are also noteworthy with Russell Hunter (Uvanov), David Collings (Poul) and Pamela Salem (Toos) turning in fine performances in exceptionally well-characterised parts.

Once again the effects are superb, and the modelwork of the sandminer on the surface of the planet is top rate. The music too is worthy of mention as composer Dudley Simpson gave the robots a throbbing heartbeat-like theme which builds the tension as they start to pick off the human crew one by one.

The Talons of Weng-Chiang (4S)

EP	DATE	TIME	DURN	VIEWERS	CHART POS
1	26.02.77	18.32	24'44"	11.3	16
2	05.03.77	18.37	24'26"	9.8	28
3	12.03.77	18.32	21'56"	10.2	22
4	19.03.77	18.32	24'30"	11.4	21
5	26.03.77	18.31	24'49"	10.1	18
6	02.04.77	18.31	23'26"	9.3	32

PRODUCTION DETAILS

Location filming: c. 13.12.76

OB: 08.01.77–13.01.77

Studio: 24.01.77, 25.01.77, 08.02.77-10.02.77 (studio unknown)

The Doctor takes Leela to Victorian London, circa 1889, so that she may see how her ancestors lived. He plans to take her to a music hall, but on their way there they witness the abduction of a man, Buller, by a group of Chinese coolies. Leela incapacitates one of the thugs until the police arrive. The Doctor then learns of other disappearances, and, intrigued, makes friends with the police pathologist, Professor Litefoot. He discovers that hairs taken from the clothing of one of the victims found floating in the Thames seem to have originated from a very large rat.

The Doctor explores the sewers and discovers that there are indeed giant rats down there. He also notes that the course of the river Fleet, which empties into the Thames, runs directly underneath the Palace Theatre which is central to the numerous disappearances.

His investigations lead him to Li H'sen Chang, a stage magician at the theatre, and from Chang to an ancient Chinese god, Weng-Chiang, who has apparently been reincarnated on Earth.

Weng-Chiang is in fact Magnus Greel, a war criminal from the 51st century whose experiments in time brought him back to 19th-century China. There, his appearance from nowhere prompted his elevation by Chang and his friends to the status of a god. The journey through time has disrupted his molecular structure and Greel needs to feed on the life force drained from human victims, the younger and more vital the better. His precious time cabinet had been lost to him, however, and his travels (aided by a locator) have brought him and his entourage to

Victorian London where he has discovered that the cabinet is in the possession of Litefoot.

Infiltrating Litefoot's home with Chang's ventriloquist doll Mr Sin (an advanced computerised children's plaything with the brain of a pig – unfortunately the pig aspect has taken over and it has become unstable and dangerous), Greel retrieves his cabinet and prepares to travel back to his own time, abandoning his long-time worshipper Chang to death in an opium den.

The Doctor, aided by Leela, Litefoot and the proprietor of the Palace Theatre, Henry Gordon Jago, go to Greel's headquarters, a warehouse lair which is also the centre of the deadly Chinese Tong of the Black Scorpion, and trap Greel before he can escape. He falls into his life force extraction machine and disintegrates before their astonished eyes. The Doctor is then attacked by Mr Sin but manages to disconnect its circuitry, rendering it inanimate.

As the London fog closes in the Doctor and Leela leave in the TARDIS. Jago and Litefoot look on in astonishment.

WHO FAX

● Novelised as *Doctor Who and the Talons of Weng-Chiang* by Terrance Dicks in 1977.

● Story released in edited form on BBC Home Video in 1988.

● Regular *Doctor Who* composer Dudley Simpson had a cameo role as the conductor of the Palace Theatre's orchestra.

● Working title: *The Talons of Greel*.

● Writer Robert Holmes said that the story was influenced by *The Phantom of the Opera* and by the numerous *Fu Manchu* films and books.

● Because the script called for Li H'sen Chang to perform some magic tricks on stage during parts one and four, two advisers, Larry Barnes and Ali Bongo, were brought in to assist.

● The making of *The Talons of Weng-Chiang* was examined in detail in *The Lively Arts* documentary *Whose Doctor Who* in 1977.

● The story was based on an idea from Robert Banks Stewart.

COMMENT

If there is one thing that the BBC does well, it is recreating London at the turn of the century. The Talons of Weng-Chiang *combines the considerable talents of some of the BBC's best designers to create a production which ranks alongside any Dickensian tale. The cast is a treat to watch with John Bennett effortlessly portraying the mesmeric Li H'sen Chang, together with Christopher Benjamin and Trevor Baxter as Jago and Litefoot. The tale transports us with ease into a murky world of intrigue, Chinese tongs, giant rats and an evil, distorted monster from the future.*

Everything about this adventure is superb, with perhaps the sole exception of the aforementioned giant rats, the costumes of which would not look out of place in a pantomime. The Talons of Weng-Chiang ranks among the very best Doctor Who adventures of all time. It's not surprising that this story topped the DWAS's season poll.

SEASON FIFTEEN

Horror of Fang Rock (4V)

EP	DATE	TIME	DURN	VIEWERS	CHART POS
1	03.09.77	18.18	24'10"	6.8	52
2	10.09.77	18.15	24'10"	7.1	51
3	17.09.77	18.18	23'12"	9.8	23
4	24.09.77	18.16	23'49"	9.9	23

PRODUCTION DETAILS

Ealing filming: 04.05.77–06.05.77
Studio: 25.05.77, 26.05.77, 07.06.77–09.06.77 at Pebble Mill

The TARDIS arrives on Fang Rock, a small island off the English coast. It is the first decade of the 20th century and the island's only inhabitants are a trio of lighthouse keepers who operate the recently installed electric light to warn ships off the treacherous rocks close by.

Earlier that evening, the youngest of the keepers, Vince Hawkins, saw a light in the sky fall in the sea, but little realised that it was in fact a Rutan spacecraft, and that the lighthouse would soon have three unearthly visitors.

The Doctor and Leela seek shelter at the lighthouse and are made welcome by Vince and old Reuben. The third keeper, Ben, disappears and his body is later discovered hidden behind the generators – he has been electrocuted.

A passing ship fails to heed the fog warnings and crashes on the rocks. The survivors stumble into the lighthouse to find that they are now all prey to an alien creature which is picking them off one by one. Ben was first, and Reuben is next. The Doctor realises that the creature can change its form and is actually masquerading as Reuben, but this realisation comes too late as the Rutan kills Vince and then the survivors from the wreck.

The Doctor fights back by blasting the Rutan, now reverted to its natural form of an amorphous jelly-creature, with a makeshift mortar bomb which kills it. However, it has been sending a homing signal to its mothership which is now close to Earth.

The Doctor rigs up the lighthouse lamp with a diamond taken from a cache held by one of the now-dead survivors of the shipwreck and creates a powerful laser beam. He focuses it on the Rutan mothership, destroying it.

The Doctor and Leela take their leave of the now deserted lighthouse, leaving only bodies and a mystery in their wake.

WHO FAX

- Novelised as *Doctor Who and the Horror of Fang Rock* by Terrance Dicks in 1978.
- The Rutans had been mentioned in two previous stories, *The Time Warrior* and *The Sontaran Experiment*, as being engaged in a long war with the Sontarans.
- One reference work used extensively by the production team on this story was E. G. Jerrome's *Lighthouses, Lightships and Buoys*.
- Louise Jameson stopped wearing brown contact lenses at the end of this story. The reason given for Leela's consequent change of eye colour was that the flash from the explosion of the Rutan ship caused pigment dispersion in her eyes, changing them from brown to blue.
- Working titles: *The Monster of Fang Rock*, *The Beast of Fang Rock*.
- At the end of the serial, the Doctor recites *The Ballad of Flannen Isle* by Wilfred Gibson.
- This is the only story in which all the characters, except for the Doctor and his companion, die.

COMMENT

Like The Ark in Space, Horror of Fang Rock *is an exercise in minimalism. Instead of a space station there is a lighthouse, the role of the Wirrn is taken by the Rutan and the cast again numbers less than ten and dropping. Considering that it was written by Terrance Dicks in a hurry to fill a gap when his planned story entitled* The Witch Lords *was vetoed by BBC management, it stands up remarkably well. The actors throw their all into the action, and the tension and sense of foreboding generated is almost palpable.*

Conventional visual effects are kept to a minimum, with electronic effects used instead to achieve the required results. Director Paddy Russell manages to get a claustrophobic feel out of her few sets, and the whole production is both memorable and a good season opener.

The Invisible Enemy (4T)

EP	DATE	TIME	DURN	VIEWERS	CHART POS
1	01.10.77	18.20	23'09"	8.6	40
2	08.10.77	18.04	25'13"	7.3	55
3	15.10.77	18.13	23'28"	7.5	65
4	22.10.77	18.13	21'22"	8.3	50
Repeat					
1	13.07.78	19.00	23'09"	4.9	60
2	20.07.78	19.00	25'13"	5.5	76
3	27.07.78	19.01	23'28"	5.1	81
4	03.08.78	19.00	21'22"	6.8	35

PRODUCTION DETAILS

Bray filming: April 1977

Studio: 10.04.77–12.04.77, 24.04.77–26.04.77 in TC6

Hovering in space around the year AD 5000, the TARDIS enters a cloud of energy which shoots lightning-like tendrils into its systems and from there into the Doctor's mind. He has been infected by the Virus, a space-borne intelligence which wishes to spread itself across the universe.

The TARDIS arrives on Titan, one of the moons of Saturn, where a refuelling station has also been taken over by the Virus. The Doctor manages to relay the coordinates of a local hospital asteroid to Leela before he collapses.

At the Bi-Al Foundation, based on asteroid K4067, Professor Marius examines the Doctor and pronounces that there is little he can do. However, the Doctor devises a plan whereby he clones himself and Leela, miniaturises the clones using the relative dimensional stabiliser from the TARDIS, and then has them injected into his body by Marius. There they have to find and destroy the Virus Nucleus.

The plan backfires as the Nucleus escapes from the Doctor in place of the clones and is enlarged to human size. The creature arranges for itself to be taken back to Titan where breeding tanks have been prepared prior to its invasion of the galaxy.

The Doctor, now cured of the Virus's influence, arranges with the help of K-9, Professor Marius's dog-shaped robot computer, for the breeding tanks to be blown up, thus killing the Nucleus.

Marius gives K-9 to the Doctor as a parting gift as the Professor is returning to Earth.

WHO FAX

● Novelised as *Doctor Who and the Invisible Enemy* by Terrance Dicks in 1979.
● Working titles: *The Enemy Within*, *The Invader Within*, *The Invisible Invader*.
● K-9 was a radio-controlled electronic robot dog designed by Tony Harding and built by the BBC Visual Effects Department. One earlier idea for realising K-9 was to use a huge robotic Doberman costume with an actor inside.
● The voice of K-9 was supplied by actor John Leeson who also voiced the Virus Nucleus.
● This story saw a return to the original-style TARDIS control room.
● The decision to keep K-9 on as a regular companion was made fairly late in the day with the result that a means had to be contrived in some of the following stories to incapacitate the dog, as he had not been included in the plot.

COMMENT

Following on from the dramatic treats of the previous season, The Invisible Enemy *comes as something of a disappointment. The much-lauded introduction of K-9 seems a definite backwards step as far as adult viewers are concerned, although the younger generation loved it. The story regrettably has a major failure in the Virus Nucleus which looks like a giant prawn and which is too immobile to do more than wave its arms about. There are other problems too, for example a wall with a barely hidden crack, down which it splits when K-9 blasts it. Frederick Jaeger's somewhat stereotyped Professor Marius, complete with fake Germanic accent, is a world apart from his sensitive portrayal of Professor Sorenson in* Planet of Evil, *and the sequences set inside the Doctor's body, while nice to look at, amount to very little in terms of plot development.*

In the story's favour is some of the best space model work seen on the series. Designed by Ian Scoones, the scenes of the shuttle being attacked by the Virus and then arriving on Titan are especially good.

Image of the Fendahl (4X)

EP	DATE	TIME	DURN	VIEWERS	CHART POS
1	29.10.77	18.12	24'38"	6.7	70
2	05.11.77	18.10	24'44"	7.5	64
3	12.11.77	18.07	24'22"	7.9	63
4	19.11.77	18.14	20'32"	9.1	46

PRODUCTION DETAILS

Location filming: 01.08.77–05.08.77
Studio: 20.08.77, 21.08.77, 04.11.77–06.11.77 in TC6

A 12-million-year-old human skull has been discovered by archaeologists and is being used by Professor Fendelman in his Time Scanner experiments at Fetch Priory on contemporary Earth. Drawn by the operation of the Scanner, the Doctor arrives as the experiments reach a peak. A strange force is called into existence when the Scanner operates, and a hiker has been killed in the woods as well as a security guard at the priory which is being used as a base by the scientists.

One of the scientists, Thea Ransome, is also affected. The skull is exerting an influence over her mind and each time the Scanner operates, the skull glows with power as the connection is strengthened.

The Doctor realises that the skull is a channel through which a powerful and ancient creature called the Fendahl will manifest on Earth. The Fendahl lives by sucking the life from others and it had been thought destroyed by the Time Lords when, following its destruction of life on Mars, it was trapped on the fifth planet in the solar system which disappeared when the Time Lords threw it into a time loop. Since then the creature has been subtly affecting and influencing life on Earth, guiding it to a point where the Fendahl could manifest. It is no coincidence that the scientist in charge of the Time Scanner is called Fendelman, nor that Thea is sensitive to the ancient skull. This is all a part of the Fendahl's plan.

Thea is transformed into the Fendahl core, and a group of acolytes assembled by Maximilian Stael, another scientist who is trying to harness the power of the Fendahl, are all converted into snake-like Fendahleen. Stael kills Fendelman and later commits suicide. The Doctor meanwhile organises the remaining scientist, Colby, together with a local wise-woman Granny Tyler and her son Jack, to defend themselves against the Fendahleen using rock salt loaded into shotgun cartridges. The Doctor then takes the skull back to the TARDIS as the Time Scanner is operated for a final time. The resultant power surge destroys the house and the Fendahl core, while the Doctor aims to dump the skull into a super nova in space and thus destroy the Fendahl's bridgehead.

WHO FAX

● Novelised as *Doctor Who and the Image of the Fendahl* by Terrance Dicks in 1979.

● K-9 appears only briefly in this story – he is suffering from corroded circuitry and stays in the TARDIS.

● Leela wore a new version of her standard costume for this adventure.

● There were two sizes of Fendahleen created for the show. Several small hand-operated versions were made for the sequence in which the Fendahl core converts her followers into the creatures, and one full-sized monster was also built.

● This was the first story in which *Radio Times* credited the lead character as 'The Doctor' rather than as 'Doctor Who'. This did not happen again until *The Power of Kroll*. With *Castrovalva* (1982), the fifth Doctor's debut story, the credit became 'The Doctor' permanently.

● When news of this story was first released by the production office, the title was misheard down the telephone by an over-eager fan, who thought it was *The Island of Fandor*. Ever since then, many people have believed this to be a 'lost' story.

COMMENT

Image of the Fendahl *has never been highly acclaimed, and this is a shame as it is a very effective story. The early sequences of the lone hiker being killed by the unseen Fendahleen are tense and gripping, while the realisation that Thea is somehow linked to the events is well established by the overlapping of the images of her face and the glowing skull.*

Tension is further built by holding back the appearance of the large Fendahleen until the end of part three, and by the slow transformation of Thea into the vengeful Fendahl core.

Once again Dudley Simpson's music adds a superb finish to the whole production which stands up very well indeed.

The Sun Makers (4W)

EP	DATE	TIME	DURN	VIEWERS	CHART POS
1	26.11.77	18.07	24'59"	8.5	48
2	03.12.77	18.05	24'57"	9.5	36
3	10.12.77	18.05	24'57"	8.9	35
4	17.12.77	18.08	24'57"	8.4	42
Repeat					
1	10.08.78	18.21	24'59"	3.2	117
2	17.08.78	19.10	24'57"	6.5	50
3	24.08.78	19.09	24'57"	6.5	49
4	31.08.78	18.46	24'57"	7.1	53

PRODUCTION DETAILS

Location filming: 13.06.77–18.06.77
Studio: 04.07.77, 05.07.77 in TC3, 17.07.77–19.07.77 in TC6

The TARDIS arrives in the city of Megropolis One on Pluto where to the Doctor's amazement there is a warm sun (one of six), oxygen, and a thriving factory community. The people, such as D-grade Citizen Cordo, are not so happy, however, as the Company that controls the planet works them to the bone, pays them a pittance and then taxes them on everything imaginable.

Cordo and the Doctor join up with an underground band of rebels, led by Mandrel, who are out to smash the system, and discovers that the power behind the Company, represented through the human gatherer of taxes, Gatherer Hade, is an Usurian known as the Collector.

The Usurians are notorious for enslaving whole planets through business ventures and then fleecing the inhabitants with exorbitant taxes and other bureaucratic means. The Collector is a particularly nasty and money-grabbing individual who has the population well and truly subjugated while the Company continues to make ever greater profits.

The citizens are kept in line by a calming gas, PCM (pento-cycleinic-methyl-hydrane), distributed throughout the complex. The Doctor manages to stop production of this gas, leaving the enslaved workers free to make up their own minds about the state of affairs.

For the Usurian Collector the Doctor has different plans. He programs the Company computer to apply a 2 per cent growth tax and the Collector, who cannot cope with making a loss, reverts to his natural form – a type of poisonous fungus.

WHO FAX
- Novelised as *Doctor Who and the Sun Makers* by Terrance Dicks in 1982.
- Robert Holmes wrote this story as a satire on the British tax system, and there are numerous in-jokes in the script.
- The part of the rebel Goudry was played by Michael Keating, later to play Vila, one of *Blake's 7*.

COMMENT
As a satire, The Sun Makers *works very well, but it works even better as an enjoyable piece of drama. Holmes's vision of a world in which everything from work to clothes and even death is taxed is very effective. Roy Macready is excellent as citizen Cordo, who finds that he cannot pay his father's death taxes and after meeting the Doctor and Leela joins the resistance.*

Like all great villains, Henry Woolf's Collector and Richard Leech's ebullient Gatherer Hade steal the show. The Collector is played as the ultimate tax official, even down to his wearing a pin-striped kaftan, while Hade is cast from the mould of the high-ranking official who promises the world but always finds a legitimate reason not to come up with the goods.

Underworld (4Y)

EP	DATE	TIME	DURN	VIEWERS	CHART POS
1	07.01.78	18.25	22'36"	8.9	50
2	14.01.78	18.27	21'27"	9.1	37
3	21.01.78	18.31	22'21"	8.9	37
4	28.01.78	18.29	22'53"	11.7	27

PRODUCTION DETAILS

Studio: 03.10.77, 04.10.77, 15.10.77–18.10.77 (studio unknown)

The TARDIS arrives on board a Minyan space craft, the R1C, commanded by a man named Jackson. Jackson and his crew are on a long quest to recover the Minyan race banks from a ship called the P7E which left Minyos aeons ago. The Minyans are suspicious of the Doctor as they know his race of old: the Time Lords shared some of their knowledge with the Minyans, who then proceeded to destroy themselves through war, as they were unable to cope with such advanced technologies.

The R1C is buried in a meteor storm but the Doctor helps the crew to free it. However, it then crashes into another newly formed planet at the heart of which is the P7E.

Inside the new planet the time travellers and the Minyans discover a maze of tunnels and passages. The Doctor eventually makes his way to the centre where the P7E's computer, the Oracle, holds court. The computer was originally programmed to protect the race banks but has gone insane and dominated the Minyan survivors and their descendants. The Oracle allows Jackson to take what appear to be the race banks, but they are in truth imitations containing fission-grenades. The Doctor realises the deception and obtains the real race banks. He then tricks the Oracle's guards into taking the grenades back to their leader. As there is no way of defusing them, they explode, destroying the planet and the P7E and boosting the R1C off on its voyage to Minyos II.

WHO FAX

- Novelised as *Doctor Who and the Underworld* by Terrance Dicks in 1980.
- The sets of the Minyan spacecraft proved much more expensive than anticipated leaving no scenery budget for the scenes set inside the new planet. To overcome this problem, Colour Separation Overlay was used in conjunction with models to give the impression of caves and tunnels.
- Herrick, one of Jackson's crew, was played by actor Alan Lake, the husband of Diana Dors.
- Imogen Bickford-Smith who played Tala, another crew member, was optimistically promoted by her agent as the next *Doctor Who* girl, as Louise Jameson had announced her intention to leave the series.
- This story was inspired by the myth of Jason and the Argonauts' quest for the Golden Fleece.
- *Underworld* came bottom in the DWAS season poll.

COMMENT

Underworld is a classic example of poor visuals ruining what is a clever and thoughtful script. The Colour Separation Overlay completely overshadows the action, with actors occasionally stepping through rocks and walls while tell-tale blue edging appears around them. The story apparently looks better in black and white, but in colour it fails dismally.

This is a great shame as the effects in the opening episode – the TARDIS hovering by a nebula, and the R1C in flight and crashing into the newly formed planet – are brilliant. Only Jackson, played by James Maxwell, stands out amongst the guest cast, as the others seem to go through their paces with little enthusiasm. In particular the Minyan descendants slaving for the Oracle are faceless and forgettable.

The Invasion of Time (4Z)

EP	DATE	TIME	DURN	VIEWERS	CHART POS
1	04.02.78	18.25	25'00"	11.2	28
2	11.02.78	18.24	25'00"	11.4	29
3	18.02.78	18.24	25'00"	9.5	47
4	25.02.78	18.25	23'31"	10.9	28

| 5 | 04.03.78 | 18.27 | 25'00" | 10.3 | 32 |
| 6 | 11.03.78 | 18.25 | 25'44" | 9.8 | 35 |

PRODUCTION DETAILS

Bray filming: 01.11.77, 02.11.77

Studio: 06.11.77–08.11.77 in TC8

Location filming/OB: 14.11.77–18.11.77

OB: 05.12.77–09.12.77, 12.12.77–16.12.77

The Doctor returns to Gallifrey after a suspicious meeting in space with a group of unseen aliens. When he arrives at the Time Lord Capitol he claims the position of Lord President which is his by right as he was the only surviving candidate to the post following the assassination of the former President (see *The Deadly Assassin*). The Doctor commandeers an office and gives orders for it to be decorated with panels beaten from lead. Leela cannot understand what has got into the Doctor as he is behaving irrationally and completely out of character.

The unseen aliens watch as the Doctor sets events in motion to have himself inaugurated as President. He is 'crowned' with a device giving him access to the Matrix and the aliens attempt to pry into this repository of Time Lord knowledge, an intrusion which the Doctor prevents by a massive force of will.

The Doctor then arranges for the transduction barriers around Gallifrey to be destroyed by K-9, and when this is done his alien 'friends' materialise in the Panopticon. They are Vardans, beings which intend to take over Gallifrey.

The Doctor maintains his mind shield against the invaders as K-9 links with the Matrix to work out where their home planet is. He plans to place a time loop around the planet but must make sure the Vardans do not suspect him until he is ready. He banishes Leela to the wastelands of outer Gallifrey as she is in danger of unintentionally jeopardising his plans. There she meets up with a group of outlaw Time Lords who organise an attack on the Capitol to fight off the invaders.

The Doctor finally springs his trap and the Vardans are banished. However, at almost the same time, Gallifrey is invaded by troopers from the Sontaran Special Space Service, who were, unknown to the Doctor, using the Vardans as a bridgehead to enable them to conquer the Time Lords.

The Doctor and Leela, with the help of a few of the Time Lords and a group of the outsiders, dispatch the Sontarans one by one once the invaders have gained access to the TARDIS.

Realising that the Sontarans are after the Matrix, the Doctor uses knowledge extracted from it by K-9 to construct a forbidden demat gun, activated by the Great Key of Rassilon. He uses this to kill the remaining Sontarans in the TARDIS and then confronts the Sontaran leader, Stor, in the Panopticon. Stor intends to destroy the Time Lords' power centre with a bomb, but the Doctor activates the gun as the charge detonates.

The Doctor survives the release of energy although his memory of recent events, including the fact that he has become President, is wiped. He decides to leave Gallifrey as he still has much to achieve in the Universe. Leela announces that she wishes to stay on Gallifrey with Commander Andred, one of the Chancellory guards, with whom she has fallen in love. K-9 also decides to stay with Leela.

As the TARDIS dematerialises, the Doctor pulls out a large box marked 'K9 MII'.

WHO FAX

● Novelised as *Doctor Who and the Invasion of Time* by Terrance Dicks in 1980.

● A great deal of the TARDIS's interior is seen in this story as much of the final two episodes is set there. Among the rooms glimpsed are a swimming pool (described by the Doctor as a bathroom), a changing-room, an art gallery and numerous corridors.

● *The Invasion of Time* was a replacement for *The Killer Cats of Geng Singh* (spelling uncertain) by David Weir, which fell through. It was written by producer Graham Williams and script editor Anthony Read and transmitted under a BBC in-house pseudonym David Agnew.

● The Sontarans in this story reverted to having three fingers on each hand rather than five, as in *The Sontaran Experiment*.

COMMENT

The Invasion of Time *starts well but goes downhill rapidly. The opening shot of a spacecraft flying overhead is similar to the opening of the film* Star Wars *and is just as effective, but when the Doctor appropriates the Presidency on Gallifrey the story starts to lose its impact, as the viewer really has no idea what is going on.*

Credibility is further lost when the Vardans finally appear, first as rather sorry-looking tinfoil shapes hanging in the air, and then as nothing more than a group of human-looking soldiers.

What raises the story temporarily is the totally unexpected and dramatic appearance of the Sontarans, but their impact is completely dissipated when Stor speaks and actor Derek Deadman's Cockney accent emerges in all its misplaced glory. The final two episodes are really nothing more than a protracted chase through the TARDIS and come over as silly. Finally, Leela's decision to stay and marry someone with whom she appears to have exchanged no more than a dozen words is plainly ludicrous.

Despite all these problems, the story won the DWAS's annual poll, proving that there must have been some attraction for the fans.

SEASON SIXTEEN

The Ribos Operation (5A)

EP	DATE	TIME	DURN	VIEWERS	CHART POS
1	02.09.78	17.44	25'02"	8.3	42
2	09.09.78	18.21	24'46"	8.1	36
3	16.09.78	18.32	24'42"	7.9	38
4	23.09.78	18.21	24'50"	8.2	36

PRODUCTION DETAILS
Studio: 09.04.78–11.04.78, 23.04.78–25.04.78 in TC4

The Doctor is set a quest by the White Guardian, a powerful being who monitors and controls time. He is to collect and assemble the Key to Time, the disguised segments of which are scattered through time and space. Once assembled, the Key will be used by the Guardian to restore the balance of the Cosmos. The Doctor has little choice in the matter and is given a new Time Lord assistant, Romanadvoratrelundar, or Romana for short, and a locator to help him find the segments and convert them into their true form.

The first segment is traced to the city of Shur on the planet Ribos where a con man named Garron and his assistant, Unstoffe, are engaged in a scam to sell the entire planet to the Graff Vynda-K, deposed ruler of Levithia, who wants to use Ribos as a base from which to plan the winning back of his throne.

The Graff is particularly interested in Ribos for it is apparently a rich source of jethryk, a rare and very valuable blue mineral vital for space warp drive. His interest is further piqued when he sees a large lump of the mineral in a display case of jewels. Unstoffe, disguised as a guard, tells the Graff an elaborate tale of hidden maps and caves full of the blue mineral, which he claims the locals call scringe-stone.

The Doctor realises that the lump of jethryk is the first segment, but before he can steal it, Unstoffe spirits it away again. (It was he who placed it in the case in the first place.)

The Graff realises the deception and sets about hunting the con men down, while they, together with the Doctor, Romana and K-9, head for the catacombs under the city.

The Graff captures the travellers and the con men, takes back his gold and confiscates the jethryk. However, before he can kill his captives, the Riban guards blow up the entrance to the catacombs. The death of his officer and friend Sholakh in the ensuing rock fall unhinges the Graff's mind. He storms into the dust to be killed by a thermite bomb with which he intended to destroy the catacombs entirely. The Doctor meanwhile reaches safety with the jethryk.

Unstoffe and Garron leave with the Graff's ship of plundered loot, and the Doctor, Romana and K-9 leave with the first segment of the Key.

WHO FAX

● Novelised as *Doctor Who and the Ribos Operation* by Ian Marter in 1979.

● The stories of the sixteenth season were linked by a continuing theme, the hunt for the Key to Time. Each story would begin with the Doctor tracking one of the six segments and would involve him, Romana and K-9 trying to retrieve it.

● Cyril Luckham appeared as the White Guardian at the start of the season.

● Romana was played by Mary Tamm for this season only.

● The Key to Time was a prop comprising six clear resin segments which fitted together to form a cube. Several were constructed for the season and a complete Key was later sold at auction for £1,300.

● Working titles: *Operation, The Ribos File*.

COMMENT

The concept of linking together a season of Doctor Who *under one umbrella theme has certain problems. For a start, the risk of alienating casual viewers is obviously a problem within individual stories, but when the 'story' comprises an entire season, the problem is magnified.*

Luckily, the sixteenth season avoids this problem by keeping the linking theme to an absolute minimum, with only the opening of The Ribos Operation *and the ending of the last story,* The Armageddon Factor, *directly connected to the quest and its resolution.*

The Ribos Operation *is a marvellous story, with some memorable characters. Garron and Unstoffe are in the same vein as Jago and Litefoot and the Collector and Hade. Writer Robert Holmes gives them all the best lines and they are played to perfection by Iain Cuthbertson and Nigel Plaskitt (better known at the time as the sniffly-nosed boy from a decongestant advertisement). Binro the Heretic, an old man who offers Unstoffe sanctuary from the Graff's men, is another superb character. Binro has been ridiculed among his own people for claiming that the lights in the sky are other stars. In a very touching scene, Unstoffe tells Binro that his beliefs are correct.*

Ironically Mary Tamm claimed in the newspapers that Romana was a tough lady, not easily frightened by alien monsters, yet the ending of the first part of The Ribos Operation *has her screaming at one of the monstrous Shrivenzales which inhabit the catacombs.*

The Pirate Planet (5B)

EP	DATE	TIME	DURN	VIEWERS	CHART POS
1	30.09.78	18.22	25'05"	9.1	30
2	07.10.78	18.22	25'30"	7.4	52
3	14.10.78	18.22	25'47"	8.2	44
4	21.10.78	18.22	25'16"	8.4	46
Repeat					
1	12.07.79	18.56	25'05"	2.8	123
2	19.07.79	18.55	25'30"	4.0	91
3	26.07.79	18.56	25'47"	3.3	104
4	02.08.79	18.56	25'16"	3.9	103

PRODUCTION DETAILS

Location filming: 01.05.78–05.05.78
Studio: 22.05.78, 23.05.78, 03.06.78–05.06.78 in TC6

The tracer detects that the second segment is on the planet Calufrax – a location with which the Doctor is less than enamoured, describing it as 'Paralysingly dull, boring and tedious'.

The TARDIS makes a very bumpy landing and when the Doctor and Romana leave to find the segment they discover that they are not on Calufrax at all, but on Zanak, a hollow planet which has been fitted with engines so that it can transmat through space and materialise around other planets, such as Calufrax, and drain them of their energy and minerals, leaving them as shrunken husks held by gravitational forces in a 'trophy room' on Zanak.

Zanak is governed from a complex known as the Bridge by the Captain, half-man half-robot, who is in thrall of his Nurse, in reality a projection of the aged Queen Xanxia whose real body is held in stasis by a time dam. She is using the power taken from the plundered planets to keep the dam operational until her new, younger form becomes stable and permanent.

The Captain prepares Zanak to 'jump' again and this time the target is a planet rich in PJX18 (quartz) which can be used to repair the engines. The planet chosen is Terra, known to the Doctor as Earth.

The Doctor realises the truth about Xanxia – that there is no amount of energy that will give her a permanent new form – and attempts to stop Zanak from destroying the Earth. In this he is aided by the Mentiads, a gestalt of telepathic dwellers on Zanak who are sensitive to the life force of the planets that are destroyed. Under the Doctor's supervision they damage the engines by using telekinesis literally to put a spanner in the works.

The Captain asserts his independence and tries to free himself from the Nurse's control but she kills him instead. The Nurse herself is destroyed by Kimus.

The Doctor obtains the key, which he has realised is the whole planet Callufrax, by dropping the compressed husks of the planets into a space/time vortex created by the TARDIS in the centre of Zanak and then picking up the key at his leisure.

WHO FAX

● *The Pirate Planet* was written by Douglas Adams, who at the time he was commissioned had only just completed the pilot episode of *The Hitch-Hiker's Guide to the Galaxy* radio series.

● Adams's original draft of the story was very complex, involving a Time Lord trapped inside a giant aggression-absorbing machine, and had to be considerably simplified at the script-editing stage.

● Vi Delmar, who played old Queen Xanxia, asked for extra money to remove her false teeth in her scenes.

COMMENT

Douglas Adams's first script for Doctor Who *contains numerous, very imaginative, and slightly surreal concepts such as a space-hopping planet, a partly robotic pirate captain and a mechanised parrot. Against this, the plot is convoluted and at times difficult to follow.*

Bruce Purchase is superb as the Pirate Captain, full of overblown superlatives at first, later counterpointed by scenes of great pathos when his second in command and friend Mr Fibuli is killed by his duplicitous nurse.

Unfortunately the remainder of the characters are weak by comparison. The Mentiads come across as particularly spineless and unable to make a decision, and the other inhabitants of Zanak are completely forgettable.

The Stones of Blood (5C)

EP	DATE	TIME	DURN	VIEWERS	CHART POS
1	28.10.78	18.24	24'20"	8.6	38
2	04.11.78	18.22	23'53"	6.6	75
3	11.11.78	18.21	24'27"	9.3	38
4	18.11.78	18.23	23'07"	7.6	66

PRODUCTION DETAILS

OB: 12.06.78–16.06.78

Studio: 03.07.78, 04.07.78, 16.07.78–18.07.78 in TC3

The third segment of the Key to Time is traced to present-day Earth, but the Doctor finds that while the tracer leads him to the Nine Travellers, a circle of standing stones on Boscowan Moor in Damnonium, the key does not appear to be there. He meets up with elderly archaeologist Professor Amelia Rumford and her assistant Miss Vivien Fay, who are surveying the site, and discovers that the circle appears to have had a variable number of stones through the years.

The Doctor decides to visit Leonard de Vries, supposedly the leader of the British Institute for Druidic Studies (BIDS) which worships at the circle. He is knocked unconscious whilst at the Hall (de Vries's home) and is subsequently saved by Professor Rumford from being the Druids' next sacrifice. He then returns to the house to speak again with de Vries only to find that the latter has been killed by one of the stones from the circle, in truth a life form from the planet Ogros in Tau Ceti called an Ogri, which lives on blood.

Miss Fay turns out to be the Cailleach, an ancient being worshipped by the Druids, and she transports Romana to a spaceship hanging in hyperspace at the same spatial coordinates as the stone circle. The Doctor builds a gun-like contraption which transports him to the ship as well. There he unwittingly releases the Megara, two justice machines which have been trapped for centuries, and they put him on trial for breaking the seal on their compartment.

The Doctor discovers that the Megara's mission was to recapture and try Cessair of Diplos for murder and the theft of the seal of Diplos. He tricks them into knocking Miss Fay unconscious (she had arrived on the ship to gloat), and when they read her mind to determine if she is injured, they discover that she is Cessair.

The machines try her and sentence her to be turned into a stone in the circle on Earth. Before the sentence is carried out the Doctor snatches from around her neck a necklace – the third segment.

WHO FAX

● Novelised as *Doctor Who and the Stones of Blood* by Terrance Dicks in 1980.
● *The Stones of Blood* was *Doctor Who*'s 100th story and a scene involving the Doctor, Romana and K-9 having a party in the TARDIS was scripted and rehearsed but not recorded as producer Graham Williams felt it was too self-congratulatory.
● Two old enemies of the Doctor died while imprisoned on the ship with the Megara. A Wirrn appeared in the transmitted story, but shots of the other creature, a Sea Devil, were lost at the editing stage.

A deactivated android from *The Android Invasion* also a~~

● *The Stones of Blood* topped the DWAS season poll.

● Working title: *The Nine Maidens*.

COMMENT

One of the nice things about The Stones of Blood *is that the story changes from an apparent horror story about blood-drinking stones to a science-fiction tale about justice machines trapped on a spacecraft in hyperspace.*

The first part of the adventure is steeped in mystery as the Doctor and Romana try to unravel what has happened to the segment the tracer has led them to. The mystery deepens as Miss Fey turns out to be an ancient goddess, and the stones in the circle start to move about of their own volition. One particularly harrowing scene involves a pair of campers finding a standing stone outside their tent one morning. As the woman touches it to see if it is real, the stone pulses with power and starts sucking her blood through her hand. Her companion then grabs hold to pull her away, but his life force is drained too. Her hand fades to a skeleton as the stone drinks its fill of her blood.

When the action switches to a courtroom drama on board the prison ship, the atmosphere lightens, the Doctor deftly sidestepping the Megara's persistent questioning and returning to his particular predicament and the question of how to escape from it.

There is one loose end, namely how the Doctor knew that Cessair's necklace was the segment, but this hardly seems worth complaining about.

Overall this is a very enjoyable adventure, aided by the welljudged casting of the late Beatrix Lehmann as the irrepressible and inquisitive Professor Rumford.

The Androids of Tara (5D)

EP	DATE	TIME	DURN	VIEWERS	CHART POS
1	25.11.78	18.22	24'53"	8.5	45
2	02.12.78	18.21	24'27"	10.1	30
3	09.12.78	18.21	23'52"	8.9	38
4	16.12.78	18.20	24'49"	9.0	45

Repeat					
1	09.08.79	18.57	24'53"	6.2	49
2	16.08.79	18.57	24'27"	10.4	43
3	23.08.79	18.56	23'52"	10.5	43
4	30.08.79	18.57	24'49"	9.6	41

PRODUCTION DETAILS

Location filming: 24.07.78–28.08.78
Studio: 14.08.78, 15.08.78 in TC6, 28.08.78, 29.08.78 in TC1

When the fourth segment is traced to the lush planet of Tara the Doctor opts for a spot of fishing, leaving Romana to find it on her own. She locates it, disguised as part of a statue, but is attacked by a Taran beast. She is rescued by Count Grendel of Gracht who sees off the beast and takes the segment from her for registration. As she tries to leave she realises she has twisted her ankle and Grendel insists on taking her to his castle for treatment. When they arrive, Grendel and Lamia, a surgeon-engineer, are all set to disassemble Romana but are astonished when her ankle is seen to be swollen. She is a creature of flesh and blood and not an android as they had thought.

The Doctor, meanwhile, is captured by Swordsman Farrah and Swordmaster Zadek, two men loyal to Prince Reynart, rightful heir to the throne of Tara. They are interested in his knowledge of science and enquire if he can repair androids. They lead him off to meet Prince Reynart who explains that his coronation as King is due to take place the following day and that Grendel will do anything to stop the ceremony as if it does not go ahead as planned then Grendel will become King by default. An android of the Prince is intended as bait to safeguard Reynart, and the Doctor is forced at swordpoint to help repair it.

Grendel kidnaps the Prince and the Doctor is forced to modify the android so that it may be crowned in place of the genuine article. The Doctor summons K-9 from the TARDIS and sends it off to Castle Gracht to check on Romana. Meanwhile he arranges to get the android Prince to the throne room in time for the coronation.

Romana is placed in a cell with the injured Reynart. The Count is also holding the Princess Strella captive (she is the exact double of Romana – hence his and Lamia's astonishment that Romana was not

110

an android) but she will not cooperate in any of his plans. Grendel now intends to marry the real Prince to Romana (persuading her to pose as Strella) and then kill him, following which he will marry Romana and then kill her, thus ensuring that he becomes ruler.

Reynart's coronation goes ahead but Princess Strella arrives towards the conclusion. The Doctor realises that this is an android copy sent to destroy the android Prince, and disables it. The ceremony is put on hold and Grendel begins plotting another way of achieving his plan. He constructs another android copy of Romana – this time equipped with a lethal ray operated by the Doctor's voice – and arranges for the Doctor to come and get her at the Pavilion of the Summer Winds. K-9 recognises the trap and saves the Doctor. Meanwhile the real Romana escapes from the castle and in her turn rescues the Doctor and K-9, who have been trapped by Grendel's men.

Grendel turns the tables when he destroys the Reynart android with a spear and recaptures Romana. He arranges for his twin marriage ceremonies to be conducted by the Archimandrite while the Doctor, K-9 and Reynart's men prepare to attack his castle.

The Doctor enters the castle via the moat and manages to disrupt the ceremony (having first found and pocketed the fourth segment in Lamia's workshop) and battle is joined as Reynart's men attack. In the confusion, Romana saves Strella from being killed and the Doctor fights with Grendel on the castle battlements. Grendel dives into the moat and swims to safety leaving the Doctor and Romana to work out a way of rescuing K-9, who is still in a boat on the moat.

WHO FAX
- Novelised as *Doctor Who and the Androids of Tara* by Terrance Dicks in 1980.
- This story borrowed heavily from the plot of Anthony Hope's 1894 novel *The Prisoner of Zenda*.
- The opening titles for this story were in a different order from others at this point in the series' history. The order was story title, episode number, writer's name, as opposed to story title, writer's name, episode number.
- *The Androids of Tara* came bottom in the DWAS season poll.
- Working titles: *The Prisoners of Zend*, *The Seeds of Time*.

111

COMMENT

As a Doctor Who *adventure, it is debatable whether* The Androids of Tara *works. As it borrows so heavily from the political intrigues of Anthony Hope's novel, many of the traditional* Doctor Who *elements are absent. The story features some marvellous location work at Leeds Castle, and a strong villain in the form of Peter Jeffrey's Count Grendel, but there is little else of note.*

If you like protracted chases, and a plot which disappears under the sheer number of kidnaps, escapes and double dealing (pun!) then you may enjoy this, but as a Doctor Who *story, it is a little too ambitious.*

The Power of Kroll (5E)

EP	DATE	TIME	DURN	VIEWERS	CHART POS
1	23.12.78	18.17	23'16"	6.5	85
2	30.12.78	18.31	23'57"	12.4	26
3	06.01.79	18.28	21'56"	8.9	51
4	13.01.79	18.27	21'58"	9.9	31

PRODUCTION DETAILS

Location filming: 18.09.78–22.09.78, 25.09.78–29.09.78
Studio: 09.10.78–11.10.78 in TC6
Bray filming: 19.10.78, 20.10.78

The TARDIS arrives on the third moon of Delta Magna and the Doctor and Romana are forced to leave K-9 behind as the ground is marshy. While they are trying to get an accurate reading on the tracer, the Doctor is shot at by Fenner and Thawn, two men from a nearby methane catalysing refinery, while Romana is captured by a group of green-skinned natives, the Swampies, who are buying guns from a gun-running human called Rohm-Dutt. Rohm-Dutt is supplying the guns as part of a plot by Thawn to discredit the pro-Swampie Sons of Earth organisation and open the way for the Swampies to be wiped out. The Swampies intend to attack the refinery on the following day and plan to sacrifice Romana to their god Kroll that evening.

The Doctor is taken back to the refinery where, hearing the sacrificial drums, he learns from Mensch, a Swampie working at the base, that someone is to be sacrificed.

The Doctor leaves and makes his way towards the Temple of Kroll to rescue Romana. This he does and he and Romana also discover a passageway in the ground, and in it a book which tells of Kroll. Meanwhile the humans at the refinery notice that the seabed is shifting and moving as if something massive is underground.

The Swampies, led by Ranquin, prepare their attack but the arrangements are cut short when an enormous squid-creature appears on the horizon. This is the creature seen moving under the seabed; it is the great god Kroll. Kroll heads for the refinery and attacks it while the Doctor, Romana and Rohm-Dutt are sentenced to be sacrificed to the god. They are to be stretched to death by being tied hand and foot to some steadily contracting vines.

A storm breaks outside and the Doctor shatters the window with a high-pitched scream so that rain can come in and slacken the vines, allowing them to escape.

As they make their way across the swamp, Rohm-Dutt is caught and killed by one of Kroll's tentacles but the Doctor and Romana manage to get back to the refinery.

Thawn plans to kill Kroll by aiming an orbital plasma rocket at it – the rockets are normally used to ship their refined product off-planet. The Doctor and Romana go to the rocket silo where the Doctor disables the missile.

Furious, Thawn takes the Doctor and Romana prisoner once more, but then the Swampies attack, killing Thawn. Kroll then attacks the refinery once again and the Doctor goes outside armed only with the tracer.

He points the tracer at the monster, which is transformed into the fifth segment. It was the segment which was responsible for Kroll growing to such mammoth proportions in the first place.

WHO FAX

● Novelised as *Doctor Who and the Power of Kroll* by Terrance Dicks in 1980.

● John Leeson, who was under contract to provide the voice of K-9, was given the role of Dugeen in this story after another actor dropped out, to compensate for the fact that K-9 was stuck inside the TARDIS and did not appear.

● The green make-up used for the Swampies proved particularly difficult to remove, causing the cast to retire to a nearby air base to

try to scrub it off, much to the amusement of the watching airmen.
● Working titles: *Horror of the Swamp*, *The Shield of Time*.
● Writer Robert Holmes was briefed to provide a serial featuring the biggest monster ever seen in *Doctor Who*. He did so even though he thought it a bad idea.

COMMENT

Despite a strong cast which includes Doctor Who *stalwarts Philip Madoc (*The War Games, The Brain of Morbius*), John Abineri (*Fury from the Deep, The Ambassadors of Death, Death to the Daleks*) and Neil McCarthy (*The Mind of Evil*), The Power of Kroll *falls down in other areas. Robert Holmes's script lacks the power of his previous contributions to the programme, and the combination of a tribe of green-skinned natives and a giant squid fails to inspire.*

Once again the location work is excellent, the Iken marshes making a suitably alien setting for the action. The Kroll creature itself is well realised, and in execution is reminiscent of the giant Krynoid from The Seeds of Doom.

The Armageddon Factor (5F)

EP	DATE	TIME	DURN	VIEWERS	CHART POS
1	20.01.79	18.25	24'39"	7.5	93
2	27.01.79	18.27	23'56"	8.8	49
3	03.02.79	18.28	25'03"	7.8	76
4	10.02.79	18.28	25'09"	8.6	60
5	17.02.79	18.26	24'42"	8.6	66
6	24.02.79	18.30	25'09"	9.6	36

PRODUCTION DETAILS

Ealing filming: October 1978
Studio: 05.11.78–07.11.78, 20.11.78–22.11.78, 03.12.78–05.12.78 in TC3

The twin worlds of Atrios and Zeos have been engaged in a long interplanetary war and the Marshal of Atrios is desperately seeking a means by which to win.

The Doctor, Romana and K-9 arrive on Atrios as the latest bombing raid by the Zeons comes to an end. They go in search of the sixth and final segment of the Key to Time. K-9 is lured into a metal recycling system and the Doctor has to go after him towards the furnace.

The Marshal is being controlled by someone else, and receives his orders from a skull-like communicator behind a two-way mirror. The Doctor makes his way to 'Zeos' and realises that it is not the opposing planet at all, but another, invisible planet, placed between the two, and known as the planet of evil or the third planet.

This world is ruled by the Shadow, who, with his servants the Mutes, is working for the Black Guardian to try to gain control of the final segment before the Doctor can find it.

The Shadow has captured Princess Astra of Atrios and is holding her under threat of torture in the belief that she can tell him where the segment is, but she does not know.

The Doctor finds that the war between Atrios and Zeos is being controlled from Zeos by a computer commandant called Mentalis, and that it is planning a final strike to counter the Marshal's similar plan. Mentalis was built by Drax, a Time Lord and old college friend of the Doctor's, who agrees to help the Doctor disable the computer before both worlds are destroyed.

To stop the Marshal, now on his way in a ship to deliver a final missile strike on Zeos, the Doctor builds a fake final segment for the Key to Time out of chronodyne, and in this form the Key has enough power to create a temporary time loop, trapping the Marshal and his ship.

Mentalis is destroyed and the Doctor realises that Princess Astra is herself the sixth segment and the Shadow converts her into the crystal. The Doctor snatches this from under the Shadow's nose and escapes to the TARDIS where he assembles the complete Key.

The White Guardian appears on the TARDIS scanner and congratulates the Doctor on a job well done. He is now to hand over the Key. The Doctor, realising that this is a deception and also that the Key is too powerful for any one being to control, orders it to redisperse itself, much to the chagrin of the 'White' Guardian who in his rage reverts to his true colour – Black. The raging Guardian swears that the Doctor will die for this. To try to shake him off the Doctor fits a randomiser to the TARDIS controls – he now has no idea where or when his travels will take him.

WHO FAX

● Novelised as *Doctor Who and the Armageddon Factor* by Terrance Dicks in 1980.

● The Black Guardian was played by the late Valentine Dyall, a role he was to reprise several times in later years.

● Princess Astra was played by Lalla Ward, who returned the following season to play Romana.

● Part one of *The Armageddon Factor* was the 500th episode of *Doctor Who*.

● Part five was interrupted by a break in transmission for several minutes. Music was played and a caption slide displayed until transmission resumed from a point just before the break occurred.

● Working title: *Armageddon*.

COMMENT

The Armageddon Factor *brings to a conclusion the hunt for the Key to Time. Of note are the two protagonists, the Marshal, played with military precision by John Woodvine, and the Shadow, an excellent portrayal of suppressed evil from William Squire.*

To counterpoint these two dramatic characters, there is a lighter element supplied by Davyd Harries as Shapp, bumbling second in command to the Marshal, and Barry Jackson as Drax, a Time Lord with a chirpy Cockney accent and matching attitude.

Perhaps most memorable is Valentine Dyall's Black Guardian who appears only at the conclusion. The Guardians proved successful enough to warrant several future rematches against the Doctor.

Perhaps the only problem with the story is that it leaves unresolved the question of the Key to Time. The White Guardian sends the Doctor on a quest at the start of the season, and when the end is reached, the Doctor deliberately rescatters the segments – nothing has been achieved. If what the White Guardian said about needing to re-establish the balance of the universe is correct then the Doctor's actions have certainly not helped unless the White Guardian was somehow able to effect the necessary change during the few moments the Key was together.

This question, and also the idea that the White and Black Guardians may have been the same being, are never adequately explained on screen. This leaves the viewer feeling slightly disappointed at the end of 26 weeks of adventure.

SEASON SEVENTEEN

Destiny of the Daleks (5J)

EP	DATE	TIME	DURN	VIEWERS	CHART POS
1	01.09.79	18.14	24'03"	13.0	28
2	08.09.79	18.10	25'14"	12.7	39
3	15.09.79	18.08	24'32"	13.8	28
4	22.09.79	18.17	26'05"	14.4	27
Repeat					
1	05.08.80	18.28	24'03"	4.9	91
2	06.08.80	18.19	25'14"	5.8	59
3	07.08.80	18.28	24'32"	7.1	33
4	08.08.80	18.24	26'05"	6.5	41

PRODUCTION DETAILS

Location filming: 11.06.79–15.06.79

Studio: 02.07.79, 03.07.79 (studio unknown), 15.07.79–17.07.79 in TC1

As chance would have it, the first place the randomiser chooses to deposit the TARDIS is somewhere the Doctor knows only too well – Skaro. After Romana has regenerated into the form of Princess Astra, she and the Doctor leave the TARDIS to investigate.

After watching a bedraggled group of slaves bury one of their dead, a Kantrian, the Doctor and Romana see a space craft land and bury itself in the sand of the planet's surface. A series of mining explosions then rock the planet and the time travellers take cover in some ruined buildings. The Doctor becomes trapped under some fallen masonry and Romana returns to the TARDIS to fetch K-9.

While she is gone, the Doctor is rescued by the Movellans, a race of robots, and taken back to their newly arrived ship.

When Romana returns (a rock fall had partially buried the TARDIS and she could not get in), she finds the Doctor missing. One of the slave workers, Tyssan, who has been following her, approaches and she backs away in alarm, falling down a duct into a lower level of the ruined city. She is soon surrounded by Daleks who take her away for questioning. Following this she is assigned to work with Labour Force

Two, a group of slave workers, clearing rocks away from the drilling areas.

Tyssan is found by the Movellans and explains what has happened. The Doctor, together with a group of Movellans, returns to the city to investigate. They meet up with Romana who had feigned death to escape from the mining team, and deep in the city find what the Daleks are searching for – Davros.

Davros is reactivated and takes command of the Daleks as the Doctor, Romana and Tyssan escape. The Movellans, now aware that the Daleks need Davros to break the logical stalemate that the Movellans' and the Daleks' battle computers are in, decide to recapture the Doctor to help them do likewise. They stun Romana and place her inside a tube containing a powerful explosive, the Nova device. This will be the bait to lure the Doctor. The trap works and the Movellans take the Doctor and Romana back to their ship, intending to destroy the planet with the bomb once they are safely clear.

Meanwhile Davros has been briefed on the problem by a computer sphere, and decides to destroy the Movellans using a squad of Daleks on a suicide mission. Each Dalek is loaded with bombs which will be detonated by Davros once they are in position around the Movellan spaceship.

Tyssan has meanwhile organised the slave workers to attack the Movellans and then to try to prevent the suicide Daleks from achieving their positions. The Doctor returns to the city and tricks Davros into inadvertently detonating the suicide Daleks before they reach the Movellan ship and Romana stops the Movellan commander, Sharrell, from detonating the Nova device by hand.

The danger over, Davros is cryogenically frozen on board the Movellan ship until he can be tried on Earth for his crimes, and Tyssan takes the ship to return the slaves to their rightful homes.

WHO FAX
● Novelised as *Doctor Who and the Destiny of the Daleks* by Terrance Dicks in 1979.
● Romana's regeneration in this story was prompted by Mary Tamm's departure at the end of the previous season. Lalla Ward was cast as the new Romana.
● Michael Wisher was not available to reprise his role of Davros from *Genesis of the Daleks* and so David Gooderson was cast instead, as

he was a voice artist and it was thought that he would be able to imitate Wisher's half-Dalek half-human cadences.

● Another interesting piece of casting was Tim Barlow, a partially deaf actor who took the role of Tyssan.

● The influence of new script editor Douglas Adams is visible when the Doctor pulls from his pocket a book, *Origins of the Universe*, by none other than Oolon Caluphid of *The Hitch-Hiker's Guide to the Galaxy* fame.

● During the opening credits, *Destiny of the Daleks*'s individual segments were called episodes, rather than parts as was the standard for all other Fourth Doctor stories.

● The other brief incarnations of Romana were played by Maggy Armitage, Yvonne Gallagher and Lee Richards.

COMMENT

Destiny of the Daleks is a story let down by the special effects. The script is strong, but contains little that is innovative. One of the better effects is the spacecraft which buries itself upon landing, and the worst has to be the procession of lightweight Daleks wobbling along the horizon towards the Movellan ship. The Movellans are a nice idea, but don't come across too well. They lack any real sense of threat, and as they can be disabled simply by detaching a power pack from their belt, are hardly invincible enemies of the Daleks!

Davros too fails dismally. David Gooderson tries hard, but he cannot match Michael Wisher's definitive portrayal. Tyssan is both wooden and uninteresting, and generally the cast seem uninspired to perform well in what has the potential to be an excellent adventure.

City of Death (5H)

EP	DATE	TIME	DURN	VIEWERS	CHART POS
1	29.09.79	18.07	24'25"	12.4	50
2	06.10.79	18.17	24'33"	14.1	44
3	13.10.79	18.04	25'25"	15.4	34
4	20.10.79	18.16	25'08"	16.1	16
Repeat					
1	12.08.80	18.26	24'25"	6.3	57
2	13.08.80	18.26	24'33"	5.5	81

| 3 | 19.08.80 | 18.26 | 25'25" | - | - |
| 4 | 20.08.80 | 18.26 | 25'08" | - | - |

PRODUCTION DETAILS

Location filming: 30.04.79–03.05.79

Bray filming: 08.05.79–10.05.79

Studio: 21.05.79, 22.05.79 in TC3, 03.06.79–05.06.79 in TC6

The Doctor and Romana are enjoying a holiday in Paris 1979 when time starts to fracture around them. The Doctor is determined to continue the holiday, but time slips again when they visit the Louvre to see the Mona Lisa. The Doctor, dazed by the phenomenon, is helped by a countess when he falls semiconscious into her lap. The Doctor takes this opportunity to slip a futuristic alien bracelet from her wrist.

Later, at a street café, the Doctor and Romana meet a private detective, Duggan, who explains that he has been investigating the Countess's husband, Count Scarlioni. All three are then 'invited' at gunpoint to visit the Count by a group of thugs. Scarlioni locks them in his cellar and the Doctor discovers that he has six Mona Lisas stored there too, all of them originals!

The Count is actually an alien called Scaroth, the last member of the Jaggaroth race. He was splintered in time when his ship exploded above primeval Earth and in his twelve aspects has been guiding the development of mankind to a point where time travel is possible. He now intends to travel back in time and prevent himself from destroying the ship.

The Doctor travels back to 1505 in the TARDIS to visit the Florentine home of Leonardo da Vinci and writes 'This is a Fake' in black marker pen on six boards, leaving the artist a note just to paint over them. While he is there he discovers that it was a splinter of Scaroth who arranged for Leonardo to produce eight copies of the painting in the first place. He then follows Scarlioni back 400 million years to primeval Earth and with Duggan's help prevents him from altering the course of time.

Scaroth's ship explodes as before and the resultant blast of radiation brings life into being in the primordial swamps below, life which will eventually develop into mankind.

WHO FAX

- Story released on BBC Home Video in 1991.
- Popular film actor Julian Glover returned to *Doctor Who* to play Count Scarlioni. He had previously appeared as Richard the Lionheart with William Hartnell's Doctor in *The Crusade* (1965).
- Catherine Schell, who played the Countess, had previously played the shape-changing character Maya during the second, 1976, season of Gerry Anderson's series *Space: 1999*.
- Part four featured John Cleese and Eleanor Bron in cameo roles as art critics who have mistaken the TARDIS for a piece of modern art. They are even more impressed when the ship vanishes in front of their eyes!
- This story came top in the DWAS season poll.
- *City of Death* was written by producer Graham Williams and script editor Douglas Adams when a script by David Fisher called *The Gamble with Time* had to be reworked due to changing production requirements. As a result it was transmitted under the name David Agnew, previously used for *The Invasion of Time*.
- Working title: *Curse of the Sephiroth*.

COMMENT

After the fairly disastrous Destiny of the Daleks, City of Death *is a return to classic* Doctor Who. *The story is helped greatly by the Parisian locations, and because of an amount of running about simply to show as much of Paris as possible, the location work helps achieve a naturalism often missing from studio-bound adventures.*

Julian Glover is perfect as the suave Count Scarlioni, and despite the shortcomings of the spaghetti-like Jaggaroth mask, manages to give the last surviving member of that race a twisted and desperate nobility. The other members of the cast also help to make this story work. Tom Chadbon as the somewhat inept detective is perfect, as is Catherine Schell as Scarlioni's unsuspecting wife.

Ian Scoones provides the modelwork of Scaroth's ship rising and exploding above the Earth, and as in The Invisible Enemy, *these sequences are flawlessly executed, adding a great deal to the production.*

The Creature from the Pit (5G)

EP	DATE	TIME	DURN	VIEWERS	CHART POS
1	27.10.79	18.02	23'32"	9.3	43
2	03.11.79	18.07	24'03"	10.8	23
3	10.11.79	18.02	23'55"	10.2	36
4	17.11.79	18.04	24'07"	9.6	36

PRODUCTION DETAILS

Ealing filming: 19.03.79–26.03.79

Studio: 09.04.79, 10.04.79, 22.04.79–24.04.79 (studio unknown)

The TARDIS picks up a distress call on its Mark III Emergency Transceiver and brings the Doctor and Romana to the planet Chloris to investigate. Chloris is a lush and verdant world but has a chronic shortage of all metals, resulting in a band of scruffy thieves organising raids on the palace of the planet's ruler, Lady Adrasta, to steal whatever metal they can get their hands on. Adrasta keeps order with her wolfweeds and guards and controls the planet's supply of metal.

The Doctor discovers that the distress signal is actually coming from a large eggshell-like structure in the forest at the Place of Death, but before he can investigate further he is taken by Adrasta's guards and sentenced to be thrown into the Pit – a fate that befalls all who oppose the Lady.

The Doctor manages to cling to the sides of the Pit when he is thrown in and makes his way safely to the bottom. There he meets Organon, formally Adrasta's astrologer, who fell foul of the Lady when she didn't like his predictions. The Pit is also home to an immense green globular creature which oozes through the passages and suffocates those who are fed to it.

The Doctor realises that this monster is not an unthinking killer, but an ambassador from the planet Tythonus. Tythonus has a lack of chlorophyll but has much metal and the Tythonians hoped to trade with Chloris. Unfortunately the first person their ambassador Erato met was Adrasta, who realised that if more metal was brought to her planet then her monopoly on it would be broken. Instead she took Erato's communicator device and trapped him in the Pit.

Adrasta is trapped and killed by Erato in the Pit. The bandits, who

122

were robbing Adrasta's palace while she was otherwise occupied, come across Erato's communicator. It exerts an influence over them when they touch it and they are compelled to carry it to the Tythonian. Erato then tells the Doctor that his own people have already retaliated for his imprisonment by setting a neutron star on course for Chloris.

The Doctor takes Erato and the TARDIS out into space, where the Tythonian spins an aluminium shell around the star and pulls it off course, thus saving Chloris.

WHO FAX
- Novelised as *Doctor Who and the Creature from the Pit* by David Fisher in 1981.
- Geoffrey Bayldon, better known for his title role as *Catweazle*, was cast as the astrologer Organon.
- Eileen Way, who had appeared in the very first *Doctor Who* story in the role of Old Mother, returned to *Doctor Who* to play Lady Adrasta's right-hand woman Karela.
- This was the last story to be directed by Christopher Barry, one of *Doctor Who*'s longest-serving contributors.
- One of *Doctor Who*'s previous directors, Morris Barry (*The Moonbase*, *The Tomb of the Cybermen*, *The Dominators*) was cast in the minor role of Tollund, one of Adrasta's advisers, who was sacrificed to the creature.
- For this story and for the rest of the season, K-9's voice was provided by David Brierley rather than John Leeson.

COMMENT
The Creature from the Pit is superficially enjoyable. The problem is that it contains elements which work against any lasting worth.

Most of the characters are very stereotyped: there is a group of clichéd Jewish bandits looking as though they have stepped directly off the set of Monty Python's Flying Circus; *Adrasta is an archetypal dictator; and Organon is a typical sage-like astronomer. The titular creature is possibly one of the worst-realised monsters ever to have appeared on* Doctor Who, *and much of the story's basis is half-baked and scientifically impossible.*

The more humorous slant favoured by script editor Douglas Adams is evident when the Doctor finds himself clinging to the side of the Pit. He rummages in his pockets and pulls out a rock-climbing textbook,

Everest in Easy Stages, *but it is written in Tibetan so he rummages again and finds a* Teach Yourself Tibetan *book.*

On the positive side, the Chloran jungle is very well realised, and both Myra Frances (Adrasta) and Geoffrey Bayldon (Organon) turn in excellent performances. Just don't think about the plot too much.

Nightmare of Eden (5K)

EP	DATE	TIME	DURN	VIEWERS	CHART POS
1	24.11.79	18.01	24'17"	8.7	41
2	01.12.79	18.05	22'44"	9.6	31
3	08.12.79	18.03	24'06"	9.6	32
4	15.12.79	17.56	24'31"	9.4	32

PRODUCTION DETAILS

Studio: 12.08.79-14.08.79, 26.08.79-28.08.79 in TC6

In orbit around the planet Azure in the year 2116, a luxury space liner, the *Empress*, and a private ship, the *Hecate*, collide as the liner emerges from hyperspace and the ships become fused together. The Doctor and Romana arrive to investigate.

The travellers meet the scientist Tryst who has a Continuous Event Transmuter (CET) machine with him. On this are recordings of many of the planets that he has visited, which continue to develop within the machine. The Doctor discovers that someone on the liner is smuggling the dangerous addictive drug vraxoin and that some Mandrels from the mud-swamps of Eden have somehow escaped from the CET machine and are running amok.

The culprits are revealed to be Tryst and the pilot of the *Hecate*, Dymond, who are planning to beam the vraxoin down to Azure, the planet below, by sending the sample of Eden from the CET machine.

Vraxoin turns out to be the material that the Mandrels decompose into when they are killed. It is also discovered that the CET machine does not take recordings of planets, but has actually displaced whole planetary areas into its recording crystals.

The Doctor prevents Tryst and Dymond from carrying out their plan, separates the two ships and returns the Mandrels to Eden.

WHO FAX

- Novelised as *Doctor Who and the Nightmare of Eden* by Terrance Dicks in 1980.
- Director Alan Bromly walked out part-way through production and the remainder of the story was directed by *Doctor Who*'s producer, Graham Williams.
- This story was the first solo *Doctor Who* project for writer Bob Baker, who had scripted many stories previously with his partner Dave Martin. Together they had created K-9.
- Working title: *Nightmare of Evil*.

COMMENT

Nightmare of Eden continues the inexorable downward slide of the seventeenth season. Here viewers are presented with the concept that a race of monsters will instantly transform into an addictive drug when they are electrocuted. Further, the idea of portions of a planet being stored on a machine for later 'playback' was previously explored in Carnival of Monsters.

The acting is not up to much. David Daker hams his way through the part of Captain Rigg, mostly under the influence of vraxoin, and Lewis Fiander plays Tryst with an accent even worse than Professor Marius's in The Invisible Enemy. *The Mandrels look daft – they are so obviously men in suits and as their arms are elongated their movements are more comic than frightening. The whole story lacks any real conviction. Tom Baker delights in playing up the comedic element. When the Doctor lures the Mandrels into the Eden projection he disappears into the undergrowth followed by two of the creatures and then the foliage rustles, clumps of grass are thrown into shot and Tom exclaims 'My fingers! My arms! My legs! My everything!'*

The Horns of Nimon (5L)

EP	DATE	TIME	DURN	VIEWERS	CHART POS
1	22.12.79	18.11	25'41"	6.0	100
2	29.12.79	17.54	25'00"	8.8	56
3	05.01.80	18.22	23'26"	9.8	40
4	12.01.80	18.06	26'45"	10.4	26

PRODUCTION DETAILS

Studio: 24.09.79–26.09.79, 07.10.79–09.10.79 (studio unknown)

The planet Skonnos is dying, and its inhabitants have been promised by an alien Nimon that he can return their empire to greatness. However, this requires sacrifices and Hymetusite crystals, both of which the Skonnons obtain from the nearby planet Aneth. The Anethans have been supplying their young and their minerals for many years and the Nimon on Skonnos has become a part of their legends.

When the Doctor and his companions arrive – Romana first on the ship with the tribute and the Doctor and K-9 later by TARDIS – they are sent into the Nimon's labyrinthine Power Complex on Skonnos to meet the creature. It turns out to be a bull-headed alien. The Nimon are like a race of intergalactic locusts. They send a representative to an unsuspecting planet, offering help and assistance, and when they have gained the trust of the inhabitants, they arrive in force and drain the planet of all its resources before moving on to another world in the same manner.

Romana travels back along the Nimon's space-tunnel to their last world, the dying planet Crinoth, which they have all but exhausted. She obtains from Sezom, the last surviving inhabitant, a staff which can be used against the Nimon.

The Doctor manages to trap the Nimon on Crinoth by destroying the Complex on Skonnos.

WHO FAX

- Novelised as *Doctor Who and the Horns of Nimon* by Terrance Dicks in 1980.
- The Nimon were originally intended to be aliens wearing bull-masks to frighten the inhabitants of the planets they invaded, but budgetary restrictions meant that the masks ended up being the real creatures.
- Before her days as a presenter of the children's programme *Blue Peter*, Janet Ellis played the part of Teka, one of the sacrificial Anethans.
- Graham Crowden, one of the actors considered for the role of the fourth Doctor and later well known for his role as Jock in *A Very Peculiar Practice*, played the part of Soldeed, the Nimon's high priest on Skonnos.

- The Nimon Power Complex was based around the idea of a giant printed circuit, the paths through which changed to trap any visitors and draw them to the Nimon at the centre.
- The story was inspired by the tale of Theseus and the Minotaur.

COMMENT

Although widely criticised for its comic portrayal of the Doctor, the overacting of Graham Crowden as Soldeed, and the appearance of the Nimon, who turned out to be men in ballet tights wearing obvious bull-masks, if the viewer is in the right mood for it the story is actually highly enjoyable because of these elements!

Former script editor Anthony Read's script is both imaginative and fun, and is treated as so by the production team. The idea of a building which operates as a printed circuit is highly original, and the transplanting of the locust concept also works.

Unfortunately, while Crowden's overacted portrayal of the Nimon's servant is enjoyable because of its excesses, the other cast members are simply dreadful. Janet Ellis and Simon Gipps-Kent are wooden and characterless as two of the hapless Anethans, and Malcolm Terris's Skonnon co-pilot is equally bad. The only other character with any credibility is John Bailey's Sezom.

The Horns of Nimon *comes as close as* Doctor Who *gets to a pantomime production. This can almost be forgiven given that it was transmitted over the Christmas period. With the loss of the much vaunted* Shada, *this is a very disappointing end to a somewhat mixed season. It came bottom of the DWAS' annual poll.*

Shada (5M)

[The following information is given for completeness only and should not be taken to imply that *Shada* is part of accepted *Doctor Who* mythology.]

PRODUCTION DETAILS

Location filming: 15.10.79–19.10.79

Ealing filming: 22.10.79

Studio: 03.11.79–05.11.79 in TC3

Planned studio: 19.11.79, 20.11.79 in TC6, 01.12.79–03.12.79 in TC3

The Doctor and Romana arrive in present-day Cambridge to visit an old friend of the Doctor's, Professor Chronotis, who has rooms at St Cedd's College. However, the Doctor is not the only one with an interest in the Professor, as a criminal called Skagra is also after him.

Skagra has a mind-draining sphere in which he hopes to trap the Professor's mind. He is also after a book which the Professor has, *The Ancient and Worshipful Law of Gallifrey*. The book, however, has been borrowed by mistake by student Chris Parsons, and Skagra leaves empty-handed.

Skagra eventually manages to get the book after his sphere chases the Doctor through the streets of Cambridge. He also kidnaps Romana. The book is the key to how to get to Shada, the ancient prison planet of the Time Lords. Skagra wants to obtain the mind of a criminal called Salyavin who was incarcerated there.

It transpires that Chronotis is Salyavin and that he escaped from Shada years ago and has been living peacefully ever since. The Doctor prevents Skagra's plans for domination by winning a mind battle against him and his alien allies the Krargs.

WHO FAX

● *Shada* was never completed due to a technicians' strike at the BBC, and was therefore never transmitted.

● BBC Video released a compilation of existing *Shada* footage in 1992 and material from the story was also used in *The Five Doctors* (1983).

● Working title: *Sunburst*.

● This story replaced another which Douglas Adams had wanted to write about the Doctor losing interest in saving the universe and going into retreat – an idea which Graham Williams forbade him to pursue on the grounds that it would send the series up too much.

SEASON EIGHTEEN

The Leisure Hive (5N)

EP	DATE	TIME	DURN	VIEWERS	CHART POS
1	30.08.80	18.15	23'33"	5.9	77
2	06.09.80	18.20	20'45"	5.0	103
3	13.09.80	17.57	21'21"	5.0	111
4	20.09.80	18.16	21'19"	4.5	111

PRODUCTION DETAILS

Location filming: 20.03.80, 21.03.80

Studio: 02.04.80–04.04.80 in TC1, 18.04.80–20.04.80 in TC3

After an abortive holiday in Brighton, Romana persuades the Doctor to take another on the planet Argolis which in the year 2290 is the location of a giant pleasure dome, the Leisure Hive.

The Argolins are dying. The radiation on their planet's surface, the result of a war with their enemies the Foamasi, has rendered them sterile. Pangol, the youngest Argolin alive, was actually created by the Tachyon Recreation Generator, a machine used to generate games in the Hive. He now secretly plans to re-create himself many times over, forming an army of duplicates to destroy the Foamasi for good.

The Hive's leader, Mena (Pangol's mother), is being persuaded by her Earth agent Brock to sell the Hive to the Foamasi who have made a good offer, but Pangol vehemently opposes this plan. As Mena grows weaker, Pangol takes command and attempts to create his army. However, the Doctor has tampered with the equipment and an army of Doctors emerges instead. The duplicates are also unstable and quickly vanish.

The Hive turns out to have been infiltrated by some Foamasi agents from their planet's government, who expose Brock and his assistant, Klout, as being renegade Foamasi members of the West Lodge. Mena and Pangol enter the TRG following the Doctor's tampering and are rejuvenated – Mena into a young woman and Pangol a mere babe in arms.

WHO FAX

● Novelised as *Doctor Who and the Leisure Hive* by David Fisher in 1982.

● John Nathan-Turner's first story as producer heralded a new title sequence and a new version of the theme music.

● K-9 was yet again incapacitated, this time by going into the sea and getting water in his circuits.

● This story made extensive use of the new Quantel image manipulation process.

● Working title: *The Argolins*.

● In the scene where the Doctor is apparently dismembered in the TRG, the various parts of his body were played by David Rolfe, Roy

Seeley and Derek Chafer as well as by Tom Baker.

COMMENT

Right from the opening moments of The Leisure Hive *it is clear that* Doctor Who *has undergone a major change. With John Nathan-Turner's arrival as producer, the series' production values have improved immensely, and the whole thing has a very glossy, expensive look to it. Lovett Bickford's direction is highly unusual and effective, and the acting is of a high standard throughout. Tom Baker's performance is particularly noteworthy, being much more subdued than in the recent past – particularly in the scenes where he has undergone a temporary ageing process, achieved with some very impressive make-up.*

David Fisher's script is far more serious than his earlier contributions to the series – largely due to it being rewritten by script editor Christopher H. Bidmead – but on close examination the plot reveals a number of gaping holes. For example, the idea that Foamasi could disguise themselves as human beings simply by donning rubber masks appears rather implausible on screen owing to the bulky nature of the monsters' costumes.

All in all, something of a triumph of style over content.

Meglos (5Q)

EP	DATE	TIME	DURN	VIEWERS	CHART POS
1	27.09.80	18.16	24'43"	5.0	105
2	04.10.80	18.17	21'24"	4.2	139
3	11.10.80	17.42	21'19"	4.7	129
4	18.10.80	17.44	19'30"	4.7	127

PRODUCTION DETAILS

Studio: 25.06.80–27.06.80 in TC6, 10.07.80–12.07.80 in TC3

The inhabitants of Tigella in the Prion planetary system have a problem: the giant dodecahedron which has powered their underground city since it fell to their planet is now failing. The surface of Tigella is covered with lush, aggressive vegetation, and the Tigellans believe that unless they can find a solution to the power loss they are doomed. The race is split into two factions: the Savants, led by Deedrix, are scientists who believe that the dodecahedron is an artifact which was manufactured, and the Deons, led by Lexa, are religious worshippers who believe it to be a gift from their god Ti.

Zastor, the impartial leader of Tigella, summons the Doctor to come and help, but on its way to the planet the TARDIS is caught in a chronic hysteresis – a loop in time.

The TARDIS has been trapped by Meglos, the last surviving Zolfa-Thuran, whose race built the dodecahedron. Meglos, whose true form is that of a xerophyte, has summoned help in the form of an unruly band of Gaztak mercenaries, led by General Grugger. They kidnap a human and Meglos takes over his body, then transforms it to look like the Doctor.

Meglos arrives on Tigella ahead of the trapped Doctor and tricks the Tigellans into allowing him access to the dodecahedron. When he is alone with it, he miniaturises and absconds with it.

When the Doctor arrives, having escaped the time loop, he is of course accused of the crime. However, he escapes and follows Meglos back to Zolfa-Thura where the cactus creature plans to unleash the power of the dodecahedron to destroy Tigella. The Doctor turns the tables and mis-sets the computers controlling the device, causing an explosion which destroys Meglos.

The Tigellans are forced to begin reclaiming their planet's surface from the vegetation and the Doctor takes home the human whose body Meglos had stolen.

WHO FAX

- Novelised as *Doctor Who – Meglos* by Terrance Dicks in 1983.
- Jacqueline Hill, who had played the Doctor's companion Barbara Wright during *Doctor Who*'s early days, returned to play Lexa, leader of the Deons.
- Some of the Gaztak costumes came from a BBC production of *Macbeth*, others from previous *Doctor Who* stories: *The Ribos Operation* and *Carnival of Monsters*.
- This story came bottom of the DWAS season poll.
- The music for most of part one was provided by Paddy Kingsland, and Peter Howell took over for the remainder of the story.
- Bill Fraser agreed to play Grugger only if he could kick K-9.
- Working titles: *The Golden Pentangle*, *The Last Zolfa-Thuran*.

COMMENT

Meglos *is perhaps the weakest story of season eighteen. The script is unoriginal and largely dull, and the direction lacks any real conviction. Aside from their respective leaders, the Savants, Deons and Gaztaks display little or no characterisation.*

The production values are also weaker here than on other stories in the season. Tigella's carnivorous plants, for example, look plastic and unreal – even though they are said to have been extremely expensive props – and it is all too obvious that the Gaztaks' costumes have been cobbled together from other productions, including some earlier Doctor Who*s.*

The overall style harks back to season seventeen, with over-the-top performances from some of the cast and a general feeling that the whole thing is being taken rather less than seriously.

Full Circle (5R)

EP	DATE	TIME	DURN	VIEWERS	CHART POS
1	25.10.80	17.40	24'23"	5.9	106
2	01.11.80	17.42	22'11"	3.7	170
3	08.11.80	17.43	22'00"	5.9	115
4	15.11.80	17.40	24'16"	5.5	127
Repeat					
1	03.08.81	18.29	24'23"	4.9	85
2	04.08.81	18.21	22'11"	4.2	101
3	05.08.81	18.21	22'00"	4.6	92
4	06.08.81	18.21	24'16"	6.4	60

PRODUCTION DETAILS

Location filming: 23.07.80–25.07.80

Studio: 07.08.80, 08.08.80, 21.08.80–23.08.80 (studio unknown)

The TARDIS becomes caught in a Charged Vacuum Emboitment, a hole in the fabric of space, and is drawn into E-Space, a smaller universe which coexists with our own.

The first planet the Doctor and Romana arrive on is Alzarius, a seemingly idyllic world supporting a happy and contented people. The

Terradonians are misplaced from their own world as their starliner crashed on Alzarius fifty years before. They live on the planet now, whilst all the time making repairs to the ship in readiness to leave.

The colony is run by three Deciders – Draith, Nefred and Garif – who periodically check on the people living outside the ship. There is also a small group of Outlers, youngsters led by Varsh who have rebelled against the elders of the colony and who live apart from the others in a cave, stealing what little they need.

The arrival of the Doctor and Romana coincides with Mistfall, a periodic event spoken about in the Terradonians' history, when the normally harmless river-fruit they harvest hatch venomous spiders and misshapen monsters rise from the misty marshes to attack the colony.

The Deciders evacuate everyone back to the starliner as the Marshmen arise and begin to advance on the colony.

It is the Doctor who works out the truth: the Terradonians all died when they first arrived, and the people who now think of themselves as Terradonians are in fact evolved Marshmen. Mistfall is just a part of the planet's ecological process, and the spiders and attacking Marshmen will eventually evolve into the humanoids who now run the ship. He further deduces that the ship has been ready for take-off for years; the problem is that none of the Deciders will face up to the awful knowledge that they simply don't know how to pilot the ship.

With the Doctor's help, the humanoid Alzarians leave the planet in the starliner. Adric, one of the Outlers, stows away on board the TARDIS rather than leave with his people.

WHO FAX
● Novelised as *Doctor Who – Full Circle* by Andrew Smith in 1982.
● This story was the first in a trilogy of sorts set in E-Space.
● The writer, Andrew Smith, was a 19-year-old fan of *Doctor Who* who finally got the opportunity to write for it.
● This story introduced the character of Adric, played by Matthew Waterhouse, also a *Doctor Who* fan.
● Working title: *The Planet that Slept*.

COMMENT
Full Circle *marks the* Doctor Who *debut of director Peter Grimwade, and the end result is a highly effective production, boasting some moody and atmospheric location work and credible, well-judged*

performances by most of the cast. The script by new writer Andrew Smith is brimming with interesting and original ideas and contains a number of very good set-pieces. Again, the detailed plotting and exposition is far from watertight, and viewers are left with a number of puzzles unresolved at the end of the closing episode.

Matthew Waterhouse, making his debut appearance as new companion Adric, is actually nowhere near as good as Richard Willis, playing his doomed brother Varsh, or indeed as June Page, playing Keara, the other principal Outler. It would perhaps have been better had one of those other characters been retained as a regular.

State of Decay (5P)

EP	DATE	TIME	DURN	VIEWERS	CHART POS
1	22.11.80	17.42	22'24"	5.8	119
2	29.11.80	17.41	23'16"	5.3	136
3	06.12.80	17.40	24'13"	4.4	145
4	13.12.80	17.40	24'54"	5.4	125

PRODUCTION DETAILS

Location filming: 30.04.80-02.05.80

Studio: 15.05.80, 16.05.80 in TC3, 29.05.80-31.05.80 in TC6

The next port of call in E-Space is another habitable world. Here the people live in fear of 'the three who rule', who live in a high tower overlooking their village. The rulers demand humans whom their guards select from the village and take to the tower never to be seen again. They also keep the villagers in ignorance although there is a small secret group of scientists who are struggling to rediscover and keep alive the knowledge of electricity and technology.

The three who rule, Queen Camilla, King Zargo and Councillor Aukon, are in fact vampires, the surviving crew of the Hydrax, a spacecraft sucked like the TARDIS into a CVE, who have been vampirised by the Great Vampire, the last of a race exterminated by the Time Lords, who is now asleep underground awaiting his next summons.

The Doctor discovers that the tower is the shell of the original spacecraft and arranges for one of the shuttles to lift off and then to plummet to the ground, staking the awakening Great Vampire through the heart. With their controlling influence removed, Camilla, Zargo and Aukon crumble to dust.

WHO FAX
- Novelised as *Doctor Who and the State of Decay* by Terrance Dicks in 1981.
- *State of Decay* started life as long ago as 1977, when Terrance Dicks's vampire story, *The Witch Lords*, was put on hold due to the BBC's own production of *Dracula*.
- This story made ingenious use of stock footage of bats in flight.
- Working titles: *The Wasting*, *The Vampire Mutations*.

COMMENT
State of Decay *is a very moody and atmospheric story, in which great use is made of music and sound effects, combined with some very effective sets.*

The 'three who rule' are marvellously portrayed by Emrys James (Aukon), William Lindsay (Zargo) and Rachel Davies (Camilla). The first acts as the liaison point between the human villagers and the vampire Lords while the Lords themselves skulk in their tower, ritually awakening, feeding, washing and sleeping until their master arises.

As often in Doctor Who, *the remainder of the characters tend to be somewhat faceless, losing out to the well-written and well-acted villains. Good use is made of the locations, but the model used for long shots of the tower and its surrounding village is obviously a miniature, and this is particularly evident when the shuttle lifts off.*

Perhaps the most unfortunate aspect is the Great Vampire. All that is seen of him when he awakes is a clawed hand blindly groping in the air before the shuttle pierces his heart and kills him. Luckily this dodgy piece of effects work is immediately followed by a superb sequence in which the three vampires crumble to dust before the eyes of the Doctor and his friends.

Warriors' Gate (5S)

EP	DATE	TIME	DURN	VIEWERS	CHART POS
1	03.01.81	17.21	22'54"	7.1	88
2	10.01.81	17.10	23'47"	6.7	93

3	17.01.81	17.11	22'15"	8.3	59
4	24.01.81	17.10	24'53"	7.8	69

PRODUCTION DETAILS

Studio: 17.09.80–19.09.80 in TC3, 02.10.80–04.10.80 in TC1

Travelling through E-Space, the TARDIS is hijacked by Biroc, a Tharil, who phases into the ship and operates the controls. He directs it to a white void at the centre of the Time Lines.

Biroc is the formerly imprisoned navigator of a ship, the Privateer, carrying many of his Tharil brothers into slavery as time-sensitive navigators. He has brought the ship to the void to try to rescue his race.

The Doctor follows the image of Biroc through the void to a strange stone gateway, wherein a dusty and deserted banqueting hall is still laid for a meal. Biroc disappears into a mirror as the Doctor watches and time begins to jump about as the Doctor finds himself back in a period when the hall was occupied. Biroc explains about his mission to free the Tharils, but then their meal is interrupted by Gundan robots, creations of the Tharils' humanoid slaves, who in turn enslave the Tharils.

The Tharils have realised the error of their formerly dictatorial ways and are now intent on escaping to continue their lives in peace.

Rorvik, the insane commander of the slave ship, tries to break out of the void by back-blasting the gateway with his engines. Instead, the mirrors reflect the blast back, and the ship is destroyed, freeing the Tharils.

Romana and K-9 elect to stay with the Tharils to help them free the remainder of their people from slavery, and the TARDIS is flung back into N-Space.

WHO FAX

● Novelised as *Doctor Who and Warriors' Gate* by John Lydecker (pseudonym for Stephen Gallagher) in 1982.

● Kenneth Cope, well known for his role as the dead Marty Hopkirk in *Randall and Hopkirk (Deceased)*, played the part of Packard.

● The story was written by Stephen Gallagher, who has gone on to become one of Britain's top horror/thriller novelists.

● Production assistant Graeme Harper directed some of this story while Paul Joyce was unavailable.

● Clifford Rose, who played Rorvik, was well known as Kessler in *Secret Army*.

● Working title: *Dream Time*.
● This story replaced one called *Sealed Orders* by Christopher Priest.

COMMENT

This story can best be compared to The Celestial Toymaker *(1966) and* The Mind Robber *(1968) in that it is completely atypical. The main setting is a white void in which stands an old-fashioned stone gateway. The narrative jumps about as time shifts within the void, and this lends the scenes of the Doctor at the banquet, and the counterpointing scenes of Romana held captive by Rorvik and his crew, a dramatic edge which would otherwise be missing.*

Paul Joyce's direction is inspired, with scenes like Rorvik's ship entering the centre of the Time Lines causing a spinning coin to slow and stop in mid-air, and Biroc's forced entry into the TARDIS, being of particular note.

The plot is very convoluted with certain explanations left vague – viewers never do really know exactly whether the Gateway is the stone structure, the mirrors within it or something else entirely.

Overall Warriors' Gate *is a visual treat, but one which requires the viewer to work at understanding it.*

The Keeper of Traken (5T)

EP	DATE	TIME	DURN	VIEWERS	CHART POS
1	31.01.81	17.09	24'05"	7.6	72
2	07.02.81	17.09	24'50"	6.1	106
3	14.02.81	17.09	23'49"	5.2	112
4	21.02.81	17.12	25'11"	6.1	103
Repeat					
1	10.08.81	18.30	24'05"	5.2	71
2	11.08.81	18.20	24'50"	4.4	93
3	12.08.81	18.30	23'49"	5.2	71
4	13.08.81	18.21	25'11"	5.0	74

PRODUCTION DETAILS

Studio: 05.11.80, 06.11.80 in TC6, 21.11.80–23.11.80 in TC8

The Doctor and Adric are visited in the TARDIS by the Keeper of

Traken, an elderly wizened man, who tells them of a great evil which has come to his planet in the form of the Melkur, a calcified statue which was once an evil entity, drawn to the goodness and tranquillity of the Union of Traken as a moth is to a flame.

The Keeper's reign is nearly at an end, and he requests that the Doctor come to Traken to prevent the evil from taking control of the bioelectronic Source which is the keystone of the Union's society.

On Traken, Consul Kassia marries widower Consul Tremas only to find that Tremas has been chosen as the next Keeper Nominate, which means that she must leave him. The Melkur whispers to her that he can prevent this, and in desperation Kassia agrees. The Melkur via various deceptions becomes the next Keeper and is revealed to be the Master's TARDIS, its operator still blackened and emaciated as he was in his last meeting with the Doctor (see *The Deadly Assassin*). The Master hopes to use the power of the Source to regenerate himself, but the Doctor manages to expel him using the servo shutoff and sanctioning programs and install Consul Luvic as a new Keeper in his place.

In a last-minute ploy, the Master traps Consul Tremas and merges with his body before fleeing Traken. Nyssa, Tremas's daughter, is left concerned as to her father's whereabouts.

WHO FAX

● Novelised as *Doctor Who and the Keeper of Traken* by Terrance Dicks in 1982.

● The role of Tremas (an anagram of Master) was taken by Anthony Ainley, cast partly because of his facial similarity to the late Roger Delgado.

● The emaciated Master was played by Geoffrey Beevers, the husband of Caroline John, who had played Liz Shaw in the seventh season.

● Although she did not join the TARDIS crew until the following story, *The Keeper of Traken* saw the introduction of Nyssa, played by Sarah Sutton.

COMMENT

The penultimate adventure of Tom Baker's reign as the Doctor is a well-directed mystery, with excellent set design and acting. The return of the Master is completely unexpected, and as the true nature of the Melkur is concealed until the last possible moment, this gives an added boost towards the end of the story.

It is not, however, explained how, if the Melkur is the Master's TARDIS (it is bigger inside than out, can move via dematerialisation and is said to be a TARDIS in the story), he can have an additional TARDIS inside the Melkur, this one disguised as a grandfather clock!

Anthony Ainley comes over well as Tremas, convincingly displaying both parental concern for his daughter Nyssa and a keen desire to see the Union of Traken preserved. His absorption by the Master (if this is what happens - again it is not fully explained) adds a last-minute jolt to a very enjoyable story.

Logopolis (5V)

EP	DATE	TIME	DURN	VIEWERS	CHART POS
1	28.02.81	17.09	24'32"	7.1	84
2	07.03.81	17.09	24'03"	7.7	57
3	14.03.81	17.11	24'32"	5.8	102
4	21.03.81	17.09	25'10"	6.1	97
Repeat (BBC-2)					
1	30.11.81	17.43	24'32"	5.5	-
2	01.12.81	17.34	24'03"	5.0	-
3	02.12.81	17.42	24'32"	6.0	-
4	03.12.81	17.40	25'10"	5.4	-

PRODUCTION DETAILS

Location filming: 15.12.80–19.12.80

Studio: 08.01.81, 09.01.81 in TC3, 22.01.81–24.01.81 in TC6

With his ship's Cloister Bell tolling, a sign of impending doom, the Doctor decides to repair the TARDIS's chameleon circuit and so goes to Earth to obtain the exact external dimensions of a real police box which can be used to reconfigure the ship correctly. While he is there Tegan Jovanka, an air hostess, en route to her new job, enters the TARDIS thinking it to be a real police box.

The Master has devised a complex trap for the Doctor and kills Tegan's aunt Vanessa. The Doctor is apparently warned of an impending ordeal by a mysterious figure in white, the Watcher, who appears to him several times. The Doctor goes to Logopolis, a planet of mathematicians, where he hopes to gain assistance in his repairs to the TARDIS. However, the Master has hitched a ride, having materialised his own TARDIS within the Doctor's, and he now starts killing the Logopolitans. The Watcher appears again, having brought Nyssa from Traken to Logopolis.

The Master's meddling causes the Logopolitans' complex block transfer computations to go wrong, culminating in his use of a sound suppressor to prevent the calculations from being spoken at all – the means by which the Logopolitans run their programs.

The Monitor on Logopolis explains that it is his people's calculations that are keeping the Universe from destruction. It passed its normal heat death years ago, and the Logopolitans' programs are holding open numerous CVEs through which the excess entropy from our Universe is draining. With the Master's interference, the CVEs will close and the Universe will be destroyed. Watching on the TARDIS scanner, Nyssa and Adric see Traken destroyed as the entropy begins to take effect.

The Doctor and the Master join forces to prevent the destruction of the Universe and hurry to the Pharos Project in Cambridge on Earth with a copy of the Logopolitan program. They intend to use a radio telescope to transmit it and thus keep the CVEs open. The Master sees an opportunity to seize power and promptly blackmails the peoples of the Universe with destruction unless they agree to his demands. The Doctor tries to prevent the Master from carrying out his threat and succeeds, only to fall from the gantry of the radio telescope.

As he lies under the telescope, Adric, Nyssa and Tegan rush to join him. The Watcher appears once more and merges with the Doctor as he regenerates into a younger form.

WHO FAX

- Novelised as *Doctor Who – Logopolis* by Christopher H. Bidmead in 1982.
- Story released on BBC Home Video in 1992.
- The lead-up to the Doctor's regeneration at the conclusion of *Logopolis* included two compilations of clips featuring old enemies and friends of the Doctor. The enemies were the Master (*The Deadly Assassin* part one), a Dalek (*Destiny of the Daleks* episode four), the Pirate Captain (*The Pirate Planet* part two), a Cyberman (*Revenge*

of the Cybermen part three), Davros (*Genesis of the Daleks* part five), a Sontaran (*The Invasion of Time* part five), a Zygon (*Terror of the Zygons* part three) and the Black Guardian (*The Armageddon Factor* part six). The companions were Sarah (*Terror of the Zygons* part two), Harry (*The Sontaran Experiment* part two), the Brigadier (*Invasion of the Dinosaurs* part two), Leela (*The Robots of Death* part one), K-9 (*The Armageddon Factor* part two), Romana 1 (*The Stones of Blood* part one) and Romana 2 (*Full Circle* part one).

- The regeneration sequence at the end of this story was repeated with different music and overdubs as a pre-title sequence before the first Peter Davison story *Castrovalva*.

- The Watcher was played by actor Adrian Gibbs, who was not credited in the *Radio Times* or on screen.

- It was decided only late in the day that Nyssa would be a continuing character, so the other new companion, Tegan, was actually cast first.

COMMENT

As an end to the seven-year reign of the fourth Doctor, Logopolis *is something of a disappointment. The epic battle between good and evil turns out to be the Master operating the controls of a radio telescope to overbalance his nemesis; and the only thing that makes this particular trial for the Doctor special is that he inexplicably sees clips from some of his previous adventures just before he falls.*

Logopolis *is a very complex story, with writer Christopher H. Bidmead bringing in some fairly detailed scientific concepts (such as the power of mathematics to affect the physical make-up of the Universe and the idea of draining entropy away through holes into other Universes) and some completely bogus ones (for instance the Master attempting to hold the Universe to ransom using what appears to be either a transistor radio or a small dictaphone).*

Like many adventures in the eighteenth season and subsequently, the plot of Logopolis *is sacrificed to a number of nice-looking set pieces, which only occasionally hang together coherently, and which tend not to tell an ordered story.*

Logopolis *is enjoyable television, but is an adventure perhaps more suited for fans of* Doctor Who *than for the casual viewer. Perhaps not surprisingly, it topped the DWAS season poll.*

AFTERWORD

'It's the end. But the moment has been prepared for.'

As the Doctor utters these words lying broken on the ground under the radio telescope he knows that a new era in his long life is being ushered in. Considering that for Time Lords to meet themselves is to contravene one of the most important Laws of Time, one must wonder what the Watcher was doing and how he did it. What information the Doctor and the Watcher actually trade is not known, but whatever it is, the Doctor throws himself wholeheartedly into saving first Logopolis, and then the Universe, from destruction at the hands of the Master. He does not hesitate when he has to venture out on to the tilting telescope gantry to try and unplug the power, and as he hangs, suspended above the ground, the faces of his many enemies flash before his eyes. After his fall, he sees and hears his past friends and companions speaking his name. But the Doctor is not ready to die and instead regenerates with the help of the Watcher into the younger, fair-haired form that is to be his fifth incarnation.

4: Rewriting the Myth

Every era of *Doctor Who* brings new elements to the series' developing mythology. Story after story, new facts are invented by the programme's writers and added to what is already known of the Doctor's universe. Some new pieces of this ever-growing jigsaw puzzle interlock neatly with what has gone before, while some fit so poorly that the viewer is forced to start rebuilding the picture from scratch. Many hardcore *Doctor Who* fans expend great amounts of time and energy trying to find an order which gives all the seemingly contradictory facts and stories some kind of logical continuity.

Plot continuity has always been a bug-bear of long-running television programmes. It could be argued that good continuity is essential in a popular soap opera for the sake of believability, but is it so important in a series such as *Doctor Who*?

In the fourth Doctor's era, countless new monsters, planets, alien races and other elements were added to the *Who*niverse. Some were so important that they would forever change the nature of the programme. Yet continuity would seem to have been fairly low in the list of priorities of the successive production teams making *Doctor Who* in the seventies, as revealed in an interview with Tom Baker and producer Graham Williams in Issue 19 of *Starburst*:

BAKER: I meet people who reel off these titles or ask my opinion about certain things and they obviously know more about the history of the programme than I do. Because I'm not really – except in the informed way of not subverting anything – interested very much in what Pat did or Jon did. We're playing it absolutely from moment to moment, holding on by our fingertips with the pressure of time and money and everything.

WILLIAMS: I mean, you and I only keep marginally in the back of our minds what we did last year . . .

BAKER: Yeah.

WILLIAMS: Let alone five years ago or ten years ago.

BAKER: Not interested in that.

WILLIAMS: The audience aren't very interested in that either.

BAKER: What those fans are conceding is they don't understand actors and programme makers. What's in the past is in the past. Each one you try to make history with – 'This one is the best one'.

WILLIAMS: If we stuck religiously to points of continuity, of what we'd done before, the series would still be exactly where it was 15 years ago. You can't change a programme overnight. I don't think any audience could be expected to wear that – it wouldn't be fair on them. But, I think, in my years with the show, the changes we've made have been quite significant. It's changed only 15% or 20% a year, so it's still within the acceptable framework of the programme, but nevertheless it's moved on.

Graham Williams seems to have been suggesting that continuity was often sacrificed in favour of good plots, and that this practice of rewriting *Doctor Who* history was acceptable provided that changes were made gradually so as not to confuse the viewer. It would not however be true to say that this was the policy of all the producers of the Tom Baker era, or – perhaps more importantly – of the various script editors who worked under them. Baker's suggestion that what had gone before his era was ignored does not stand up to close scrutiny. Many links with the series' past were apparent during his time with the programme. Even if one chooses to ignore the fact that his first story, *Robot*, was a very typical UNIT tale which could arguably have slotted in at any point during Jon Pertwee's tenure as the Doctor, there is no denying the fact that the remainder of his debut season also drew heavily on the series' past. His third story, for instance, saw the reuse of a monster race – the Sontarans – which had made its own debut as recently as the previous season. This was clearly an attempt by departing producer Barry Letts and the Sontarans' creator, script editor Robert Holmes, to keep continuity between the adventures of the new Doctor and those of the old.

Field-Major Styre, the Sontaran in *The Sontaran Experiment*, appears identical at first sight to the original Sontaran, Linx, seen in *The Time Warrior*. In fact the same actor – Kevin Lindsay – played both parts. A number of minor differences are worthy of note, especially as they serve to illustrate some of the factors which can underlie departures from strict continuity.

First, although the Sontarans are supposedly a race of genetically identical clones, Styre's facial features are slightly different from Linx's. These changes were the result of a need to make the costume more comfortable for Lindsay to wear; the original mask had been made from heavy fibreglass matting coated with a thin surface layer of latex and had caused breathing problems for the actor (who suffered from a heart condition). The new mask was lighter and better ventilated – an example of a departure from continuity caused by a practical necessity.

Secondly, Styre has five fingers whereas Linx had only three. When asked about this discrepancy at a convention, one-time script editor Terrance Dicks joked that Sontarans probably found it easier to break human bones with five fingers! However, this change was probably the result of a simple mistake or oversight by a member of the design staff. If this change had been carried forward into subsequent Sontaran stories, it would no doubt have become accepted that Sontarans have five fingers, but in their next appearance in *The Invasion of Time* they had reverted to having only three fingers, leaving Styre the odd man (or Sontaran) out.

In *The Sontaran Experiment* it is also revealed that when exhausted, the Sontarans need to recharge themselves. This new fact is introduced as a plot device which allows the Doctor to defeat Styre, and is an example of a deliberate addition to *Doctor Who* mythology.

In terms of character, Styre and Linx are very similar. This is not surprising, as writer Bob Baker recalled in an interview in *In-Vision* that the Sontarans' creator Robert Holmes had given him and his writing partner Dave Martin a very detailed introduction to the monsters:

'Bob had given us the most incredibly deep briefing on the life and breeding systems and defecation systems of the Sontaran (I think he must have met one at some time). We just had to stop him, he was going on so much. It was very funny actually. He was under a bit of a strain, I felt, and this was manifest in the way he was talking about the Sontaran.

'So he said, "There's the character, in you go and put the story for two episodes around that." As far as cramping our style goes, it was just a brief – just like the Doctor is already a character. We didn't feel we were being fobbed off with a Sontaran. A story is a story, and we did get our own little monster in it.

'The script was printed, rushed down to the location, and shot. I think Bob changed three or four words – about the Sontaran. "He wouldn't do that. He wouldn't say that." "Oh all right then, change it Bob. It's your monster."'

In the very next story after *The Sontaran Experiment*, the fourth Doctor encountered another old foe, in fact the oldest of all – the Daleks. Dalek history comprises a major part of the *Who*niverse, and in the twelve years prior to their appearance in *Genesis of the Daleks* their mythology had already undergone a number of subtle changes and developments. From radiation-spawned mutants trapped inside metal casings, powerless to move outside the confines of their metal-floored city, they had been transformed into a space- and time-faring army, sweeping through the galaxy to conquer and enslave countless other worlds.

In *Genesis of the Daleks*, the Daleks' creator, Terry Nation, sought to tell the story of their origins. Naturally enough, he set the action on the creatures' home world, Skaro, which had first been seen in their introductory story, *The Daleks*, back in 1963. In *The Daleks*, the Doctor and companions had learnt from the history records of the planet's humanoid inhabitants, the Thals, that the Daleks had once been a race of scientists and philosophers called the Dals. A terrible nuclear war between Dals and Thals had led to the creation of the horribly mutated Daleks. This view of Skaroine history is confirmed in *Genesis of the Daleks*, although the Dals are replaced by the Kaleds as the Daleks' ancestors and a new character is introduced as the Daleks' progenitor. This character, Davros, creator of the Daleks, stole centre stage from the Daleks themselves and would continue to do so in many subsequent Dalek tales, long after the end of the fourth Doctor's era.

It was perhaps inevitable that any story about the origins of the Daleks would focus primarily on the situation which had existed before their creation, showing the transition to the state of affairs on Skaro which viewers had seen in *The Daleks*. Davros was the personification of the transition. Half-human, half-Dalek in appearance, he exhibited the evil cunning which he would eventually instil in his creations. Meanwhile, the prototype Daleks appeared almost inanimate, being switched on and off like radio-controlled models. It was only at the end of the story, when they apparently exterminated Davros and seized control of their own destiny, that they revealed their sentience.

Although *Genesis of the Daleks* appears to fit fairly well into previously established Dalek history, a few continuity errors do surface. The most obvious of these is the fact that the prototype Daleks are seen to operate outside the Kaled Elite's bunker, far from any metal floors, and even attack the Thal city. Yet in *The Daleks*, which must have been later in the Daleks' time stream, they were unable to leave their city, a disadvantage which the Doctor was able to exploit. Also the 'prototype' Daleks from *Genesis of the Daleks* resembled those from much later periods of Dalek history rather than those seen in their debut story.

In *Destiny of the Daleks*, the Daleks' second and last appearance during the fourth Doctor's era, Davros was resurrected. There was of course no overriding need for him to have reappeared for the sake of continuity, as he had already been established to have died at the very beginning of Dalek history. Yet, although *Destiny of the Daleks* is presumably set many hundreds of years after the events in *Genesis of the Daleks*, the character is brought back to aid his progeny in their battle with the Movellans.

The Movellans are humanoid robots whose thinking is perfectly logical in all respects, including their battle strategy. The Daleks' battle computers are also totally logical, and the resulting impasse sends the Daleks scurrying back to Skaro to excavate and revive their creator in the hope that he will be able to break the deadlock – a hope which proves well founded, as Davros realises that the required solution is for one of the sides in the battle to make an intuitive, illogical move. This plotline is flawed, however, as the Daleks should have been able to break the stalemate without Davros's help, simply because they are by nature illogical and emotional, conditioned to respond to situations with hate and anger.

Yet the Daleks in *Destiny of the Daleks* are subtly different from the Daleks of old. Several times during the story they are referred to as robots; and at one point the Doctor himself mentions in passing that they were once organic life forms, perhaps inferring that they no longer are. Is this the 'destiny' to which the title of the story refers – the evolution of the Daleks into the robots the general public and media have often mistakenly assumed them to be? Whether this suggestion of a radical change in the nature of the Daleks was intentional on the part of the production office is, however, uncertain, especially in the light of subsequent stories in which the Daleks reverted to their original nature as organic mutations within metallic casings.

Tom Baker's first season ended with a story featuring a race of monsters absent from the programme for seven years. The Cybermen had last appeared in the Patrick Troughton story *The Invasion*. It is perhaps not surprising then that many changes were apparent when they returned in *Revenge of the Cybermen*.

For one thing, there were a number of differences in the Cybermen's appearance. This was not unusual, as there had been some degree of variation in the costumes in every previous Cybermen story, ranging from very subtle touches to radical redesigns. The introduction of the Cyber Leader into the Cybermen's command structure was another important factor added in *Revenge of the Cybermen*. Previously the viewer had seen only the Cyberman Controller in *The Tomb of the Cybermen*, the Cyber Planner in *The Wheel in Space* and the Cyber Coordinator in *The Invasion*, the latter two of which had been not even humanoid in shape but more like partly organic computers.

The concept of the Cyber Leader (his rank denoted by the black colouring of the sides and back of his head) was an innovation which militated against a view of the Cybermen as being just a horde of identical silver zombies, raising the possibility of Cybermen trained, or rather programmed, for specific tasks. However, it was in the characterisation of the Cybermen that *Revenge of the Cybermen* differed most from previous stories. Before, the Cybermen had not really had individual characters as such. They were merely machine men, without emotions or personalities to distinguish one from another. In *Revenge of the Cybermen*, the Cybermen – and in particular the Cyber Leader – display a wide range of emotions, including anger, pride and fear.

The premise of the Cybermen being vulnerable to gold dust, which plates the respiratory apparatus in their chest units and effectively suffocates them, was an important and interesting development in their history. *Revenge of the Cybermen* can in fact be seen as the final end of the Cybermen, their race having been reduced to a mere handful of survivors by an earlier cataclysmic war with humanity. Their plan to destroy Voga, the 'planet of gold', seems born of desperation, and at one point the Doctor taunts the Cyber Leader over his race's depleted state:

> You've no home planet, no influence, nothing. You're just a pathetic bunch of tin soldiers skulking about the galaxy in an ancient spaceship.

It is indicative of the level of emotion with which the Cybermen are endowed in this story that the Doctor's goading seemingly causes the Cyber Leader to lose his temper to the extent that he physically attacks the Time Lord, even though the latter's survival is, for the time being, essential to his plan.

Reinforcing the impression that these were unusually emotional Cybermen was the treatment of their voices. In previous stories their dialogue had been delivered by a voice artist who, in most cases, used a small electronic palate device inside his own mouth to give the voices a machine-like monotone: a process which effectively removed any sense of emotion from the resulting voice. In *Revenge of the Cybermen*, however, the actors playing the Cybermen provided the voices themselves, with only a slight electronic treatment. The resulting voices were still very human-like, and in the case of the Cyber Leader, played by Christopher Robbie, a slight trace of a South African accent was detectable.

After the death of Roger Delgado in 1973, it seemed unlikely that the Master, the evil Time Lord he had so memorably portrayed, would ever again pit his wits against the Doctor's. In 1976, however, *The Deadly Assassin* did see the Master return, albeit in a much-altered form.

The Master had originally been presented as a character very similar to the Doctor; he was of the same race, of comparable intelligence and capable of exhibiting equal if not greater charm. Yet whereas the Doctor had always been driven to help the underdog and to combat injustice wherever he encountered it, the Master saw only the possibilities for exploitation and corruption. During the Pertwee era, viewers witnessed the Doctor thwarting many of the Master's evil schemes. Each successive defeat would no doubt have fuelled his adversary's sense of frustration and resentment. It is not surprising, therefore, that by the time of his reappearance in *The Deadly Assassin*, the Master has clearly become unhinged. Although he retains his cunning and guile, and his penchant for the grand scheme, his veneer of charm has gone. Moreover, nearing the end of his natural life, having used up all his regenerations, he is now a twisted parody of his former self. His body is emaciated and blackened, the result of a terrible accident on the planet Tersurus, and he is clinging to life only by virtue of his amazing willpower and his hatred of the Time Lords – and especially of the Doctor.

Writer Robert Holmes included in his script for this story some evocative stage directions for the Master, describing his features as 'the crawling face of death' and his hands as '. . . belonging to skeleton, the remaining withered skin hanging in strips'. The fact that the BBC chose to bring the Master back in this deteriorated form is a testament to the strength of the public's association of Roger Delgado with the role of the evil Time Lord. Producer Philip Hinchcliffe could simply have regenerated the character, in much the same way as the Doctor himself had been transformed on three previous occasions, but would the public have accepted a new actor in the part? The idea of depicting the Master in a decrepit state allowed the production team to resurrect the character in a way which would minimise such audience resistance while at the same time leaving open the possibility of a proper regeneration at a later date. In the publicity material sent out to the press prior to transmission of *The Deadly Assassin*, the BBC went out of their way to stress that this was not the straightforward return of an old foe:

'Although publicity along the lines of "The return of the Master" will help us, please bear in mind that Roger Delgado who formerly played the Master died tragically in a car accident several years ago. The actor playing the new Master, Peter Pratt, is only ever seen wearing a mask.'

It would be another four years before the Master would return in *The Keeper of Traken*, the penultimate story of the fourth Doctor's era. Still initially in his decayed form, he attempts to gain control of the Keepership of the Traken Union and the vast powers which accompany it. His plan is only partially successful, as the Doctor's intervention forces him to abandon the Keepership. However, the residual effects of his time in the Keeper's chair apparently enable him to steal the body of Keeper-elect Tremas, giving himself a new lease of life. (This is not explicitly stated in the story, but if he had already possessed the power to take over another person's body, he would presumably have done so before this point.)

The actor cast as the Master's new incarnation was Anthony Ainley, who had also played Tremas. Whereas each successive incarnation of the Doctor had been given a different and distinctive image, Ainley was intentionally chosen and made up to resemble Delgado. And in *Logopolis*, the story in which the new Master really established himself, it quickly became apparent that Ainley's interpretation of the role also owed much to Delgado's original. The Master seemed to have regained the calm and self-confidence of his earlier incarnation, albeit now tinged with a streak of pure insanity from his degenerated period.

The Master's plan in *Logopolis* involves disrupting the Logopolitans' calculations, which are holding open a number of Charged Vacuum Emboitments (CVEs) – gateways into other universes. This was in itself a clever piece of story continuity, as CVEs had been previously introduced as part of a linking theme to the stories of season eighteen.

As so often before, the Doctor eventually defeats the Master in the story's closing moments. In doing so, however, he sacrifices his own fourth incarnation and regenerates. And this is by no means the end of his troubles with the Master . . .

With such interesting characters, it is hardly surprising that *Doctor Who* viewers and writers alike were fascinated by the society which spawned them. Of all the new elements of *Doctor Who* mythology introduced during the fourth Doctor's era, those revolving around the Time Lords and their planet were arguably the most important in terms of the series' future development.

When first introduced in *The War Games*, Patrick Troughton's final story as the Doctor, the Time Lords had been presented as a mysterious and rather aloof race possessing awesome powers. Then, in their occasional appearances during the Jon Pertwee era, a little more had been learnt about them and they had come to seem rather less alien. In *The Three Doctors*, they had even been seen to be vulnerable to attack, albeit by one of their own kind – namely Omega, the stellar engineer who had originally given them the power they needed for time travel. The Time Lords seen here had appeared to be a technocratic race, heavily reliant on science for their position of power. They had also been shown to have a hierarchy, with a President and a Chancellor taking charge of the emergency.

The Three Doctors had still however failed to reveal any great detail about Time Lord society, leaving a residual air of mystery surrounding them. Viewers had not in fact even learnt the name of their home planet Gallifrey until season eleven's opening story, *The Time Warrior*.

The first season of the fourth Doctor's era added little to this previously established history of the Time Lords, although a single emissary did appear to the Doctor at the beginning of *Genesis of the Daleks* to assign him the task of attempting to alter the Daleks' future. It wasn't until the next season, the thirteenth, that any significant new information came to light.

The Brain of Morbius cast still further doubt on the original view of the Time Lords as invulnerable, near-immortal beings. In particular, it revealed their need to use a substance known as the Elixir of Life to get them through difficult regenerations. Something else which became apparent during the course of the story was that Time Lord society might not be as idyllic and well ordered as had previously been suggested. It was recounted that revolutionaries had in the not-too-distant past attempted to overthrow the Time Lords' rulers and their policies of non-intervention in the affairs of other worlds. Morbius, believing that his race should dedicate itself to conquest, had raised a large following to aid him in his quest for power. He and his supporters had however been defeated on the planet Karn, where he had eventually been tried and sentenced to be vaporised.

Morbius was by no means the first renegade Time Lord to have featured in *Doctor Who* – there had previously been the Monk, the War Chief and the Master, amongst others. The fact that so many Gallifreyans want to rebel against their rulers' authority tends to suggest that there is something rotten at the core of their society. This was certainly the view taken by script editor Robert Holmes, who presented his own interpretation of Gallifreyan life in *The Deadly Assassin*, the first adventure to be set entirely on the Doctor's home world.

Holmes's Time Lords were a race gone to seed, more concerned with etiquette and rituals than with the science which had made them so powerful in the first place. Their superior knowledge in fact appears to have allowed them to slip into complacency, spending their time worrying about petty politics rather than about the affairs of the rest of the Universe.

This depiction came as a bit of a shock to many fans who had grown accustomed to the idea of the Time Lords as a race of almost omnipotent beings. The President of the fledgling *Doctor Who* Appreciation Society wrote a strongly critical review of the story, condemning it for not following the established Time Lord mythology. In a letter to the fanzine *Gallifrey*, Holmes explained his reasons for departing so radically from previously perceived notions of the race:

'I'd noticed that over the years they had produced quite a few galactic lunatics – the Meddling Monk, the Master, Omega and Morbius. How did this square with the notion that the Time Lords were an omnipotent bunch of do-gooders? Could it be that this notion had been put about by the Time Lords themselves?'

Holmes claimed that the main inspiration for the plot of *The Deadly Assassin* was the film *The Manchurian Candidate*, from the novel of the same name by Richard Condon. This told the tale of an American war hero secretly brainwashed by the Chinese and sent back to America to assassinate key political figures, including the president. The mention in *The Deadly Assassin* of a secretive Time Lord organisation known as the CIA (Celestial Intervention Agency) is a clear reference back to Condon's tale of political intrigue. *The Deadly Assassin* also has many plot similarities to the real-life assassination of President John F. Kennedy in Dallas on 22 November 1963.

The system of Time Lord government as depicted in *The Deadly Assassin* seems to have its basis both in scholastic and in religious organisations. The Lord President is the figurehead, and beneath him are the Chancellor and the Cardinals, the heads of the Time Lord chapters, three of which – the Prydonians, the Patrexes and the Arcalians – are specifically named in the story. Each of the different chapters is distinguishable by the colours of its ceremonial robes: orange and scarlet for the Prydonians, green for the Arcalians and heliotrope for the Patrexes. The Doctor is revealed to be a Prydonian, and this is apparently the most important and influential of the chapters, having provided more Presidents than all the others put together. The true seat of power on Gallifrey however rests within the High Council, a body on which the most high-ranking of the Cardinals sit.

These facts about Time Lord society are presented to the viewer primarily by way of the dialogue of the character Runcible, one of the Doctor's peers from his days at the Prydonian academy. He is a Commentator for public access video, covering the important Presidential resignation ceremony held in the Panopticon, the central chamber of the Time Lords' city, the Capitol.

Below the Cardinals there are other ranks of Time Lords, including the Castellan, an official responsible for law and order, who is in command of the force of Chancellory guards. There is also the Coordinator whose duties are akin to those of a librarian, watching over the APC Net and the Matrix – the repository of all the knowledge and experience of deceased Time Lords. In *The Deadly Assassin*, it is to Coordinator Engin that Castellan Spandrell goes when he wishes to access the Doctor's biog-data extract.

Engin comments to Spandrell that the Castellan usually deals with more plebeian classes than Prydonian renegades, a remark which suggests that although all Time Lords are Gallifreyans, not all Gallifreyans are necessarily Time Lords. The evidence seems to suggest that the majority of the populace of Gallifrey do not share the great powers of their rulers – a possible cause of the unrest which is hinted at, especially by Cardinal Borusa's insistence that Chancellor Goth's treachery be covered up to avoid the Time Lords being seen in a bad light.

The Time Lords certainly would have looked foolish if it had become commonly known that they had forgotten the true significance of the Sash and the Great Key of Rassilon, which they had believed to be merely symbolic regalia of the Time Lord President. As the Doctor discovers, these artifacts are in fact devices which give access to the Eye of Harmony, a monolith hidden beneath the floor of the Panopticon which holds stable the core of a black hole and thereby acts as the source of all the Time Lords' power.

Like Omega, Rassilon is described as a legendary Time Lord figure who lived at the dawn of their civilisation. Coordinator Engin reads to the Doctor from the Book of the Old Time, which records that Rassilon was originally an engineer and an architect before the Time Lords abandoned the barren road of technology – a rather strange statement considering that, however ignorant they may be of the workings of the technology which powers their world, they are still very much dependent upon it. It seems odd, too, that although the APC Net supposedly holds the sum total of all Time Lord knowledge, they still have to turn to such obscure texts as the Book of the Old Time to find out about their early history.

Underworld gave viewers a little more information about that history, explaining in the process the reason for the Time Lords' non-interventionist policies. It reveals that the Time Lords once aided a race called the Minyans by giving them the technology with which to build an advanced society. The Minyans treated the Time Lords as gods, but were not advanced enough to cope with the new power they had been given. They used those gifts to create powerful weapons, and ultimately destroyed themselves in a cataclysmic war. The Time Lords vowed that from that time onwards they would never again interfere in the affairs of other races.

It was in *The Invasion of Time*, the story which immediately followed *Underworld*, that the Time Lords themselves were next seen in *Doctor Who*. This story essentially confirmed the Robert Holmes view of Gallifreyan society, while at the same time adding a number of new elements.

One of those elements was a female Time Lord, Rodan, who – with the sole exception of the Doctor's own grand-daughter, Susan – was the first female Gallifreyan ever to be seen in the series. Rodan was a very junior Time Lord, whose responsibilities included monitoring the approach of spaceships to Gallifrey and controlling the transduction force field barriers which protected the planet from possible invasion.

Another important addition was that of a group of Gallifreyans who had turned their backs on their former comfortable lifestyle and now lived a more primitive existence in the wastelands outside the Capitol. It has often been speculated by fans that these people were the Shabogans, a group of trouble-makers mentioned by Castellan Spandrell in *The Deadly Assassin*, but there is no evidence to suggest that the two groups were connected.

A slight oddity in *The Invasion of Time* is that the rod-like artefact referred to in *The Deadly Assassin* as the Great Key of Rassilon is described here as the Rod of Rassilon, while another Key of Rassilon is introduced which does actually look like a conventional key. The Key proves to be a vital component of the Demat gun, a weapon so powerful it can remove its target from time and space altogether.

The sixteenth season of *Doctor Who* also introduced a number of important new elements; and the fact that it had an umbrella theme was in itself an innovation. The Doctor's search for the Key to Time was initiated by the White Guardian, a being representing the forces of good, who was implied to be in an eternal power-struggle with the opposing Black Guardian, representing the forces of evil. The Guardians were created by *Doctor Who* producer Graham Williams essentially to meet the series' need for a race of powerful, omniscient beings – a role vacated by the now-flawed Time Lords – and they would become an important aspect of the series' development over the next few years.

For one thing, the White Guardian provided the Doctor with a new companion, a female Time Lord by the name of Romanadvoratrelundar, or Romana. This was the first time the Doctor had had a companion who was his intellectual equal. Romana had in fact gained higher grades than the Doctor at the Time Lord academy. But her aloof nature and her lack of practical experience of the Universe outside the transduction barriers of Gallifrey often led her to stumble into dangerous situations.

Romana's relationship with the Doctor was often strained by their competitive natures, and this may perhaps be why, after they had successfully collected all six segments of the Key to Time, she chose to regenerate. This regeneration was quite different from those which viewers had previously witnessed the Doctor undergoing, in that Romana was able to choose her new form. She paraded a number of alternatives before the Doctor, before overcoming the Doctor's resistance at her adopting the likeness of Princess Astra, the living being who had embodied the final segment of the Key. In her new incarnation, her relationship with the Doctor seemed to improve greatly. The Doctor was clearly deeply saddened when she elected to leave him to remain with the Tharils in E-Space at the end of *Warriors' Gate*.

Three stories during season eighteen took place within this mysterious realm of E-Space, a universe smaller than our own, which the TARDIS inadvertently entered through a CVE. It was in one of these stories, *State of Decay*, that a further piece of information about the ancient history of the Time Lords surfaced. The Doctor finds himself battling the last of the Great Vampires, the ancient enemy of the Time Lords from the time of Rassilon. It is revealed that the Time Lords formed a fleet of bow-ships to hunt down and destroy the Vampires, but one of the creatures escaped and fled into E-Space. Rassilon then ordered that a special instruction be placed within all time capsules to the effect that the operator should make every attempt to destroy the Vampire if ever its whereabouts were to be discovered.

Further facts would have been added to Time Lord history in *Shada*, but as industrial action at the BBC prevented its completion, it is arguable whether or not these should be regarded as bona fide elements of *Doctor Who* mythology. We have chosen not to regard as valid anything which was not televised.

The Doctor's TARDIS had played an important part in the programme's history from the first episode onwards. During seasons twelve and thirteen there were actually very few scenes which took place within the TARDIS, but in *The Masque of Mandragora* the Doctor was seen to take Sarah Jane Smith on a tour through some of the many rooms of his ship, including the enormous boot cupboard. The most interesting discovery is the TARDIS's secondary control room, a wooden-panelled affair with a smaller central console on a raised dais, also in wood. This new control room set was used for the whole of the season, and was intended to be a permanent replacement for the now fairly tatty original console and set. However, the panels of the new set warped whilst in storage, and were unusable come the beginning of the following season. Hence the original control room was rebuilt, and it made its reappearance in *The Invisible Enemy*.

Another new fact revealed about the TARDIS in *The Deadly Assassin* was that it was a Type 40 TT Capsule, and the only one of its type still in operation.

Perhaps the greatest tour of the TARDIS ever undertaken was during *The Invasion of Time*, when the Doctor and his friends were chased by the Sontarans through the many rooms of the ship. A laboratory and a swimming pool (described as the bathroom) were amongst the sections shown.

In *Logopolis*, the existence of the Cloister room is revealed. This is a large chamber containing ancient stonework covered in overhanging plants. Another addition is the Cloister Bell, presumably located somewhere within the Cloister room. The tolling of the Bell indicates the approach of some catastrophe for the TARDIS.

Throughout the fourth Doctor's adventures, new elements were continually added to the evolving myth that is *Doctor Who*. This process of development was the end result of many individual and collaborative decisions by the writers, script editors and producers who worked on the series during this period, each leaving his own personal mark on it. Some writers went to great pains to weave their tales into the existing legend, whereas others ignored the restrictions of established facts and concentrated on producing exciting and watchable television.

Doctor Who's strength as a series has always lain in its flexibility. As the Doctor can travel anywhere in time and space, the only limits for a writer are those of his imagination. It would be a shame if any writer felt so burdened by the programme's past that he could not create new characters and situations because of a fear of contradicting previous stories. If, however, a fact were to be established in one story only to be contradicted in the next, the viewer would quickly become disoriented and lose interest. As Graham Williams recognised, major changes must be carried out over a period of time to allow viewers to get used to them.

Fans of course have a rather different perspective from other, less committed viewers. They are much more concerned about the minutiae of continuity. However, they can plug almost any gap with their own theories to explain apparent inconsistencies. Some even take up their pens to write their own versions of events to link two or more unconnected bits of *Who* mythology. Perhaps if the whole history of *Doctor Who* had been meticulously planned in advance to allow no departures from strict continuity, the programme would not be so exciting to write for, and, of course, to watch.

PART THREE – FACT

5: Production Development

The production of a TV drama series relies heavily on teamwork, with many different people – script editor, writers, directors, designers and actors among them – all influencing the form and content of the finished product. Probably the most influential contributor of all is the producer, who has overall responsibility for the programme. During Tom Baker's time as the Doctor, *Doctor Who* had four producers – Barry Letts, Philip Hinchcliffe, Graham Williams and John Nathan-Turner - each of whom brought his own particular approach and style to the series.

Barry Letts had been appointed to the producer's job in 1969, and had been in charge throughout Jon Pertwee's successful five-year stint as the third Doctor. In 1974, when he came to cast Tom Baker as the new lead actor, he had almost reached the end of his time on the series; *Robot*, recorded back to back with Pertwee's swan song *Planet of the Spiders*, was in fact the last story on which he received the producer's credit.

Save for the new Doctor himself, there was little in *Robot* to distinguish it from the *Doctor Who* to which viewers had become accustomed in recent years. It took place in near-contemporary England – the setting used for the majority of the Pertwee stories – and featured not only the Doctor's established companion, Sarah Jane Smith, but also the familiar characters of Brigadier Lethbridge-Stewart, Sergeant (now Warrant Officer) Benton and UNIT. Interviewed in

1981 for *Doctor Who Monthly*'s Winter Special, Barry Letts explained the thinking behind this:

'Because the audience has not yet accepted the new Doctor, their sympathies are with the characters they know, and they are identifying with these characters as they react to the new and eccentric Doctor. The old characters – the Brigadier, Benton and Sarah – are there to reassure the viewing public that they are still watching *Doctor Who*.'

This was a philosophy which underpinned much of Tom Baker's debut season, season twelve. Although *The Ark in Space*, *The Sontaran Experiment*, *Genesis of the Daleks* and *Revenge of the Cybermen* followed the trend of the latter Pertwee seasons by moving away from the tried and trusted UNIT set-up and into more unfamiliar territory, continued viewer reassurance was provided by way of the inclusion of a parade of popular returning monsters – Sontarans, Daleks and Cybermen. Then, in *Terror of the Zygons* – planned as the final story of season twelve although ultimately made as the first of season thirteen – the Doctor, Sarah and Harry Sullivan were brought back to Earth for another UNIT adventure.

Speaking in 1987 to *In-Vision*, Letts recalled this period of transition between himself and Hinchcliffe:

'The cross-over period was quite lengthy. While I was still producer, Philip hung around; and then after he became producer, I hung around to hand over. So I was there during *The Sontaran Experiment* and I was there for *The Ark in Space* and made various comments.

'*Planet of the Spiders* was far more my epitaph than *Robot*. I had far more input and directed it myself, and we said goodbye to Jon. With *Robot*, the main thing was to try to get a good exciting show for the first one of the new Doctor, so that I could hand the success over to Philip Hinchcliffe.'

Although Letts was not physically present for the whole of the season, all the scripts had been commissioned while he was still producer, so his influence continued to be felt. However, much of the responsibility for the content of the season fell to new script editor Robert Holmes, as Philip Hinchcliffe told *In-Vision* in 1987:

'Bob Holmes had quite a large influence. He was very much anti-UNIT – he thought it was all rather silly, running around shooting at monsters. It had had its day.

'When I got there, they'd commissioned a Dalek story from Terry Nation, a Cyberman story from Gerry Davis, and from Bob Baker and

Dave Martin they'd commissioned one about a Sontaran – which was a character that Bob himself had invented. Although those stories were not completed – the Sontaran one had been written, and the Dalek one was half written – they were on the go. Bob didn't like the idea of using the old monsters, but he was enough of a showman to know that probably it was a safe bet to beef up the season.'

Despite the presence of some reassuringly traditional elements, these stories contained strong hints that *Doctor Who* was undergoing an important change of style at this time. *Robot*, for all its military hardware, gun battles and explosions, had been essentially cosy, fantasy-based family drama, very much akin to most of the Pertwee-era UNIT tales, but productions like *The Ark in Space* and *Genesis of the Daleks* had a harder, grittier, more realistic quality. *The Ark in Space*, for instance, had a Gothic horror flavour in its portrayal of people becoming physically and mentally possessed by the Wirrn, while *The Sontaran Experiment* depicted the brutal torture of a group of human spacemen. *Genesis of the Daleks*, with its themes of warfare, racial hatred and genetic experimentation, was even more graphic and disturbing, provoking complaints from some viewers and from TV watchdog Mary Whitehouse's National Viewers and Listeners Association.

The new, more adult style was welcomed and actively encouraged by Philip Hinchcliffe, who shared his script editor's view that there ought to be, in tandem with the change of Doctor, a change of direction for the series as a whole:

'Although we'd got these old favourites in the first season – in the bag, as it were – both Bob and I felt that we'd like to move the show away from what had been the "Barry Letts formula". Not because we didn't rate that – I think Barry was a terrific producer of the show, and Jon Pertwee was a very good Doctor . . . But I felt that that was now slightly played out.

'I felt that we could move the show in a different direction – more into genuine science fiction and fantasy. We didn't want to be so reliant on monsters in funny masks all the time, but in a way to take the audience on a genuine journey of fantasy by creating an atmosphere in the stories. And that tied in with Bob's idea of not relying totally on monsters that weren't very interesting and didn't have very interesting motives. I thought we could add a bit more power – I was quite interested in doing something in the science fiction area which, okay, would be *Doctor Who*, but we could balls it up a bit!'

The new, more 'ballsy' style was readily apparent in seasons thirteen and fourteen – the two seasons for which Hinchcliffe was fully responsible. The stories of these seasons are generally regarded as amongst the most frightening in the series' history. Incidents often cited as having been particularly horrific include: the dropping of Morbius's brain on the floor in *The Brain of Morbius*; the man-to-Krynoid transformations and Harrison Chase's death in the compost grinder in *The Seeds of Doom*; the strangulations perpetrated by *The Robots of Death*; and the various grim and violent fates suffered by characters in *The Talons of Weng-Chiang*.

The National Viewers and Listeners Association's earlier condemnation of *Genesis of the Daleks* proved to be just the first of many such attacks on *Doctor Who*; and in one instance, when the Association complained about a scene at the end of *The Deadly Assassin* part three in which the Doctor appears to be on the point of being drowned, they even won a written apology from BBC Director General Charles Curran. Curran wrote that the scene in question had in fact been cut down prior to transmission but that, with hindsight, 'the head of department responsible would have liked to cut out just a few more frames of the action than he did'. Although expressed in relatively mild terms, this apology marked a significant change of policy by the BBC, where at one time Mary Whitehouse had been very much *persona non grata*. It represented a minor landmark in the perennial debate about the portrayal of violence in TV drama, and was to have a long-term and arguably damaging impact on *Doctor Who* itself.

In an interview with *Daily Express* journalist Jean Rook, published on 11 February 1977 under the title 'Who do you think you are, scaring my innocent child?', Robert Holmes answered some standard criticisms of the programme's new style:

'Of course it's no longer a children's programme. Parents would be terribly irresponsible to leave a six-year-old to watch it alone. It's geared to the intelligent 14-year-old, and I wouldn't let any child under ten see it.

'If a little one really enjoys peeping at it from behind the sofa, until Dad says "It's all right now – it's all over", that's fine. A certain amount of fear is healthy under strict parental supervision. Even then I'd advise half an hour to play with Dad and forget it before a child goes to bed.

'That's why we switched the time-slot from 5:15 to after 6:00, when most young kids are in the bath.

'When *Doctor Who* started, as a true children's programme, the monsters were rubber and specific and you saw them almost at once. What horrifies far more is the occasional flash of monster – bits and pieces of one. People are frightened by what *might* come round the corner or in at the window.'

When challenged about the portrayal of death in the series, Holmes told Rook:

'They're strictly fantasy deaths. No blood, no petrol bombs, nothing a child could copy. We're not in business to harm children. We learned our lesson years ago, with some plastic daffodils which killed just by spitting at people. We didn't consider that people actually have plastic daffodils in their homes. They caused screaming nightmares, so we scrapped them. You must never attack the security of a child in its home. If you make something nasty, you don't stick it in a nursery.'

In fact, Holmes's memory was slightly at fault here: seasons thirteen and fourteen did feature both blood and (in *The Seeds of Doom*) petrol bombs. However, it would be wrong to assume that the impact – and undeniable success – of *Doctor Who* under Hinchcliffe and Holmes relied solely on the presentation of a succession of gory or shocking images. Much more important were the chilling concepts underlying the stories and the realistic and frequently Gothic style in which they were produced.

Hinchcliffe explains what he and Holmes were aiming for:

'We'd already decided that we wanted to take the Doctor away from Earth, to go out there to other worlds. So that was one principle. Alternatively, if Earth was involved in some way, it would not be just a case of having a monster invading and then getting the soldiers out to come and shoot at it!

'What I wanted to do were stories that had a powerful concept behind them. Stories which had depth and menace, in terms of science fiction or horror or literature generally.

'We wanted to develop themes – like nemesis, a man trapped in something he doesn't really understand and he's really fighting himself. Those very basic mythic themes were things that I wanted to try and get in. And Bob and I wanted to incorporate them into things we'd either seen before, or which we had read about.'

This derivation of inspiration and ideas from other sources such as popular myths, literature, TV and, in particular, cinema films was another of the distinctive features of seasons thirteen and fourteen. It had not been unknown for *Doctor Who* to draw on such sources in the past – some of the early Pertwee stories, for instance, had paid homage to the BBC's science-fiction serials of the fifties featuring Professor Bernard Quatermass, while Tom Baker's debut adventure, *Robot*, had been in some respects a reworking of the *King Kong* idea. In these two seasons, however, the practice was taken further than ever before, as Tom Baker recalled when interviewed in 1991 for *Doctor Who Magazine*:

'We used to see lots of movies at that time and often, like actors and directors do, we adapted scenes from films – recalling a scene from a film and doing our version of it. If anyone out there loved the film as much as we did, we wanted to send them a sort of signal. Likewise, when I had to say the co-ordinates of something I often used the BBC telephone number and the *Doctor Who* office extension, and no-one ever noticed!

'Of course the stories Philip Hinchcliffe and Robert Holmes worked on were all film pastiches and of course we spotted them. In fact, sometimes I was extremely rude about it if they didn't come clean about where they were nicking the idea from! Like good comedians, you thrash around anywhere for material and steal and adapt, trying to perform that alchemy, transmuting one thing into another.

'If people recognise the influence, it adds a certain pleasure, it's another little level. You don't have to see those things, but there were lots of little nudges and winks that people who were going through time and space were able to send to their watchers, little signals like an astronaut might send, which mean one thing to one listener and something else to another.'

The eclectic referencing of such sources added great depth and resonance to the stories of seasons thirteen and fourteen, and helped to create the suspenseful and often Gothic atmosphere for which Hinchcliffe and Holmes were aiming. These stories also benefited from the fact that they were made during a period now widely regarded as a golden age of BBC drama, with extremely high production values being achieved across the Corporation's entire range of series, serials and plays. Having reached an almost unprecedented level of popularity, *Doctor Who* was at this time regarded as one of the BBC's flagship programmes, and the production team were able to call upon not only the highest real-terms budget the series had ever had but also on some of the cream of the BBC's considerable creative talent to help bring it to the screen.

Contributors included such experienced directors as Douglas Camfield and David Maloney, both of whom had been responsible for many well-remembered *Doctor Who* stories in the past; costume designers of the calibre of James Acheson, later to win Hollywood Oscars for his work in films, and John Bloomfield; and top-flight set designers such as Roger Murray-Leach, another subsequent Oscar winner, and Barry Newbery. Another important contribution to the programme's overall style was made by composer Dudley Simpson, who supplied a succession of distinctive and acclaimed incidental scores. Amongst the writers who provided scripts were Robert Banks Stewart, later to be responsible for such hit series as *Shoestring* and *Bergerac*, and Louis Marks, a playwright and later a distinguished BBC producer.

Unsurprisingly, the stories of this period are now generally agreed to have been some of the most outstanding in the series' history. However, the long-term success of *Doctor Who* has always depended on change and innovation, and as season fourteen drew to a close another important development was imminent. Having been offered the job of producer on a new, hard-hitting police series called *Target*, Philip Hinchcliffe left *Doctor Who*, handing over the reins to the man who had earlier created *Target* – Graham Williams.

Williams's arrival marked the start of another change of direction for *Doctor Who*. One important reason for this was that he wanted to tone down the level of violence in the series, as he told *In-Vision* in an interview shortly before his death in 1990:

'With Philip Hinchcliffe, Bob Holmes had been spoofing Hammer films for years, and I saw no reason to discourage this practice. Hammer had been going for years in this country and had hardly drawn a breath of comment from the infamous Mrs Whitehouse. I suppose because so much of it was set in the 19th Century and in foreign countries it was deemed to be the acceptable face of horror – which is as far down that road as I wanted to go. To me, a lot of what Philip had done went too far. When I learned I was taking the show over, I made special efforts to watch it. One of the ones I saw – *Genesis of the Daleks* – had Lis Sladen climbing up a rocket gantry, being shot at by guards with rifles. She almost falls once, and then on reaching the top she gets caught, and is deliberately tripped by her captors and left dangling in mid-air while they laugh.

'I had by then just become father to our first son, and so was more aware that if children were going to be watching *Doctor Who* at 5:25 then a lot of this sadism and deliberate shock-horror, which Bob and Philip took a particular glee in producing, was not very defensible. I did not think Philip was right to let the drowning sequence in *The Deadly Assassin* go through, because the violence was too realistic and therefore could be imitated. Even on *Z Cars* you did not show a fight using a broken bottle for precisely that reason.'

Even had Williams not wanted to reduce the level of violence, this was an area in which he had little room for manoeuvre as senior BBC executives were keen for him to 'clean the series up' following the persistent criticisms which had been made during Hinchcliffe's tenure. As he would later reflect, this was the most difficult problem he had to face during his first year as producer:

'I was happy to tone down the realistic horror and gore. But then the BBC told me to go further and actually clean it up. It was over-reaction, of that I am sure, but it did not help that in my first year I was under a directive to take out anything graphic in the depiction of violence.'

While some of Williams's earliest productions, notably *Horror of Fang Rock* and *Image of the Fendahl*, retained the Gothic quality of the Hinchcliffe seasons, it was not long before his new policy took effect. This gradual removal of the series' more horrific elements left a void which was filled in part by an increased use of humour, particularly after Anthony Read succeeded Robert Holmes as script editor midway through production of season fifteen. The lighter tone at first manifested itself in the way stories were directed and acted, Tom Baker taking the opportunity to inject a lot of his own ideas and dialogue into scenes during rehearsals to make them more off the wall and amusing. Robert Holmes's own *The Sun Makers,* however, was an exception to the rule in that the script itself had a distinctly humorous slant, with its satirical references to the British tax system; and as time went by the series' writers increasingly picked up on the new, less serious approach and tailored their work accordingly, incorporating deliberately comedic scenes and dialogue.

This trend gained an added impetus when humorist Douglas Adams, later to enjoy great success with *The Hitch-Hiker's Guide to the Galaxy,* took over from Anthony Read as script editor for season seventeen, which culminated in stories such as *The Creature from the*

Pit and *The Horns of Nimon*, which came complete with ludicrous monsters, slapstick sound effects and scenes of the Doctor giving K-9 artificial respiration and talking directly to camera.

'It was inevitable that the style of *Doctor Who* would change once Tony Read took on the burning torch,' Williams later reflected. 'But of course one can never predict how in advance. In all honesty, and with no detriment implied either to Tony Read or to Douglas Adams, I have to say that I would have been a very much happier chap had I had Bob Holmes as my script editor throughout all my seasons, as Philip had done. I certainly felt I was on more of a wavelength from the word go with Bob than I was with either of the others. It took working towards with the other two, but Bob truly had found the natural slot for *Doctor Who* in the television universe.'

During Williams's time on the series, Tom Baker's Doctor increasingly took centre-stage and dominated proceedings with his wise-cracking, larger-than-life personality. This is not to say, however, that the producer exercised no restraint at all over his lead actor. Baker's more outlandish suggestions – such as replacing Leela with a talking cabbage perched on the Doctor's shoulder – were instantly discounted, and major disagreements occasionally occurred. Perhaps the most serious of these arose towards the end of production on season sixteen, when Baker threatened to quit unless given script, casting and director approval for the following year's stories – something which Williams, not surprisingly, was unwilling to concede. Fortunately this dispute was amicably resolved when, after high-level discussions and a meeting between Baker, Williams and the BBC's Head of Series and Serials, Graeme MacDonald, Baker dropped his demands.

At the time, the change of style which occurred under Williams was viewed less than enthusiastically by some of the series' fans – particularly those who had enjoyed and grown accustomed to the relatively serious Philip Hinchcliffe productions. There were wry suggestions from some quarters that *Doctor Who* ought now to be renamed *The Tom Baker Show*, or even *Tom Baker's Comedy Half Hour*. It would however be a mistake to imply that the stories of these seasons were in any way crass or simplistic. On the contrary, the liberal use of humour often disguised the fact that the scripts were, on the whole, highly literate and intelligent. They exhibited a knowing, postmodern playfulness with the traditional conventions and clichés of *Doctor Who* and of TV drama in general, and were realised with a kind of tongue-in-cheek camp unique to this period of *Doctor Who*'s history.

The cleverness and sophistication of these stories have become much more widely appreciated in recent years, and Williams's contribution to *Doctor Who* has been reassessed in a much more positive light. In any case, as far as the general viewing public were concerned, there was never any doubt as to the success of his new approach – they lapped it up!

Although not as consistent as during Hinchcliffe's time, the series' ratings remained generally high while Williams was producer, often breaking the 10 million barrier and, in the case of *City of Death*, reaching an all-time record story average of 14.5 million viewers per episode, albeit with the help of a strike which blacked out ITV. Clearly *Doctor Who* was still very much a high-profile series, and an important element in the BBC's Saturday evening programming.

On the minus side, many critics felt that there was a decline in production values during Williams's three-year stint. What they perhaps failed to recognise was that the further the series moved away from the realms of naturalistic drama, the less appropriate it became for it to have 'realistic' sets, props, costumes and so forth. The visual aspects had to reflect the increasingly larger-than-life, fantastical nature of the stories. In those instances where the production did fall short of expectations, this could almost always be attributed to the sheer scale and ambition of what was being attempted. Take, for instance, the case of *Underworld*, in which whole sequences were created through the use of CSO – by far the most extensive use ever attempted in *Doctor Who* of this electronic effect. These scenes have been widely dismissed as unconvincing, but they could equally well be viewed as a praiseworthy effort to push back the frontiers of the series' visual effects work. During its long history, *Doctor Who* has often been at the forefront of technical advances in television, and if the experiment had proved successful it would no doubt have been hailed as a great triumph.

A further example is provided by the brick-walled TARDIS interior as seen in *The Invasion of Time*. Again, some have cited this as a lapse in production standards which undermined the credibility of one of the series' most important icons. Looked at in another light, however, Williams's decision to have these scenes shot on location is a daring one, creating the opportunity for an exciting chase sequence which would have been impossible to achieve in the studio. If anyone was at fault here, perhaps it was those critics who were unable to suspend their disbelief during the scenes in question. After all, if the TARDIS's chameleon circuit can change the outer shell of the ship into a mundane, everyday object like a police box, why shouldn't it also change the interior to give it brick walls?

Throughout his time as producer Williams consistently pushed the series to the limits of what could be achieved, striving to make it as good as possible given the various difficulties with which he was faced. A particular problem, as he later reflected, was a shortage of money:

'During those three years, inflation was running at breakneck speed. We were almost hourly being told that costs had just gone up by another ten per cent. The knock-on effect was like compound interest, with everything spiralling up into quite lunatic sums. I had several long and very severe conversations with the bosses upstairs, to the effect that they didn't care how I spent my money as long as it was money from that year. Once that was gone, there was no question of over-funding. I would just lose episodes – end of argument. Philip Hinchcliffe had not left me with too much of a reputation, because so many of his *Doctor Who*s had gone massively over-budget on scenery.'

Another stumbling block Williams had to face right at the outset was the loss of the story which should have been his first production for the series – Terrance Dicks's vampire tale *The Witch Lords*. This had to be dropped at virtually the last minute on the insistence of Graeme MacDonald, who thought it might be construed as a send-up of a prestigious BBC adaptation of *Dracula* which was then in the pipeline.

The loss of *The Witch Lords* not only necessitated the hasty commissioning of a replacement script, which Dicks himself provided in the form of *Horror of Fang Rock*, it also completely disrupted the production schedule for the early part of the fifteenth season. *The Invisible Enemy*, which should have been second into the studio, had to be recorded first, and consequently ended up looking rather rushed. *Horror of Fang Rock* then followed, but had to be recorded at the BBC's Pebble Mill studios in Birmingham – making this the only *Doctor Who* story so far to have had its studio work done outside London – as it transpired that no studio space was available at the usual Television Centre facilities on the dates when needed. All in all, as Williams put it, this was 'a punishing baptism of fire'.

Williams's headaches did not end there. Throughout his time on the series he was dogged by problems arising from industrial action within the BBC. Although *Doctor Who* had been affected by such action even as far back as the sixties – the 1968 story *The Wheel in Space*, for example, had been hit by a scene-shifters' strike, necessitating several last-minute changes of studio – never before had it suffered to this extent. Inevitably this also had an impact on the stories as transmitted.

'On each of the three years I did *Doctor Who*,' reflected Williams, 'at exactly the same point in time (which was about mid-November), we had the *Crackerjack* Clock dispute. *Crackerjack* Clock is the generic title for a dispute, in those days of some fourteen years standing, about demarcation as to whether it was the props department or the electrics department who turned on the clock to start the children's programme *Crackerjack*.'

It was one such dispute which resulted in the cancellation, only part-finished, of what should have been Williams's swan song production, *Shada*; and the preceding story, *The Horns of Nimon*, was also badly hit, making for a somewhat unsatisfactory conclusion to his tenure as producer.

Such were the difficulties involved in making *Doctor Who* at this time that Williams had repeatedly requested the appointment of an associate producer to help ease his burden. Although this request had been turned down, Graeme MacDonald had instead given former producer Barry Letts a 'watching brief' over Williams's final season. When Williams left, to be succeeded as producer by the inexperienced John Nathan-Turner (formerly Williams's production unit manager), Letts was officially appointed executive producer for season eighteen. His role was however largely advisory, fulfilling a function usually performed by the head of department, and he has since confirmed that Nathan-Turner was fully responsible for the day-to-day production of the season. Letts therefore had only a limited influence on the style of the stories made at this time.

Nathan-Turner later recalled his aims in taking *Doctor Who* into the eighties:

'I think you really have to look at the expectations of an audience. The late seventies and the early eighties, and indeed the late eighties, have seen a level of sophistication in television and the movies which no-one could have foreseen. Children particularly now, possibly due to the advent of computer games and so on, have very high expectations of television programmes in our genre. My idea was simply not to attempt to compete with the likes of *Star Wars*, but to use the resources that were available to us to the best possible effect. In that way, we would appear to be moving with the times.'

The resources available for season eighteen were in fact greater than for season seventeen, as Nathan-Turner was able to win a modest increase in budget. This meant that he could improve the series' production values and give it a noticeably more polished, up-to-date look than in recent years. One aspect of this was his commissioning of a new title sequence and a more modern arrangement of the theme tune. He was also successful in arguing for an extra two episodes to be added to the season – making it the longest since the sixties – so that he could schedule seven stories at what he regarded to be the optimum length of four episodes each. The direct responsibility for the form and content of these stories fell however to the new script editor, Christopher H. Bidmead, who took over from Douglas Adams.

Interviewed by *Doctor Who Monthly*, Bidmead recalled his initial discussions with Nathan-Turner and Barry Letts:

'I had to confess to both John and Barry that I didn't actually want to do *Doctor Who*, as it had got very silly and I hated the show. They agreed with me – Barry wanted to go back to earlier principles and to find a way of familiarising children with the ways of science. You can understand how deeply that idea had been subverted.

'Two things were going wrong, as we saw it. One was the panto-mime element and the other was the element of magic which had come in. Magic is entirely contrary to science and to my mind the Doctor's view of the world is that he looks at a problem objectively and then tries to apply laws derived from experience to reach a scientific solution.

'So often in the past, it had been a case of the Doctor effectively waving a magic wand which amounted to teaching children that the scientific way of looking at things was nonsense. It was a sort of infusion of late sixties hippie ideas that derived from Third World cultures which had filtered its way down into *Doctor Who*. Now, John liked the idea that it was going to be as different from the previous era as possible. In other words I got the job on the premise that we would go back to basics.'

In line with this approach, and drawing on Bidmead's own writing experience in the scientific and technical fields, the stories of season eighteen had a much firmer scientific basis than those in the earlier part of Tom Baker's era, dealing with such ideas as tachyons, charged vacuum emboitments, E-Space, block transfer computations and, perhaps most significant of all, entropy. *Doctor Who* at this time was certainly more science-fiction than science-fantasy. This season also had an unusually high degree of conceptual and thematic coherence and a greater level of complexity in its plotting than had others in the recent past, suggesting that the series was being aimed at a more adult audience. Consistent with this, K-9 – originally intended to appeal to the younger child audience which Graham Williams felt had been lost as a result of the horrific nature of many of the Philip Hinchcliffe productions – was now written out.

Another feature of season eighteen was its generally sombre mood. The Doctor himself was considerably more subdued than before, and the stories – particularly towards the end of the season – had a dark, brooding atmosphere. Events such as the reappearance of the Master, the destruction of Nyssa's home planet Traken and the manifestation of the mysterious Watcher in *Logopolis* created an air of impending doom. This was in fact quite appropriate, given that they led up to the Doctor's 'death', his latest regeneration.

Although well received by the series' fans, season eighteen was less popular with the general viewing public: it was by some margin the lowest rated of the Tom Baker seasons, averaging only 5.8 million viewers per episode. A new era was, however, just around the corner which would see *Doctor Who* being moved to a twice-weekly time slot, enjoying a significant ratings revival, and, of course, featuring a new lead actor: Peter Davison.

6: From Script to Screen –
The Brain of Morbius

Introduction

To try to analyse comprehensively the development of a *Doctor Who*
adventure is not an easy matter. A television production is the result
of many months' work by a large number of people, and what is
ultimately seen on screen may have been affected and influenced in
greater or lesser degrees by all of them.

Unless one is afforded a fly's-eye view of every production
meeting and every aspect of the creative process, any attempt to try
to dissect the production is limited by the memories and personalities of those people to whom one speaks.

Bearing all this in mind, this chapter presents an in-depth look at
just one of the fourth Doctor's stories, revealing the process of
creating a *Doctor Who* story at this point in the series' history and
some of the behind-the-scenes discussions and thought which go
into a production, a factor common to every story.

The production chosen for this case study is *The Brain of Morbius*,
the penultimate story from the thirteenth season, first transmitted in
1976.

For our fly's-eye view of the story we are grateful to several people, in particular the director, Christopher Barry, and the designer, Barry Newbery, who recalled, scene by scene, the work which went into it.

The Scripts

Every *Doctor Who* adventure which appears on screen starts life as an idea, which may be in the mind of a writer, the producer or the script editor, or developing out of a discussion between two or more of these people.

Once the initial contact has been made, a story outline or synopsis will generally be commissioned from the author. Assuming that all is well when that is delivered, one or more of the actual scripts will be commissioned. Depending on the status of the writer, these stages may be compacted or expanded. In the case of *The Brain of Morbius*, the idea was given to an experienced author and so the synopsis stage was more a formality than a necessity.

The original idea for *The Brain of Morbius* came from *Doctor Who*'s producer, Philip Hinchcliffe.

Hinchcliffe had mentioned to his script editor, Robert Holmes, that there had not been an attempt at a serious robot story in *Doctor Who*, and he was keen to try a story which treated the human/robot relationship seriously. Holmes took this basic idea to writer Terrance Dicks, who had been script editor of *Doctor Who* during the Troughton and Pertwee eras as well as having written several scripts for the show, and discussed it with him.

Terrance Dicks takes up the story: 'We'd been talking about various myths, and one of them was the Frankenstein myth of a man making a monster. I came up with the idea of a galactic super-criminal who has a super robot assistant – a sort of devoted robot Jeeves. The criminal, Morbius, is fleeing from his enemies, and his spaceship crashes.

'Morbius is smashed up to the extent that the robot can only save the head. And having been saved like this, he demands a new body. The robot is well intentioned, but limited as robots are. Now for some reason, spaceships do crash on this planet. So the robot goes out, scoops up the remaining bits of alien life forms and whacks them together into a roughly functioning body, on to which he puts Morbius's head. But as Morbius has always been something of a handsome Greek God, he is far from pleased.

174

'That was the story – it is gruesome, macabre, and funny. But it is also logical: the robot would do that. Bob and I worked out the story, and I wrote a set of scripts which he seemed happy with.'

Some of the ideas used by Dicks were actually lifted from his script for the 1974 stage play *Doctor Who and the Daleks in Seven Keys to Doomsday*. These included the name of the planet Karn, together with images such as a single-clawed creature, a brain in a tank, a mind battle and a desolate citadel clinging to a windswept cliff. What happened next is, surprisingly, something which had happened only once before in *Doctor Who*'s history: the scripts had to be rewritten without the writer's consent or input and the writer objected to the rewrites to the extent that he asked for his name to be removed from the transmitted episodes. The previous time this had happened was on Mervyn Haisman's and Henry Lincoln's story for *The Dominators*, then under its working title of *The Beautiful People*. The disagreement over this story back in 1968 caused Haisman and Lincoln to forego any further work on *Doctor Who*, but in Dicks's case the disagreement was short-lived with – eventually – no bad feelings on either side.

Dicks: 'The mistake I made was in delivering my final scripts on the day I went away on holiday! During subsequent discussions, I was out of the country and could not be contacted. And Philip Hinchcliffe turned against the robot. I can sympathise with him more now that I'm a producer than I could then. He thought that the robot would be too expensive to realise. So Bob was instructed to remove it from the story.

'Now, the robot is the whole core of the story. Poor old Bob, in a state of some desperation he came up with a mad scientist instead. It was not the most original idea in the world, but it was the only one available. He invented Solon.'

What remained after Holmes had removed the robot was the basic idea of creating a body. He couldn't just replace the robot with Solon as they would not have had the same motivation. Holmes had to go through Dicks's script and rewrite every scene in which the robot appeared. This involved a total change of dialogue as well as shifts in characters and plot to keep the whole thing hanging together.

Terrance Dicks was less than pleased when he returned from holiday and eventually received the revised scripts. 'I rang up Bob and shouted at him down the telephone. He was apologetic, but asked what else he could have done. Eventually I said, "All right. You can do it, but I'm going to take my name off it." (This was the ultimate sanction!)

"Not because it's a bad show, but because it's now much more you than me."

'He asked: "Well, what name do you want to put on it?" I said: "I don't care. You can put it out under some bland pseudonym," and slammed the phone down.

'Weeks later, when I saw the *Radio Times*, I noticed it was "*The Brain of Morbius* by Robin Bland" – that's Robin Bland's only existence in life. By then I'd cooled down, and the joke disarmed me completely.'

Pre-production

While Dicks may not have had much to do with the scripts as they finally appeared, Holmes certainly did, and it seems that he even carried the mythical Robin Bland into the production meetings as director Christopher Barry remembers:

'The scripts were all there and available by the time I joined the team. And as for Robin Bland; Holmes said: "Oh, well, he's the scriptwriter." As a director, I seldom met the scriptwriters, particularly on a show like *Doctor Who*. On *The Dæmons* Barry Letts was the scriptwriter as well as the producer, again hiding under another name [Guy Leopold]. But the scripts had to be written and virtually finalised long before the director joined and so generally you didn't get to meet them.'

The director would normally be one of the first people to join the production team for a *Doctor Who* story, but often the producer would have previously sent out scripts to the various design departments for them to be able to allocate resources and to get started on the creative process. Usually the producer would have checked with the intended director to see if there were any specific people he or she wanted to work on the show, and then tried to arrange for them to be available. In the case of *The Brain of Morbius*, Hinchcliffe wanted an experienced director and designer to work together to bring the challenging script to life on a studio-bound production as there was no location work budgeted for.

Barry Newbery certainly recalls that, 'I was told! I had no choice in whether I wanted to do the show or not, and the gentleman's agreement of the producer, director and designer talking at an early time didn't really come about until later.'

Once the director was appointed, he would initially liaise with all the other departments as Christopher Barry explains: 'As a director joining, it's really a question of you working out your need to get in touch with all these people with their need to get in touch with you. By the time the director joins the programme, he's one hundred per cent committed. But all these other people are working on other programmes, finishing them off, and like as not, you ring them up and say you need to have a chat and they say they haven't had time to read the scripts yet but they'll look at them over the weekend and see you on Monday for a preliminary check. It really was a case of you having to fit them in when their schedules allowed. Therefore, although it would be sensible to talk to the designer first, it often turned out that this was not possible.'

With all television being made to a strict deadline, both Christopher Barry and Barry Newbery found their work cut out for them from the start.

CB: 'Working in the Series and Serials Department, we always used to complain about the Plays Department having so much time to put on a play; they seemed to have weeks to rehearse. However, in Series and Serials we never had enough time.'

BN: 'The usual time given at that point to design the settings for a thirty-minute recording was nine days. There would be extra allowed for any filming. This is the time in which all tasks have to be completed if settings are to be created and ready in studio for rehearsal and recording.

'This particular *Doctor Who* story was four episodes without any film. I therefore had just 36 days – four of which were spent in the studio – to complete my work. Thinking about all the things that had to be done before the first studio, that is in four weeks, I find it incredible now that I managed to do it. But of course that goes for everyone else as well.'

Christopher Barry certainly agrees with this view: 'If we'd had filming, things would have been even more difficult.' In fact, *The Brain of Morbius* was atypical in that it had no filming or OB work. Almost every other *Doctor Who* story up to this point had featured some material shot either on location or at the Ealing Film Studios (normally modelwork or sequences calling for fire or water or where the story required sets which were either larger than normal or with other specific requirements – for example in *The Creature from the Pit*, Ealing was used for all of the forest scenes and those involving the top of the pit into which people were thrown).

If there was to be some location work, then this would normally be completed prior to the studio recordings. Because of costs, the location filming tended to be within easy travelling distance of London, but occasionally would be further afield (for example to North Wales for *The Abominable Snowmen* and to Paris for *City of Death*) where the additional costs could be contained.

Even though *The Brain of Morbius* did not have location filming, there was still a great deal of work to be completed before the show was ready to be recorded.

CB: 'I had to put incredible pressure onto Barry because I needed to know all his design thoughts, sizes of sets and complete floor plans in time to do my preparation work: prepare a camera script; prepare for planning meetings, meaning that I had to have the production visual- ised in my mind: how I was going to shoot it; every effect; everything I wanted to discuss at the planning meetings. Ultimately I needed to produce a pro-forma camera script. I always went into rehearsal, unlike most younger directors, with a camera script that could work if I suddenly fell ill. The reason for this was that I had started my training in live television. If something happened to me then my production assistant could step in and put the show on. We used to go into rehearsal with a camera script and be utterly willing to adapt that to the exigencies of the rehearsal. If an actor didn't like something for any reason then you resolved the problem. You'd explain the effect you were after, why people were positioned as they were, and then either arrive at a compromise or change your script. In order to do that effectively, you had to have worked it all out beforehand.'

As part of the process of working out who would be doing what and by when a planning meeting per episode would be held between all the departments who would be contributing to the show.

These would include:

the designer (in charge of the overall look of the show, together with all the sets)

the director (who has to pull everything together to come up with a transmittable production)

the costume designer (responsible for every costume seen)

probably **make-up** (designs and executes all the make-ups on all the cast)

the visual effects designer (handling explosions, special props, models and other effects which must be achieved 'live' during the recording)

electronic effects designer (looks after Colour Separation Overlay (CSO) and other effects produced electronically rather than on the studio floor)

lighting (works out and arranges all the studio and location lighting requirements)

sound (handles the sound recording of all the scenes)

the technical manager (basically in charge of the studio)

the production assistant (secretary to the director, looking after the typing of scripts and continuity)

assistant floor manager (another of the director's assistants, looking after the ordering of special effects and hand props, the artistes and generally in charge of the rehearsals, who, before the rehearsals begin, also marks up the sets on the rehearsal room floor using a different colour for each set)

production manager (acts as a deputy to the director and looks after the studio floor during recording).

All these people would meet to listen to the director outline his plans for the show and to discuss how to achieve the various things that he wanted doing. Often ideas would be changed and expanded upon as each person was able to suggest other ways of getting the production to meet the director's standard. The producer would not be directly involved at this stage, unless it was the first episode of a new show, or there was a specific reason for the producer to be there.

Following the planning meeting, the next stage was the outside rehearsal which took place at the BBC's rehearsal rooms in Acton.

CB: 'The normal procedure was that about two days before you went into studio there would be a technical run-through at the rehearsal rooms. All the people who attended the planning meeting would come along, as well as the senior cameraman (responsible for the cameras and their positionings based on the director's plans), the whole camera crew if you could get them, the scenic supervisor (ensures the sets are available when required for studio) and the prop buyer (looks after everything which appears on the set which is not a part of the constructed set or a visual effect). This was to allow everyone to see how the programme was shaping up, and to ask any questions. There would be quite a crowd at the rehearsal rooms and they would all be wandering around with huge floor plans in their hands on which all the sets were overlaid. Another point is that you would usually have been rehearsing the show in scene order but at this rehearsal you may well have put everything into recording order for the first time. This could cause problems but generally it was very useful and a lot of work got done and time was ultimately saved in the studio.

'About the same time, although not necessarily on the same day, the producer and script editor, and possibly the writer [although in the case of *The Brain of Morbius* the writer was not available], would come to see a run-through of the episodes at the rehearsal rooms. This was in story order and would give the actors a chance to show the producer what they could do. The prime purpose from the producer's and script editor's point of view was to check that the performances and story points were being brought out, and discussing with the director as to how he or she was intending to shoot certain sequences. From the director's point of view, although some of the comments made could be niggly, this run-through was extremely useful as it gave the opportunity for someone (the producer) who had been at arm's length on the production to see if things were going right. Often the director became too close to the production to see the overall picture.'

In Studio

Eventually, the programme would go into the studio and would be recorded over a number of days and a number of recording blocks. *The Brain of Morbius* was recorded in two two-day blocks, on 6–7 October 1975 in TC1 and 20–21 October in TC3 respectively, with an additional one-and-a-half-minute scene for part four, between Solon, the monster and Morbius's voice, recorded on 24 October. Recording would be done in an order worked out by the director, based on which sets would be available for use in each studio. All the scenes which used one particular set would generally be recorded together, and then the crew would move on to the next set and record the scenes there, and so on. In this way, an actor could find him or herself performing his or her big death scene before he or she had recorded his or her entrance. There were two alternative ways of recording in studio. First was the rehearse/record method, where the director would rehearse each scene immediately before recording it. The other would be when all the rehearsals were carried out in studio during the day, and the evening was spent recording them. The method used was generally up to the individual director depending on the facilities available.

The actual recording of a story was always a very time-restricted process, with much being achieved by all the creative staff in getting the material required by the director actually recorded. Recording had to stop in the evening at ten o'clock sharp, and unless the director had sanction to go into overtime (an expense which had to be agreed), at ten o'clock the studio house lights would go on, even if the cast were in the middle of a scene, and the cameramen and other technical personnel would leave for the night. Unless all the sets were required in studio the following day, then the scene-shifters would come in and take down (strike) those sets which were not required, and erect those needed for the following day's work.

To indicate some of the considerations involved in making a *Doctor Who* story during the Tom Baker era, what follows is a scene-by-scene summary of *The Brain of Morbius*, taking in comments from Christopher Barry, Barry Newbery and the costume designer Rowland Warne, as appropriate.

Part One
An alien planet where an alien insect-like humanoid (John Scott-Martin) is crawling over a hexagonal rock formation as thunder and lightning crash and flash around. The creature is being watched by Condo (Colin Fay) who rises up from behind the rocks. Condo's left hand is missing, replaced with a metal hook. Raising a small machete knife in his good hand, he falls on the alien creature whose screech of surprise and pain is abruptly cut off.

CB: 'The insect alien was an old mutt costume from *The Mutants* back in 1972, which Jim Acheson had designed and I had directed.'

RW: 'We found the costume in stock, and the Visual Effects Department did quite a few repairs on it for me.'

Inside his citadel, Solon (Philip Madoc) is admiring a bust of

Morbius when Condo arrives with his prize – the head of the alien. Solon berates Condo as the head is not suitable; he needs a warm-blooded humanoid to complete his work.

CB: 'I'd not worked with Philip Madoc before but I'd seen him in a black and white series, a BBC Sunday afternoon Classic Serial, probably *The Three Musketeers* or something. I know he was playing a French d'Artagnan-type character. He had a slightly manic quality but didn't overact doing it. It's in his voice and his eyes, a certain intensity. He really is magnificent, I can't think of any other actor who could have played that part so well.'

BN: 'I hadn't really paid much attention to Philip Madoc until I worked on this. I'd seen him on films and things, and you're used to a certain competence on television, but with this, I became a fan of Madoc. I think he's terribly under-used as an actor.'

CB: 'Colin Fay was an opera singer; he just happened to write in for a job at about the right time. He said he was over six foot tall, and I wanted a big fellow to play Condo. He hadn't done any television so he was cheap. He was a huge man, and like so many big men was incredibly gentle. Yet he played this backward creature who could be both fearsome and vulnerable.'

Elsewhere on the planet, the TARDIS arrives, and the Doctor emerges, shouting angrily to the skies at the Time Lords who appear to have pulled him off course. Sarah (Elisabeth Sladen) decides to explore and sees a graveyard of spacecraft off in the distance, lit by the flashes of lightning.

BN: 'That shot was comprised of a number of elements. The background was a cyclorama skycloth and a cut-out of the mountains in the distance. In front of that was a four-foot stretch of plain dotted with model spacecraft from other productions which I obtained from Visual Effects. The plain was seen as middle distance, the nearer part being hidden by foreground rocks and plants on the set.'

The Doctor feigns complete disinterest and Sarah goes off to explore further. When she cries out upon discovering the beheaded alien, the Doctor comes running. Looking about them, they see a castle atop a mountain in the distance illuminated by a flash of lightning.

CB: 'It's a lovely shot, but it's not there long enough ... it's under three seconds ... it could have been twice that!'

BN: 'The castle was not a model nor was it painted on the cloth. It was done as a cut-out so that it could be silhouetted against a bright sky.'

CB: 'We could have lit it a bit better – we should have had a tiny spotlight on it or something, just to pick it out. It's such a fine structure and it helps justify the interior architecture that we're going to see.'

The Doctor and Sarah make their way up to the castle. It starts to rain torrentially, and standing watching their progress is Ohica (Gilly Brown), one of the red-robed Sisterhood of Karn.

CB: 'That's not real rain. We hired a six-foot film loop of rain and ran that superimposed on to the main picture.'

In his laboratory, Solon is experimenting on the mutt head when the generator blows and the lights go out. He calls for Condo to fetch lamps.
Maren (Cynthia Grenville), the leader of the Sisterhood, is informed of the Doctor's and Sarah's arrival on Karn. Maren fears that they may have arrived to take the elixir of life from the Sisterhood. She shows Ohica that the sacred flame which they tend is growing weaker by the day. Soon there will be no flame and no elixir. The Sisterhood will be no more.

BN: 'Maren's chair had Genoese velvet draped over it. It was actually a curtain pelmet and I wrapped it around the chair which had been hired in.'

CB: 'I don't remember any discussions about the colour scheme of the Sisterhood being all red: the girls are dressed in red and the decor is all red too. I don't think it was a coincidence, somebody must have said something.'

RW: 'The Sisterhood had hats which were made very cheaply and decorated with coloured latex. The skirt fabric was in two layers, and made ragged and sprayed with wood dyes to give it texture. They wore bodices which were fabric covered in latex, with plastic tea-spoons from Winnie the BBC tea lady, laid into it.'

BN: 'The inspiration for the Sisterhood's flame room came from China. I was working from Chinese wall and panel decoration and that was where the predominance of the colour red came from. The basic idea derived from the design in Buddhist temples.'

CB: 'The bit when they reveal the sacred flame received its share of criticism I gather, but it's due as always to the lack of man hours to get the perfect finish. I think the sacred flame needed to be low, as at this point you're trying to show that this fact is desperately dangerous for them.

'I cast Cynthia Grenville as Maren for her wonderful lined, craggy face and for her strong, but old, voice. She seems to be timeless and that was the quality I wanted to bring over. Gilly Brown I liked for her suppressed nervous energy, suggestive that she is realising the critical situation that she is in. The other members of the Sisterhood were cast as being good-looking women with dancing experience. Janie Kells was brought in by Geraldine Stephenson, who supervised the movement and dances of the Sisterhood, because she was a professional dancer. This comes down to cost again. Because dancers cost more to hire than extras or walk-ons we had one real dancer and the rest copied her.'

In the main hall of the citadel, Solon finds Condo looking for his missing arm. Solon tells him that he will get the arm back once his work is finished.

BN: 'I decided that the formal structure of Solon's citadel would be unlike traditional Gothic structures in that it would have supports on the inside instead of buttresses on the outside. Hence the radiating pattern of struts – the sloping columns which leaned towards the walls. I intended it to look as if each had a gigantic steel ball and socket joint at their base to allow for movement of the structure.

'It has been said that I based the designs on the work of Antoni

Gaudí but that's not so. I didn't use Gaudí at all – although I did look at his buildings in my research. The only place in which that influence did perhaps show through was in the shape of the window in Solon's laboratory.

'My starting point was to try to think of ways in which a civilisation parallel to that on Earth – one which had the same genetic make-up and lived on a planet nearly identical in its circumstances – would develop at the same rate but solve its problems differently. So the architecture was inside out.'

CB: 'I can remember talking to Barry about it and saying I didn't want Gothic in the terms of ecclesiastical architecture, I wanted Gothik with a k. I thought something like that would have a macabre quality, something out of a Grimm fairytale, or a drawing by Arthur Rackham; that kind of atmosphere.'

The Doctor and Sarah arrive at the citadel where Solon greets them enthusiastically, commenting on the Doctor's magnificent head. After Sarah has warmed herself at a blazing fire they sit at a table and Solon orders Condo to get the wine.

CB: 'This time, as they stood outside the door, we used "fully practical" rain – water falling from pierced "sparge-pipes" rigged up over the doorway. They result in a lot of unwanted rainwater noise, because it is uncontrollable, unlike rain noise off disc, and much mess on the floor, and as a result they are commonly resisted by all concerned.'

BN: 'Those chairs were originally made for the designer Norman James, for a television production of *Canterbury Tales* back in 1959.'

CB: 'Designers always give you a table bigger than you want because they want you to get back wide enough to see the whole set!

'The shot from behind the fire appears very self-conscious. But I wanted to get behind the fire to establish it, firstly because it goes out in a minute, and I also wanted to show warmth and hospitality. It wasn't just done to be clever.'

BN: 'Note that Chris wanted to give a feeling of warmth and hospitality because that was the only thing the set deliberately didn't have!'

Back at the Sisterhood's headquarters, the Sisters are chanting and gesturing as Maren concentrates on the Doctor's TARDIS, transporting it to their throne room.

CB: 'The Sisters' movements came in discussion. I remember talking to Geraldine about this and saying I wanted a sort of ritual. The words "Sacred flame, sacred fire" were in the script but it was my decision to have them delivered as a chant, overlapping the sounds and also overlapping the visuals, cross fading, making it more mysterious.

'The TARDIS's appearance was not achieved with CSO. The camera pulled back and then was fixed in position (locked off) and then we did the superimposition on the side of the shot.'

Having confirmed that the TARDIS is a Time Lord vessel, Maren decides to locate its occupant. The Sisterhood form a circle and begin to chant again.

CB: 'Directing scenes which involve a number of people can be difficult, as you have to work out the positioning. While they're moving there's no problem as you have choreographed them and it's just a question of where you cut your shots. But when you get to a static position with lots of people, it's then a question of how to make the most of it. You've paid for them to be there so you don't want the characters to be hidden either by each other or by the scenery and props. That takes time in rehearsal to get the artistes to hit their marks and to be seen. This planning is dead easy with one camera but when you are involved in a multi-camera shoot, as with all the *Doctor Who*s, you've then got to ensure that all the camera angles are correct.'

Back at the citadel, the Doctor has recognised the bust that Solon was working on as being Morbius. The Sisterhood pay a telekinetic 'visit', making the doors fly open, the fire snuff out and a chandelier fall from the ceiling.

CB: 'I'm rather ashamed of that shot of the chandelier. It wasn't actually dropped, it was run through a gloved hand with baling rope so it wouldn't break itself on the studio floor. Once it hit the ground they didn't even let go of the rope so the rest of the chain doesn't come down. In retrospect I should have cut the shot a few frames earlier.'

*The Doctor falls down unconscious; the wine has been drugged.
Sarah pretends to succumb as well (she has not been drinking). Solon
and Condo take the Doctor to Solon's laboratory where Solon examines him prior to the operation to remove his head.*

CB: 'As far as I recall, Solon's laboratory was to be a mixture of what
you would find in a fairly well-equipped medical laboratory and in a
museum. Old and new together. It's plainly a cod laboratory, it's just
got a few pipes and tubes bunged in. It's not a physician's lab, nor a
physicist's nor a chemist's but a bit of everything.'

BN: 'Yes. Basically as a scientist, I saw him as a bit of a wally.'

*When Solon and Condo leave to repair the generators, the Doctor
is transported to the Sisterhood's headquarters in the same way as the
TARDIS. Sarah enters the room just after he vanishes. She notices the
curtained-off bed and assumes that the Doctor is on it. She pulls open
the curtain to reveal a monstrous headless body (Alan Crisp) which
twitches and tries to sit as she stares in horror.*
(End of Part One)

CB: 'The intention here was to show the monster as late as possible. It's
rather like in the first Dalek story: just show a little bit of it, but hold
back from revealing the whole thing. All monsters are better if you only
suggest them; let the viewer's imagination build a picture of what it
looks like in its totality. Look at Ridley Scott's *Alien* for example.

'The design of the monster came from the script. I think it described
it as a pot-pourri, a hotchpotch. We came up with the idea that it would
be built from bits and pieces of other creatures but that became rather
difficult to realise. Rowland Warne thought we could have panels of
flesh without being specific as to their origin. What we specifically
didn't want to use were any metallic or non-organic panels, because the
only thing we wanted to look false and inorganic was the head that gets
fitted later.'

RW: 'We cut up lumps of foam and stuck them on to a cotton jumpsuit
which had been layered with textured latex and foam rubber. We then
covered the foam with terylene wadding dipped in latex. We built
muscles down the spine – which in fact were to conceal the zip – and

I used real surgical clips on the body, and also coffee beans to give the skin the right texture.'

Solon and Condo return to find the Doctor missing. Realising that the Sisterhood must have taken him, Solon determines to get him back.

The Doctor awakens in the Sisterhood's throne room to find himself tied up. Maren informs him that he will die at the next sun and that he should confess his guilt. The Doctor realises that Morbius is still alive, but Maren says this is impossible as she saw him die, and that the Doctor will soon join him.

A pyre is prepared and the Doctor is placed in its centre as the sun bursts through the window.

CB: 'That light flare is a deliberate light, that's the sun coming in and hitting the Hele Stone, like at Stonehenge. It comes through a hole in the set and hits the post where the Doctor is tied. It was a difficult effect to get right.'

The Sisters dance around the Doctor, leading up to his sacrifice. As they dance, their torches spring into life. The ceremony is inter-rupted by Solon who first offers Condo in exchange for the Doctor and then pleads for the Doctor's head to be spared. Maren dismisses him and the sacrifice continues, but this time the dancing Sisters have been joined by Sarah who followed Solon and Condo. She releases the Doctor's hands before the pyre is lit, and as the flames leap higher, the Doctor seems to vanish from within them.

CB: 'There's a procedure laid down at the BBC that you must inform the fire department through the studio manager if you will be using any form of flame in the studio. It goes for smoking too: if someone's going to light a cigarette it has to be down on paper and agreed. If a fireman hasn't been notified and he happens to be on the set watching somebody light up a cigarette, then he can step in and stop the rehearsal. Studios are strictly non-smoking, cast, crew, everybody.'

BN: 'Because we had fire in the studio, and I was fairly worried about it, I took into the studio a number of those big black carbon dioxide fire extinguisher cylinders. The scene boys were standing by with these, and the fireman came in and told us to take them away as only he was allowed to use extinguishers!

'The fire was designed and built by the visual effects designer John Horton on the scenery podium provided as part of the set. The lower platform was six feet in diameter and the upper central platform three feet in diameter giving enough room for the Doctor to stand tethered to a central post.

'The flames came from self-igniting burners within the brushwood to which gas was fed through hidden pipes. And of course everything had to be very heavily fireproofed.'

CB: 'Tom was in the middle and there was a gap at the back because Sarah had to come up to cut him free. There had to be a place where she could crawl up and get close to him.

'In the end we had to go for two takes on it because it got out of hand. The flames leapt so high that Tom had to get out early, but not without reason!'

RW: 'I wasn't told before we got into the studio that the Sisterhood were going to carry genuine burning torches. So, I had to fireproof their costumes on the day with a substance which could have caused skin irritation.'

As the Doctor and Sarah run from the Sisterhood, Maren fires her ring at Sarah, blinding her.

CB: 'I wasn't happy with the effect of the ring firing. I would have preferred it to have been more directional rather than an uncontrolled blast.'

Solon has returned to his citadel where Condo threatens him with death unless he gives Condo back his good arm and takes the hook away.

CB: 'Colin Fay had quite a lot of make-up on to play this part. He had things behind his lips to plump them out and I think there was probably a bit of collodian (latex) pulling his eyes down at the sides. He was given big bushy eyebrows and I think his nose was slightly disfigured too.'

The Doctor discovers that Sarah has been blinded and realises that the only person to whom he can go for help is Solon.

CB: 'Acting blind is a very difficult thing to do, it's terribly hard to be convincing. Some of it I think Lis (Sladen) does well, some isn't so good. The difficult thing is to not use your eyes. If you watch people who are really blind, like for example David Blunkett the MP, they're always blinking. But that's somebody who's congenitally blind. Sarah is just temporarily blind and I thought it would be similar to staring at the sun for too long. You get an after-image burnt on your retina and I think it makes you stare a bit.'

Solon has descended into a basement laboratory where he is speaking with an unseen person, eventually identified as Morbius (Michael Spice). Morbius is impatient to be free again but Solon is reluctant to proceed.

CB: 'I chose Michael Spice to play the voice of Morbius as I'd met him previously when he was working on radio. He had a good strong voice and radio actors are used to doing all their acting through their voice. Peter Hawkins, who provided the Daleks' voices for me, was again primarily a voice-over actor.'

Solon returns to the main hall when Condo announces the arrival of the Doctor and Sarah. Solon examines Sarah's eyes and tells the Doctor that there is no hope. Solon suggests that the Elixir of Life could help and the Doctor leaves to obtain it. Solon sends Condo on ahead of the Doctor with a message for Maren.
Meanwhile Sarah, left alone, hears Morbius calling from below. She heads in the direction of the voice. She stumbles down the stairs into the downstairs laboratory where she advances on the source of the voice – a flashing brain, bubbling in a tank.
(End of Part Two)

CB: 'The brain in the tank came about because I wanted this Grand Guignol feel. It was partly the settings, the visuals from Barry's design, but wherever I could extend the feeling through details, I did.

'That's one of the things I think is so astonishing about this programme, we always managed it on such a small budget.'

Solon enters behind Sarah and throws her out of the room. She listens while Solon outlines his plan to use the Doctor's head to complete his body for Morbius.

CB: 'This idea of a brain in a tank had featured in another *Doctor Who* before this [*The Keys of Marinus*]. I'm just talking of sources and unoriginality, because this reminds me of the Steve Martin film *The Man with Two Brains*.'

When Solon says that he has sent the Doctor into a trap, Sarah pulls the door shut and locks it, trapping Solon. Sarah hurriedly makes her way up the stairs and out the main door to warn the Doctor.

CB: 'That is total rubbish! She's never been there before, yet she knows how to shut and lock the door, and she's blind! That's my fault, that's bad direction. Often you get the script and find inconsistencies like this in rehearsal. You stop and discuss it for five minutes, but time is pressing, and eventually you just have to accept it and move on. Either that or you get in touch with the script editor and explain the problem – I've had to do that on occasion as well.

'If you were worried to the point that you couldn't continue rehearsals if it wasn't resolved, then you would telephone the script editor and explain the problem. The script editor would either settle it himself in discussion with the producer or, if he felt it was of prime importance and needed referring to the writer himself, he would get in touch with him and finally let you know. In the meantime you carried on rehearsing the rest of the scenes. This procedure was used throughout BBC Drama, particularly in Series and Serials.'

Five of the Sisterhood are ritually sipping the last of the elixir. Maren denies herself the liquid despite Ohica's concern about what will ultimately happen to her.

BN: 'This ritual is fairly typical; many religions have this kind of thing. But look at that! Maren tips that empty cup into the Sister's mouth . . . now she does it to the next one, and she doesn't get any either!'

CB: 'The idea was that there's a sticky liquid in there and there's so little of it that they're supposed to put their tongues in and just touch it.'

BN: 'When I first came into television I wondered why they never ever put any liquid into teacups or mugs or whatever. They were either empty or else just had a token amount inside.'

CB: 'Apparently it's because the artiste's hands shake when they pass the saucer! That said, I should have had more liquid in the chalice than I did, but it's the pressure again. Unless you have been there, you just don't appreciate the pressure! I think I'm known as a director who stops for most details but you simply cannot cover everything all the time.'

Solon's message arrives and Maren prepares for the Doctor's arrival.

Sarah stumbles through the rocks on her way to warn the Doctor.

CB: 'This is highly unlikely. I'd have loved to have been able to shoot this from very low, looking right up so it would look like she's really up high. Had we had some location budget, I would have shot it outdoors with the sky behind her to make it feel high, but you can't shoot upwards in the studio because there is no ceiling to the sets – all you would see would be the lights and gantry above.'

The Doctor arrives at the Sisterhood's domain and asks for Maren's help. Maren explains that the blindness is not permanent and that Solon knew this. The Doctor explains that he believes Morbius still lives, and discusses Morbius's crimes with Maren.

BN: 'I have been thinking about the colour of the flame room and Maren's chair. The fact that the chair was also in red was not planned. It was sheer serendipity that on one of my buying trips I found such a chair in red velvet and the cut velvet Italianate pelmet I used to dress it.'

CB: 'The scene of the Doctor and Maren walking round the flame-room whilst talking was difficult to shoot. This whole story is very static with long dialogue scenes. There are some nice opportunities in that subterranean vault at Solon's citadel: I use the set twice to give movement. Solon walks all the way round the columns and back, and later the Doctor does the same thing. On this scene, I decided to have Maren and the Doctor walk round, complicated by the fact that it's in procession, and additionally complicated by a cutting point in the middle of the scene. What I've done there is to jump frame. The Doctor is on the left as they start the walk, and we left the cut until as late as possible. If you look closely you can see that one of the Sisterhood masks the Doctor on the cutting point, and what has happened is that Maren and the Doctor have swapped positions. Luckily it works and you get away with it. I was trying to find movement because otherwise this whole scene would be completely static as it is all dialogue.'

The Doctor offers his help to the Sisterhood, but there must be no more drawing of ships down on to Karn to their doom.

Sarah is found by Condo who picks her up and takes her back to Solon.

The Doctor checks the sacred flame as he thinks he might be able to solve the problem of the lack of elixir. He realises that the flame heats the rocks which produces the elixir. The Doctor takes from his pocket a small firework which he lights and inserts into the crack from which the flame emerges. The flame dies but then there is a small explosion and the flame bursts out anew, higher and stronger than before.

CB: 'That was a firework, an ordinary sparkler, the sort you can get in a Christmas cracker, but Visual Effects produced the little bang at the end. Then there's the big flame, again produced from a gas jet.'

BN: 'The walls of the sacred flame's niche were made from fibreglass which had been fireproofed pretty heavily.'

Solon secures Sarah in his laboratory and returns to the cellar to inform Morbius of the impending operation. He lets slip that the Doctor is a Time Lord. Morbius is horrified and suggests that the Doctor has been sent by the Time Lords and is working with Maren to destroy him. Morbius insists that Solon gets him into the body as soon as possible using an artificial brain-case which Solon had earlier constructed and rejected. Solon reluctantly agrees.

BN: 'All of the bubbling vials and equipment were provided by John Horton. The bubbles in the bottle were done with air jets, with the air lines out of sight somewhere controlled by the effects team. John had two assistants, one of whom was John Brace, who later became a designer in his own right, and there was also someone else there who I think was more like a visual effects operator than an assistant.

'The walls on this set were textured with sawdust taken off the workshop floor and mixed in the paint. Another way to create texturing, which I didn't use on this occasion, was to spray glue over the wall and then throw sawdust and Polyfilla at it, painting it once it had dried.'

CB: 'I decided that the brain was going to flash just to indicate that it was talking; a little like the lights on the Daleks flashing for the same reason. I know a flashing brain is crazy, but I'm not a rational man!'

The Sisterhood carry an apparently dead Doctor up to the citadel. Meanwhile, Solon and Condo carry the tank containing the brain up to the laboratory. Condo sees the patchwork creature that Solon has built and recognises his own arm attached to it. Condo attacks Solon who shoots him in the stomach. They struggle and the brain is knocked off the table on to the floor. Solon carefully picks it up and places it into the artificial brain-case.

CB: 'Now this is the scene that I, in retrospect, regret. I don't regret it for the same reasons as Mary Whitehouse, but I can see what she was getting at. It was in the era of the bloody Sam Peckinpah films and I knew what Sam Peckinpah was getting away with and I didn't feel that this *Doctor Who* scene was violent at all. But seeing it again, I can see why it is totally wrong because it suddenly ceases to be science fiction and becomes naturalism. It was an error of judgment. I think somebody explained about Solon having a gun, and then someone else probably suggested seeing a red splat when Condo is hit by the bullet. I agreed without really thinking about it. If the producer had questioned this, then I probably would have argued with him for a moment and then given in. Watching it today, I don't like it any more and it does seem wrong.

'On the other hand, I have no regrets about when the brain falls to the floor. I loved the effect.'

Solon unties Sarah and forces her to operate a pump while he performs the operation to connect Morbius's brain to the body.
The Sisterhood arrive at the base of Solon's citadel and carry the Doctor up the steps. Thunder and lightning crash about.

CB: 'This is one of my favourite shots in the show. Flashes of lightning can be done various ways. It used to be with two poles and a carbon arc across them, but here it was an electronic flash.'

In his laboratory, Solon finishes connecting the brain-case to the body when he is called away to greet the Sisterhood who have arrived at his door. Remaining in the lab, Sarah finds that her eyesight is returning as the creature on the operating table (Stuart Fell) begins to stir. It lurches to its feet behind her and moves towards her.
(End of Part Three)

CB: 'That claw really is monstrous. Stuart Fell, who played the creature, was marvellous. I always used him for stunts and he's worked with me on numerous occasions.'

The monster chases after Sarah, knocking over a bunsen burner and setting fire to some liquid and its claw in the process. The creature comes across a mirror and smashes it in frustration on seeing its reflection.

CB: 'The floor was coated in preparation for the flammable liquid spilling on it, and just out behind the camera there are three firemen with extinguishers. After the sequence with the claw alight, we stopped to put out the fire before proceeding with the rest of the scene. You can see the claw still smouldering in the next shot.

'That was real glass in the mirror. Usually you don't have real glass for obvious safety reasons.'

BN: 'I would probably have had three more mirrors off set ready for any retakes.'

Solon enters and the monster crushes him unconscious before lurching out of the room. The Doctor and Sarah meet it and it knocks the Doctor down before chasing Sarah again. The wounded Condo comes to her aid and she falls down the stairs to the basement lab as Condo fights off the creature. It grabs Condo by the neck and throttles him before leaving the citadel.

BN: 'To shoot the scene where Sarah falls down the stairs, we had a crane set up to follow behind her as she fell. The landing at the top of the stairs was twelve feet high and because there was no handrail around it, the fireman stopped us shooting until one was fitted!'

CB: 'Lis's stunt double, Jenny Le Fre, was at the top of the stairs without handrails, ready to fall down, and the fireman was saying that it was not safe up there.'

BN: 'So many things have to be done even during camera rehearsals to make the sets ready for recording. This was one of those occasions when we didn't actually get it all done in time – the chippy was supposed to have put the handrail in but probably was not allowed time to do it because of other priorities. In the end we had to wait until the chippy had fixed the handrail before we could continue.'

CB: 'Condo's death here is like opera, and Colin understood the basis – you go on dying for half an hour after you have been mortally wounded. That's straight out of *Rigoletto*, an operatic death!'

Solon recovers and loads a dart gun with tranquilliser. He recruits the Doctor to help him stop Morbius. They find and immobilise the creature, but not before it has killed Kelia, one of the Sisterhood. The Doctor tells Solon that the brain must be detached and returned to the Time Lords. He picks the creature up and returns to the citadel.

CB: 'This scene is interesting. There is a very slow pace here, long pauses as we see first Solon and then the Doctor, building deliberately until the monster appears, and then a pause as it attacks the Doctor before Solon comes to the rescue. I love the sequence where Solon is only concerned about his creation, not whether the Doctor has been hurt.'

Back at the laboratory, the Doctor gives Solon five minutes to disconnect the brain and leaves to check on Sarah in the basement. Solon follows and locks them in. The Doctor explains Morbius's history to Sarah and discovers too late that they are locked in.

CB: 'The Doctor walks around the set again here – I should have had him go the other way round from Solon. This sort of sequence can pose problems for the sound people. They may well have asked me to arrange for Tom to pause behind the column so they can pick the sound up from a microphone on that side, and then pick up the sound on another microphone from the other side, otherwise there would be a dead patch on the soundtrack.

'The columns in Barry's set were a great bonus; you get all sorts of interesting angles and compositions to shoot through and around.'

BN: 'In this instance, it wasn't something I'd consciously thought of. I was simply trying to make the structure of the room echo the constructional principle of internal buttressing. However, Christopher looked at it visually, and two lines at an irregular angle are always going to make the picture look more interesting than two parallel ones.'

CB: 'In terms of past *Doctor Who*, on *The Romans* the set was full of columns, which gave me ample scope for using them to shoot round and behind. Often in the preliminary discussions about sets with designers, you ask for items to be placed in the foreground, some columns or things like that.'

Solon repairs the brain connections while the Sisterhood discuss what should be done. Ohica persuades Maren that they should go to the citadel to help the Doctor. Trapped in the basement, the Doctor creates a cyanide gas which he wafts up a duct to Solon's laboratory. The gas affects Solon just as he puts the finishing touches to the creature, but the creature itself survives as it has specially adapted lungs. It heads off to the basement as the Sisterhood climb the steps to the citadel.

BN: 'Those poor girls! They all climbed up the steps but there was nowhere for them to go when they reached the top!'

CB: 'I had to cut the shot before they started backing up on the stairs.'

Morbius arrives in the downstairs laboratory and faces the Doctor and Sarah. The Doctor baits the creature and challenges him to a mind-bending contest. They take their places and the battle commences. As they fight we see all the past incarnations of, first the Doctor, and then Morbius appear on a screen.

CB: 'We got into trouble with Equity because we used non-Equity people for the mind-bending sequence. The photos are of George Gallaccio (production unit manager), Robert Holmes (script editor), Graeme Harper (production assistant), Douglas Camfield (director), Philip Hinchcliffe (producer), Christopher Baker (production assistant), Robert Banks Stewart (writer) and me. The picture of Morbius was a photo of the clay bust upstairs which was then retouched. Basically we couldn't afford to hire actors to do it so we tried to get away with it. In the end we had to give a fee to Equity's benevolent fund.'

There is a small explosion inside Morbius's brain-case and he staggers out of the room. In the citadel's main hall he encounters the Sisterhood brandishing flaming torches. They herd him out on to the mountain where he falls and plummets to the ground far below.

CB: 'This fall was quite a remarkable thing for Stuart Fell. He actually fell about eight feet on to mattresses. You see him take one look round to see where he's got to go and then over he goes! He actually hits the camera which is why the picture bumps as he goes out of shot, but I didn't mind that. The shot of him falling away into the distance was just one take. We put him on a blue turntable, with a high camera looking down on him, zooming out, so he appears to get farther and farther away, then that image is inlaid on a photograph from the BBC's slide library of a high shot of a canyon somewhere in California.'

Back in the Sisterhood's flame-room, the Doctor is given the few remaining drops of Elixir to prevent him from dying. Maren, having denied herself the Elixir for too long, enters the flame and as she dies she appears young again.

The Doctor and Sarah enter the TARDIS, leaving Ohica with another two fireworks. The TARDIS vanishes in a flash of light and a cloud of smoke.

(End of Part Four)

CB: 'I read somewhere that we used a double for this because Maren couldn't get in the flames, but she didn't need to get in the flames, it's a superimposition. What they mean is that the younger girl replaced Maren as her younger self.

'The TARDIS's dematerialisation in a puff of smoke was my little joke. We were using pyrotechnics in the story, the script had the Doctor reciting what was written on the firework: light the blue touch paper and stand clear, and off goes the firework. It was a joke which may offend *Doctor Who* purists.'

Post-production

While the filming and recording of a *Doctor Who* adventure accounts for what is eventually seen on screen, production does not end there. Many months can elapse between a writer first submitting his script and the story being transmitted, and the actual recording takes only about one day per episode. The proportion of time spent in studio is very low indeed compared with all the work carried out both before and after the recording sessions and this was as true in the Tom Baker era as it is today.

The early part of this chapter covered the pre-production work on *The Brain of Morbius*; now Christopher Barry describes the post-production process: what actually happened once the programme had been recorded.

'While we were in studio recording the scenes, the production assistant, Pauline Silcock, had been keeping a log of every take and retake and had noted where the best takes were and where the faults were. All the recorded tapes were then put on to a Japanese machine called a Shibaden, which was an early form of helical scan video recording machine, which could be stopped and started at random and which displayed a time code on the picture. We would go into the Shibaden Room in Television Centre, play through the tapes and note down where the edits needed to come. In those days this was called Shibadening but nowadays it is called off-line editing. You basically construct your finished programme as a sort of rough cut. It wasn't as accurate as cutting on the exact frame, you tended to cut within a second of where you actually wanted.

'With that as your guide, together with all the notes made whilst doing it, you would go in to do the final edit knowing exactly what you were going to do, how all the scenes and takes fitted together and the exact frames for editing it all together. You might even change what you had previously edited on the Shibaden, because the Shibaden showed the pictures in black and white on a tiny screen and you might have missed small details which render a take unusable – say a microphone boom was slightly in shot. You could decide on balance that one of the other takes was better than the one chosen.

'Once you had constructed a good edit, time was also a factor. The show had to run for the required time, 25 minutes in *Doctor Who*'s case. Therefore you logged where you could make cuts and you had to offset one cut against another. You traded and juggled your cuts until the running time was as required. That was then the final edit.

'Another Shibaden copy was then run off and given to the composer, Dudley Simpson. I would have talked to him beforehand about where I wanted the music to fall and as I was preparing the preliminary Shibaden, I would have been noting down the time codes of the sequences where I wanted music, sometimes specific to the frame. Dudley would then come in to the BBC, because Shibadens were huge machines and were not very portable, and he would play it through and get his exact timings from a new time code which was put on the tape after editing. He would then go away and write the music.

'We would then have a recording session to record the music, at which the director would be present; we'd record each piece, and after each piece we'd play it back. I would make any comments and so we carried on until all the music was complete. There was always the pressure of time because of the musicians. You would try and record the score in a three-hour session. If you went a minute over time, the musicians would want twice the money.

'Once the music had been recorded, the tape would be given to the sound and grams operators, who would arrange a pre-sypher session. (Sypher stands for *SY*nchronous *P*ost dub with *H*elical scan and *E*ight-track *R*ecorder.) This involves putting the music and other sounds on to the final edited visuals. They would get Dick Mills's special sound, which had been worked on separately by Dick in the same way as Dudley. The pre-sypher session would probably take place in the morning in a small studio containing tape decks and a monitor, and they would look through and log everything that needed doing in the way of adding music, effects and special sounds. We would then go into the proper sypher suite for probably six or eight hours for one episode. It was a rock-and-roll procedure like film dubbing: you'd go backwards and forwards through the story until you had everything right. This process has steadily become more and more computerised over the years, and is now very sophisticated indeed.

'Out of all this work would come your final programme.'

Transmission

The Brain of Morbius was eventually transmitted on consecutive Saturdays from 3–24 January 1976 and was well received by the general public. It received an average viewing figure of 9.7 million viewers per episode (compared with the season average of 10.1), which was very respectable, and its position, compared with the other BBC and ITV programmes on at the time, was on average 28th in the weekly chart.

Complaints were levelled at the show by the National Viewers and Listeners Association (NVALA), particularly because of the scene in which Condo is shot by Solon with an old-fashioned pistol and blood is seen to fly from his stomach. During this period *Doctor Who* was always subject to close scrutiny by the NVALA, and there were several instances when their complaints were taken further.

The Brain of Morbius was popular enough to warrant a repeat on 4 December 1976, but rather than repeat the whole story, the BBC edited it down into a one-hour omnibus version, thus removing a quarter of its original running time. This edit was done without the participation of the director, and both he and the fans felt that it did not do the story justice, as it lost much of the depth and characterisation of the original.

When *The Brain of Morbius* was chosen as the second release from BBC Video in 1984, they decided to release the cut-down version. It was subsequently rereleased complete (save for a short piece of incidental music as Sarah enters Solon's laboratory at the end of part one) and unedited in 1990.

The only other area of contention surrounding this story has already been touched on above. The BBC were taken to task by Equity for their use of non-members during the mind-battle sequence. The BBC had to make a special payment to Equity as a result.

Today the story still comes across as an impressive piece of storytelling. Knowing the background to the scripts it is easy to sympathise with Robert Holmes and Terrance Dicks, as the obvious solution to Solon's problem of having a brain and no body was to put Morbius's brain in the Doctor's body. This does not apparently occur to Solon and instead there is a rather ungainly monster crashing about the place. The acting is of a uniformly high standard, with Philip Madoc and Cynthia Grenville deserving special plaudits, but with mentions also to Colin Fay and Michael Spice. Overall *The Brain of Morbius* is everything a good piece of drama should be: entertaining, enjoyable, effective, and emotive.

7: Effects Development

Doctor Who has always put a great deal of emphasis on its special effects. The creation of the numerous monsters, space craft, explosions and futuristic weaponry has taxed the ingenuity of the programme makers from the series' beginnings. During the latter part of the seventies, *Doctor Who* benefited not only from an experienced, talented and enthusiastic team of behind-the-scenes technicians, but also from the burgeoning of television technology. This allowed ever more complex effects to be achieved in ever shorter spaces of time. *Doctor Who* was indeed at the forefront of these developments, as it was seen by many within the BBC as an important proving ground for new techniques and ideas.

With colour television firmly established in Britain by the mid-seventies, the BBC's technical staff, having got used to the technology, began to experiment with the possibilities of the medium. It was felt that the area of electronic effects – producing something electronically from the images relayed by the TV studio cameras and recording it directly to tape rather than achieving it through a physical prop or model – was one which could benefit from a greater investment of time and money.

Responsibility for producing the early electronic effects at the start of the seventies was held by a small group within the BBC called inlay operators. There were only three inlay operators at any one time and the posts were held by cameramen seconded for a three-month period before returning to the main camera department. An inlay operator's job was to combine images from two or more video sources (camera or pre-recorded tape) to create a single, combined image. Traditionally the technique was used to provide the opening and closing titles for programmes as well as more elaborate effects when images of models or paintings were combined with live action.

Many cameramen seconded to the position found the job highly tedious and were only too happy to move on once their allotted time was up. However, particularly with the advent of colour, ever greater demands were made of and expectations placed on the inlay operators. One of the cameramen seconded at this point was A. J. 'Mitch' Mitchell, who spent much of his three-month stint in the department working on *Doctor Who*'s eighth season. Mitchell remembers this period as chaotic as there was no one person overseeing the production of the electronic and photographic effects, and this often led to productions over-running their allotted studio time.

Mitchell became so interested in the possibilities offered by electronic effects that he extended his stay in the department to six months. By the end of his time there, he and his fellow inlay operators had begun to plan out the effects and things were slowly becoming more efficient. Mitchell eventually returned to his job as a cameraman, but his interest in electronic effects did not end there. He submitted a report suggesting that the BBC create the role of special-effects cameraman. Four years later, the post was indeed created, although with the title Electronic Effects Operator. Into this embryonic department came Mitchell, together with Dave Jervis and Dave Chapman. The first *Doctor Who* work credited as being performed by the Electronic Effects Department – as opposed to inlay operators – was on *The Seeds of Doom*. Since then, electronic effects have become a staple part of *Doctor Who*'s creative arsenal.

During the sixties most effects seen on British television were achieved either through inlay or overlay or were of a mechanical nature, based on the types of trickery the film industry had been using for years. These included glass paintings, mattes, scaled-down and forced-perspective models and other forms of trick photography. Some of these effects relied on the nature of celluloid film, which meant that in order to use them for television, the sequences had to be shot on film rather than recorded on video. By the early seventies, in addition to these mechanical effects, experimentation in the field of video had given rise to a bag of tricks unique to that medium. Perhaps the best-known video effect is Colour Separation Overlay, or CSO, which was used extensively in *Doctor Who* during the Tom Baker era.

CSO, or Chroma-key as it is known by ITV companies, allows one picture to be inserted electronically into another. A colour (usually blue, but any colour can be used) is chosen as the key and this is used for all the areas of the first picture that are to be replaced with the other picture. If an actor stands on a full CSO set (usually just a large coloured curtain hung behind and extending over the floor, covering all areas of the image to be recorded) he can be electronically superimposed against a different background provided by any other video source.

The colour information from the camera recording the actor is matrixed to produce a black and white key signal to be fed to a video switch. The nominated CSO backdrop becomes black and all the other colours in the picture become white. This key signal is then used to combine the original CSO camera's picture with any other background, whether it be video of a model, a painting or photograph or an image being taken by another camera. Of course, the actors and any props which are to remain in the combined image cannot contain any of the selected key colour, which would make them disappear. This is one reason why blue is often chosen, as it does not feature in most human skin tones.

The earliest use of CSO on *Doctor Who* can be found in the 1970 story *Doctor Who and the Silurians*. Subsequently during the seventies it was used increasingly as a way of combining monsters and models in scenes with actors and of creating fantastic landscapes. In *Robot*, it was employed to achieve the effect of Kettlewell's creation growing to mammoth proportions, and this was just the first of many examples from the Tom Baker years. It became the standard way of realising effects involving monitor screens and spacecraft and was used particularly effectively in a number of stories such as *The Robots of Death*, where it provided a buzzing 'live' pattern on the active Laserson Probes, and made the Robots' eyes glow red when they were converted to the cause of Taren Capel. Generally speaking, however, the electronic effects operators were happiest when their work went unnoticed by the viewers, as this meant that they had achieved what they intended – the creation of a totally realistic effect.

In *The Deadly Assassin* some very clever combinations of camera work and video effects were used to populate Gallifrey, and particularly the Panopticon set. By mixing together a number of recordings of the same scene with the twelve extras standing in a different area of the set each time, the impression was given of a far greater number of Time Lords than the story's budget could actually stretch to. The apparent size of the set was also increased by a similar effect. The upper galleries were a repeat of the lower ones, recorded separately and then electronically grafted on in the appropriate place. More traditional uses of CSO in this story included the inlaying of images on to the Time Lords' wrist communicators.

Video effects were also used for the scene where the TARDIS is transducted to the museum. A pattern generator, originally created by the effects staff for the Saturday morning children's show *Multi-Coloured Swap Shop*, was used. A shot of the TARDIS was fed through the device which broke the image up into many little squares in primary colours. The police box was then removed and the signal from the pattern generator faded out, giving the impression that the TARDIS had been converted into some form of digital pattern which had then been transmitted elsewhere. To make the TARDIS appear in the museum, the process was simply reversed.

CSO was a cheap and relatively simple technique, but was also fairly inflexible. It could not be used for panning shots, for example, as anything which had been superimposed on to the picture would remain static. The only way to achieve good results was to have all the cameras locked in position.

This limitation was one of the main reasons why the most ambitious use of CSO in *Doctor Who*, in the season fifteen story *Underworld*, was largely unsuccessful. All the chase and fight scenes had to be recorded with locked-off cameras – there could be no pans, zooms, tilts or tracking shots – and this resulted in a very static production. Added to this, the sheer quantity of CSO used, and the tell-tale blue outline it often left around the actors (a result of interference between the signals from the two camera sources), resulted in highly unconvincing images. *Doctor Who* relies on the suspension of disbelief of the viewer and in this case that suspension was very difficult to achieve. CSO generally works best when used subtly and sparingly.

These restrictions were later partly overcome with the introduction of a technique which the BBC called Scenesync. This was first used on the *Doctor Who* story *Meglos*, for the CSO-created scenes set on Zolfa-

Thura. When General Grugger and his band of Gaztak mercenaries emerge from their ship and walk between the giant screens on the planet's surface, the camera follows their progress – even as they pass behind one of the struts supporting the screens.

The principle of Scenesync is quite simple. There are two sets. The first is a model on to which the actors are to be placed via CSO. The second is the studio set through which the actors will walk in real life. The studio set must match exactly the architecture of the model set, with one important exception – it must all be in the CSO key colour. The movement of the camera focused on the actors is electronically linked to that of the camera focused on the model, so that they will move in unison. Thus, for the scene in *Meglos*, when actor Bill Fraser, playing Grugger, walked under the blue mask of the screen's supporting strut on the live-action set, the camera on the model followed exactly the same movements, providing an overlay image of the model strut.

Ironically, at about the same time as solutions were being found to the problems posed by CSO, the whole process was about to become virtually obsolete.

New developments in computers and in digital technology had resulted in electronic equipment capable of creating effects similar to those achieved through CSO, but without the use of blue screens, and without any of the problems associated with that technique. An added advantage was that digital images could be manipulated in any way conceivable. They could be flipped, reversed, broken up, re-formed and generally tailored to whatever the director wanted. This new technique was called Quantel Image Processing and, once again, *Doctor Who* was one of its pioneers.

In *The Leisure Hive*, Quantel was used to create the effects of the Tachyon Recreation Generator in the scenes where characters are seen to break into several pieces. A far more subtle use of the technique, however, was witnessed in the scenes where Mena speaks to Brock via an apparently holographic image floating in the centre of a table. Not only did the camera pan past the image as the scene progressed, but people and objects could be seen through the image too. This was a good example of something which worked so well that the viewer could easily forget that it was an effect. Another of this story's claims to fame is that it was the first in which the camera moved during the TARDIS's materialisation – an effect likewise achieved using Quantel.

Tom Baker's regeneration scene was another which benefited from digital effects. As actor Adrian Gibbs, playing the Watcher, moved towards Baker's prone body, the image was distorted to make it appear as if the two figures were merging together. An overall glow was also added to the scene in which the image of Baker's face slowly dissolves into that of the Watcher's, then blends into a shot of Peter Davison wearing Watcher-like make-up, and finally mixes into Davison's true features.

The advent of video effects might have made life a lot easier in some respects, but for the Visual Effects Department, responsible for all the series' mechanical effects work, the Tom Baker era was very much business as usual. The basic tools of their trade remained essentially the same tried and trusted techniques that they had always used. Apart from advances in film cameras and the increasing miniaturisation of electric and electronic components, the visual effects in *Logopolis* were produced in pretty much the same way as those in *Robot* over six years earlier.

By the mid-seventies, the Visual Effects Department boasted a team of highly skilled individuals, who were responsible for the great variety of effects seen during the Tom Baker era. Many *Doctor Who* scripts called for spaceships to be seen in flight, including sequences of the TARDIS spinning through space. Visual Effects were also called upon to produce any special props which could not be obtained from stock or brought in from outside the BBC. These included laser guns of all types, communicators, and even futuristic coinage. If weapons had to be seen to cause damage, controlled explosions would be placed to provide the desired effect without endangering the actors involved. Most often these pyrotechnics would be combined with a ray or pulse of light created via electronic effects to give the ultimate appearance of a laser rifle which really did fire bursts of energy and which could, say, burn a hole in a door.

The contributions of some of the visual effects designers are particularly noteworthy. The stunning model work in *The Invisible Enemy* and *City of Death* was courtesy of Ian Scoones; the numerous effects showcased in *The Stones of Blood* – spacecraft, mobile stone aliens, a flashing wand and a futuristic beam machine which made the first major use of microchip technology in *Doctor Who* – were all provided by Mat Irvine, as was the filmed model sequence of the destruction of the Gateway in *Warriors' Gate*; while arguably *Doctor Who*'s best-known effect of all, the creation of a designer called Tony

Harding, was K-9, the Doctor's robot dog companion, originally built for the story *The Invisible Enemy*. One condition of K-9's continuation as an ongoing character was that Visual Effects had to be able to supply a prop which would function well enough to be used regularly and which would survive the rigours of television production.

When first introduced, K-9 suffered a few teething problems. Difficulties arose because the radio-control frequencies used to control the dog interfered with the operation of the television cameras and vice versa. This led to K-9 going haywire on set and crashing into things. Further problems surfaced when K-9 was taken on location. Camera cables and door sills had been difficult enough for the robot to get over in the studio, but the rougher terrain of grass or quarry floors proved completely insurmountable. In many cases, K-9 was pulled along on a piece of carefully concealed twine, or wooden boards along which the dog could travel were laid on the ground out of shot.

Following *The Invisible Enemy*, several modifications were made to the dog. The first was to change its drive from rear-wheel to front-wheel. The introduction of newer cameras in some of the studios also coincidentally resolved the problems over the radio-control frequencies. However, it is to the credit of the various visual effects designers, and the talents of a radio-control specialist, Nigel Brackley, who was brought in specifically to look after K-9, that it was able to appear in as many stories as it did.

The next major overhaul came during the eighteenth season. Following *The Leisure Hive*, which saw K-9 conveniently write himself out by going for a dip in the sea off Brighton beach, the dog was completely stripped down and rebuilt internally by designer Charlie Lumm, who specialised in mechanical effects work. The wheels were enlarged, with those at the front given independent drives to achieve greater power and control, and the radio control was updated from the AM frequency band to newer FM frequency models.

The first story in which the new, improved K-9 appeared was *State of Decay* – but despite all the time and money which had been invested in the prop, it was then written out in the following story, *Warriors' Gate*.

The introduction of K-9 coincided with the release of a film which was to have far-reaching repercussions for *Doctor Who* and for television science fiction in general. George Lucas's *Star Wars* redefined the audience's expectation of what could be achieved on the screen. With its spectacular visuals and breathtaking dog-fights in space, *Star Wars* made almost everything else pale by comparison. The problem was that, in terms of effects, this film set the standard for all that was to come after it, and to try to match that standard required far more money and resources than the BBC could muster. The effects staff at the BBC did their utmost with the materials and budgets at their disposal and achieved some remarkable results. The space scenes in *The Invisible Enemy*, *Underworld* and *The Invasion of Time*, and the creatures created for *Full Circle* and *Warrior's Gate*, were every bit as good as those presented by George Lucas's film. However, the advantage of powerful computer control was not available to the BBC at this point and *Doctor Who* had to wait until technology could provide a cheaper counterpart. This was not to happen until the early eighties.

It was not only the visual aspect of *Doctor Who* which changed as the series progressed. Technology also improved in other areas, most notably in that of radiophonic sound and music. *Doctor Who*'s signature tune had been realised by the BBC's Radiophonic Workshop back when the show began, but during the sixties and the early seventies only a very small proportion of the series' incidental music had been electronic.

Although Carey Blyton (*Revenge of the Cybermen*) and Geoffrey Burgon (*Terror of the Zygons*, *The Seeds of Doom*) also provided some scores, Dudley Simpson was the principal composer for the fourth Doctor's stories, and his music came to epitomise the feel of *Doctor Who* during this period. For the eighteenth season, however, incoming producer John Nathan-Turner wanted to get away from the traditional themes and to update the show for the eighties. One of his decisions was to allow the Radiophonic Workshop to handle the incidental music as well as the special sounds. Therefore the orchestral arrangements of Simpson gave way to the electronic compositions of Peter Howell, Paddy Kingsland and Roger Limb. Their music was generated on the latest synthesisers and complemented the more glossy and hi-tech look Nathan-Turner gave the series.

Another change for the eighteenth season, again intended to update the show's image, was the altering of the title sequence. Ironically, the new titles, showing the Doctor's face being formed from clusters of stars and then disappearing, used a technique which was actually far older and less innovative than that of the version which they replaced. Bernard Lodge's 'tunnel' graphics, first introduced for the eleventh season in 1973, had been completely unlike anything else the BBC had produced up to that time. Lodge had created the patterns using a version of the technique pioneered by Douglas Trumbull for the film *2001: A Space Odyssey*. This process, called slit-scan, was very time-consuming but gave excellent results. The titles for the eighteenth season, created by Sid Sutton, were simply animation. Numerous cels (sheets of plastic) were created, each showing an advancement of the image from the previous one, and when viewed together formed the completed title sequence.

The fourth Doctor's era came to an end just as computer technology was revolutionising the creation of both electronic and other effects on British television. The effects created for *Doctor Who* during the fourth Doctor's era were, however, the most innovative of their time. Without programmes like *Doctor Who*, which has always encouraged innovation, it is doubtful whether television as a whole would now be reaping the benefits from ever-more sophisticated technology.

8: On Location

There are a number of common misconceptions concerning the physical media on which television programmes are actually made. During the sixties *Doctor Who* was recorded on videotape in an electronic studio, with a small proportion of 16mm or 35mm film inserts generally copied on to the tape during the studio day. These inserts would consist of stock footage, model or live action work shot at Ealing Film Studios or material filmed on location. As the series moved into the seventies it started to benefit from more advanced technology. By the time Tom Baker took over as the Doctor, it was possible to record on to video on location (termed Outside Broadcast or OB) as well as in the electronic studio. Despite this, until the eighties it was still normal to take film cameras on location and then transfer the film to video to produce the final programme.

The decision to take a programme like *Doctor Who* on location can be made for a number of reasons. There are artistic considerations – to try to achieve, say, a forest or a cave system effectively in the studio would simply not work, and that to go to a real forest or cave would give far better results. There are also budgetary considerations – studio recording and location filming have different costs, and therefore it can occasionally work out cheaper to go on location than to stay in a studio. This however is the exception rather than the rule, as location costs usually far exceed studio costs.

Of course, on a science-fiction production such as *Doctor Who*, it is not always possible to find what is required within easy reach – there are not too many underwater Zygon spacecraft, for example, and snow-blown, bleak ice plateaux are not the most hospitable or accessible of places to travel to in real life. Occasionally, however, an alien planet or citadel can be created from the most mundane of settings, and the humble quarry has become one of the most versatile and popular locations for planets from Gallifrey to Skaro.

When *Doctor Who* began, hardly any location filming was done. The first season had just a few short sequences filmed for *The Reign of Terror*; but following that, the amount of location work steadily increased.

Part of the problem in the sixties was that the technical equipment required for filming was big, bulky and expensive to move about, and it was far easier to create what was wanted in the electronic studio through clever and imaginative sets and effects. As *Doctor Who* moved into colour at the start of the seventies, so location work increased, but the locations tended to be fairly close to the BBC's London base with only one or two longer journeys made, such as to Cornwall (*The Smugglers, Colony in Space*), Wales (*The Abominable Snowmen, The Green Death*) and Cheshire (*The Time Warrior*).

Season Twelve

The fourth Doctor's debut coincided with the first use of OB cameras for the series' location work. For *Robot*, director Christopher Barry had the use of an OB unit which could record everything straight to video. One of the major advantages to this was that the whole story could have a uniform look to it – a switch from film-originated material to material recorded directly to tape is always accompanied by a noticeable change in picture quality.

Aside from the more practical advantages of OB over film – it is cheaper and the results can be viewed immediately – another advantage to using all-video for this particular story was that the script called for the eponymous robot to grow to giant size and go on the rampage. Obviously this could not be achieved in reality and the use of video enabled the effect to be achieved through Colour Separation Overlay (CSO).

The need to use CSO on *Robot* was, according to departing producer

Barry Letts, the reason a bid was put in to use the OB facility in the first place. The sequences were recorded first on location without the robot present. The actors had to pretend that they were shooting at and running from a rampaging behemoth without it actually being there. Then that video footage, some of which had been taken from the giant robot's point of view, was married in studio with the robot, played by Michael Kilgarriff, performing in front of a blue screen. Some scenes also called for a further CSO pass to be done, when the giant robot was in the distance and some foreground action was required. Christopher Barry remembered the set-up when interviewed for the fanzine *The Frame* in 1987: 'One big advantage we had was that all the backgrounds had been shot on video rather than film which meant that the colour balances were good and the horizontal hold was absolutely rigid, so the background and foreground fitted together better than usual.'

The only problem with the CSO was that the metallic robot reflected the key colour from the CSO backcloth, and therefore parts of the creature were occasionally replaced by the background video image.

The location used for *Robot* was the BBC's engineering training centre at Wood Norton near Evesham. It was chosen, according to Christopher Barry, 'because there is an underground bunker there, which I thought we could use as the entrance to the underground area in the story. But suddenly somebody at the BBC clamped up and said, "Sssh, you can't have that seen, it's secret." This was despite the fact that if you drive down the road you can see it! But we couldn't show it on television. So we had to build a rather unconvincing entrance into the side of a hill, rather similar to what we had done with the tumulus in *The Dæmons*, as a way into the underground area.'

Coincidentally, *Robot*, the first story to be originated entirely on video, was shortly followed by *The Sontaran Experiment*, the first story to be recorded entirely on location, again using OB cameras. The move to complete location came about because *The Ark in Space* required a high design budget as the ambitious sets which comprised the Ark had to be created from scratch; to keep costs down, it was decided to make *The Ark in Space* and *The Sontaran Experiment* almost as one six-parter, with the former all in studio and the latter all on location. Another factor was that a six-part story would usually have just one week of location filming, and so *The Sontaran Experiment* had to be completed in that week. The use of OB cameras allowed the necessary versatility and speed in the recording process, and therefore script editor Robert Holmes was able to request *The Sontaran Experiment*'s writers, Bob Baker and Dave Martin, to keep the costs down and to set it all on location.

The location used, at their suggestion, was Dartmoor. In story terms it represented Piccadilly Circus in the far future, returned to grass and moorland, as they explained to *In-Vision* in 1988: 'We chose Dartmoor because the cast and crew could travel and stay and shoot it there – keeping the cost down to a minimum and therefore invention up. We'd been there many times.'

Although Dartmoor may have been an ideal location from the setting point of view, recording in October did not guarantee the best of weather, as actor Glyn Jones, who played Krans, recalled in *Tardis*: 'Filming on Dartmoor in October was enough to freeze the proverbial brass monkey. Looking at it on the small screen one doesn't realise that, for the most part, the sleet and rain were pelting down. And I wondered why I looked so large until I realised that under my spacesuit I had enough tracksuits and sweaters to fit out the entire crew of an oil rig.'

The only other major location shoot during the twelfth season was for *Revenge of the Cybermen*, as the location work for *Genesis of the Daleks* had been restricted to a few scenes shot in the Fullers Earth Quarry near Reigate.

Revenge of the Cybermen made use of Wookey Hole, the world-famous cave system in Somerset. Oddly, this is the only time *Doctor Who* has been to this particular location, as it offers a remarkable variety of backdrops and tunnels which it would be difficult to reproduce within a studio. A story like, for example, *Underworld*, which ended up through budgetary problems being recorded against CSO models of tunnels, would certainly have benefited greatly by use of such a real location. Michael E. Briant, the director of *Revenge of the Cybermen*, told *Doctor Who Magazine* an interesting story of one of his visits to check out the location site: 'I wanted to spend about a day in the caves where we were going to film, but the authorities weren't keen on me being down there while they were showing guided tours around. They asked if I would mind going down after closing time, about seven o'clock. I said "fine" but pointed out that I'd have to be there until midnight at least. They agreed saying that they'd lock both entrances as normal, giving me a key. With my wife I duly set off into the caverns and after about two hours of wandering about, taking notes, somebody came up. I thought at first he was a security guy but then I saw he was dressed in a wet suit. I asked him how he had got in and he said, "Oh, I always come in. Can I borrow your torch?" I refused, because I needed it to see with and the man said, "Right you are," before going off into the gloom. Shortly afterwards, we heard a little Irish tune whistling from the shadows and both my wife and I began to feel a bit scared. I decided to call it a night, even though I hadn't finished, but first I asked the caretaker who the man had been and why he had been let in. I was told "We didn't let anyone in. He was an Irishman who died down there pot-holing, three years ago." Of course I couldn't tell anyone, because my film unit would never have worked there.'

AT-A-GLANCE SEASON TWELVE LOCATIONS

Robot	BBC engineering training centre, Wood Norton, Nr Evesham, Hereford & Worcester
The Sontaran Experiment	Dartmoor, Devon
Genesis of the Daleks	Fullers Earth Works, Reigate, Surrey
Revenge of the Cybermen	Wookey Hole, 1 mile off A371 between Wells & Cheddar, Somerset

Season Thirteen

The opening story of the thirteenth season, *Terror of the Zygons*, was supposed to be set in Scotland around Loch Ness and the mythical village of Tulloch. It had originally been intended that some filming would take place in Scotland, but this was eventually ruled out on cost grounds and director Douglas Camfield had to find some Scottish-looking locations closer to home.

The place chosen was the small picturesque village of Charlton, near Chichester in Sussex, and further scenes were shot on a small stretch of beach and sand dunes south of Climping, between Bognor Regis and Littlehampton on Britain's south coast. The other major location was yet another quarry, this time with a large lake in it which doubled for the shores of Loch Ness for the scenes of the Zygon spaceship emerging from the water. Actor John Woodnutt, who played the dual roles of Broton, the leader of the Zygons, and the Duke of Forgill, recalled for the fanzine *Shada* working on the story: 'It was shot just outside Bognor and in fact one village was very cleverly adapted by the scenic designer, who just stuck bits on that looked Scottish, just on the outsides of buildings. We took all the Sussex signs down and stuck up odd things that made you think of Scotland. It's not a bad location for it in fact because outside you do have quite a lot of conifers which look awfully like those in Scotland. One conifer looks very like another and when you put a bit of bagpipe music in the background, everyone assumes you're actually in Scotland.'

Charlton was ideal for the village of Tulloch, and Camfield elected to retain the name of the village pub, 'The Fox Inn' (later renamed The Fox Goes Free, presumably when the pub became one of a chain whose trademark was names ending in '. . . Goes Free'), rather than change it as Christopher Barry had done in a similar situation in *The Dæmons*.

Another real pub was featured and retained its original name in *The Android Invasion*. This was the Fleur de Lys in the picturesque village of East Hagbourne in Oxfordshire. The village and its surrounding countryside became the Kraals' duplicate English village while the unopened Harwell Atomic Research Centre nearby became the base on Earth infiltrated by androids at the story's conclusion.

Both *Pyramids of Mars* and *The Seeds of Doom* called for a large country house to be used. For *Pyramids of Mars,* Stargroves, a house near Newbury owned by Mick Jagger, with the additional benefit of a stable block which doubled for Laurence Scarman's cottage, was chosen by the director Paddy Russell.

The Seeds of Doom used Athelhampton House, about six miles east of Dorchester in Dorset. Again, this is privately owned although it is open for public viewing. Yet another quarry made an appearance in this story too: this time a sand and silicon quarry near Dorking. Another well-known building, surprisingly one not often used as a location by the BBC, was also used: their very own Television Centre in London. The script called for short scenes of characters entering and leaving the headquarters of the World Ecology Bureau, and rather than travel miles, the crew simply used one of the side entrances to the BBC.

AT-A-GLANCE SEASON THIRTEEN LOCATIONS

Terror of the Zygons   Charlton, off A286, Nr Chichester, W Sussex; Climping Sands, between

	Bognor Regis and Littlehampton, W Sussex; Littlehampton Quarry, W Sussex
Pyramids of Mars	Stargroves, East End, Nr Newbury, Hants
The Android Invasion	Bagley Woods, Oxfordshire; Radley, Nr Abingdon, Oxfordshire; East Hagbourne, B4016 Oxfordshire; Harwell, Atomic Research Labs, Harwell, A417 Oxon
The Seeds of Doom	Dorking Quarry, Surrey; Athelhampton House, Athelhampton, A35 Dorset; Outside BBC TV Centre

Season Fourteen

The fourteenth season contained more filmed location work than *Doctor Who* had ever had before, with every story bar two (*The Face of Evil* and *The Robots of Death*) having a large proportion of its scenes shot out of doors. The season started with one of the most impressive UK locations used on *Doctor Who*. Portmeirion in North Wales is very well known both as a tourist attraction and as a television location, as the Patrick McGoohan adventure series *The Prisoner* was filmed there during the sixties. Sir Clough Williams-Ellis's baroque mock-Italian village, based on the Italian village of Portofino, opened in 1926. It is situated on a forest-covered headland which also overlooks the wide expanse of a river delta fed by the Trawsfynydd Lake and the river Glaslyn amongst others, east of Porthmadog. Sir Clough Williams-Ellis died in 1978, but Portmeirion remains open to the public, and as it is a holiday village, one can stay in this remarkable place.

Designer Barry Newbery recalled working in Portmeirion for *Doctor Who Magazine*: 'I was disappointed when I discovered we were to film in Portmeirion, mainly because I was looking forward to doing some filming in Italy! But I fell in love with the place when I got there, and it approached how I imagined parts of Italy would look. Since then, I've been to Italy and realise now that it doesn't look like that at all. We built the remains of a temple close to one of the lakes and Williams-Ellis actually asked if we could leave it there when we finished. We couldn't because it was stock scenery made of lightweight jabolite – if there had been a strong wind the whole thing would have just blown away.'

For *The Hand of Fear*, a power station was required, and the writers, Bob Baker and Dave Martin, as with their previous story, *The Sontaran Experiment*, had already decided on a place which could be used. In this case they had even gone there to scout it out before writing their scripts. The location chosen was the Oldbury Nuclear Power Station on the Severn Estuary in Avon.

The Deadly Assassin's location footage is well remembered, and so it should be, for over nineteen minutes of part three's running time was given over to location film. Robert Holmes, the writer and script editor, wanted to present 'a technically innovative script with subjective and surrealist sequences that I felt widened the vocabulary of the programme'. Therefore part three was written as a nightmare dream experience for the Doctor. Sequences at the close of part two featuring the Doctor falling off a real cliff-edge, a Samurai soldier, a man in surgical gowns holding a huge hypodermic needle, and soldiers on railway lines were all filmed at Betchworth Quarry and its adjoining goods yard. All the material in the jungle and river was filmed in the gardens of the Royal Alexandra and Albert School with a short sequence in the school's swimming pool for the scene when the Doctor's face is held under water. Finally, the filming of a bi-plane attack was achieved using miniatures at Redhill Aerodrome. It took five full days to film all the required material for this one episode, compared with the six days it took to shoot two complete episodes' worth of material for *The Sontaran Experiment*.

As previously mentioned, there was no location work for *The Face of Evil* or *The Robots of Death*. However, the programme again pushed itself to the limit to create a gloomy fog-bound late nineteenth-century London for the final story of the season, *The Talons of Weng-Chiang*. Wapping was lovingly taken back in time and dressed in Victorian style, as director David Maloney remembered in *Doctor Who Magazine*: 'We were due to film in and around a set of Victorian houses in Wapping. We had posted letters to all the owners of the houses, asking them if they'd all please remove their motor cars because we wanted to bring a carriage through the square. When we got there, there was a Porsche still parked in full view and it was really going to ruin everything we wanted to do, so Roger Murray-Leach, my designer, had the very clever idea of putting a tarpaulin over the car and covering it with hay.' Other scenes involved the Doctor and Litefoot heading down the Thames in a rowing boat. All the material outside Litefoot's house was filmed in Twickenham.

As well as using film for all this location footage, director David Maloney decided to use OB cameras to record on video the remaining location work, all of which took place indoors. The first port of call was the Northampton Repertory Theatre, which was to become the inside of Henry Gordon Jago's Palace Theatre. This was chosen by Maloney 'because it's still got the original Victorian flying area above the stage and we had a big chase there'. Philip Hinchcliffe was also impressed by the results achieved in his final credited story as producer: 'All that behind-the-scenes stuff looked really classy, because it was obviously not a studio.' From there the OB cameras moved to St Crispin's Hospital where Litefoot's mortuary was set up, as well as the Palace Theatre dressing room where Chang leaves a hypnotised cleaning girl who is found by Leela.

AT-A-GLANCE SEASON FOURTEEN LOCATIONS

The Masque of Mandragora	Portmeirion, A497, Nr Porthmadog, Gwynedd, N Wales
The Hand of Fear	Oldbury Nuclear Power Station, Avon; ARC Quarry, Thornbury, B4461 Avon; Cul-de-sac, Thornbury
The Deadly Assassin	Gardens of Royal Alexandra and Albert School, Nr Merstham, Reigate, Surrey; Redhill Aerodrome, Surrey; Betchworth Quarry, Nr Dorking, Surrey; Reading, Berks
The Talons of Weng-Chiang	The Royal Theatre, Northampton, Northants; St Crispin's Hospital, Northampton; Square and Streets, Wapping, South London; Houses, Twickenham, West London

Season Fifteen

Compared with that of the previous season, the fifteenth season's location work seems positively frugal. Only one story, *The Invasion of Time*, made major use of location filming, some of it pre-planned but some because a strike at the BBC forced it out of the studios.

Image of the Fendahl was, like *Pyramids of Mars* and *The Seeds of Doom* before it, set in and around a large country house, and the production team returned to Stargroves to do the location work required.

One particular problem was that *Image of the Fendahl* required a lot of night-filming. Whereas filming during daylight often requires only a minimum of additional lighting (spotlights for artistes' faces, white boards to reflect the sunlight and so on), when night-filming, the lighting of all the scenes becomes particularly crucial and the time required to set up each shot is increased accordingly. Elmer Cossey, the film cameraman, recalled for *In-Vision* an incident which occurred while the crew were setting up to film for *Image of the Fendahl* at two o'clock in the morning: 'The Doctor and Leela were running down through this wood, with mysterious lights in the background. We got it all ready to go, and one of the dressers came up and said, "Your generator's on fire." The gaffer said, "Oh don't be silly, a joke's a joke." And the dresser said, "No, honestly, your generator's on fire!" I said, "Hang on a moment," and we looked round. Over the top of this hill was a red glow and smoke. Suddenly there was a bang, and all the lights went out. There were frantic 'phone calls back to London to the lighting company – a little difficult at two o'clock in the morning. But by about 4 a.m. we had another generator down, and fortunately there was still plenty of darkness.'

The Sun Makers posed its own problems for director Pennant Roberts and his team in scouting out the locations. The scripts called for lengthy corridors along which protracted chases in electric buggies could be staged. Roberts knew that Cambden Deep tunnels, which connect various ducts, tunnels and passages between North and West London, would be suitable as they were far cheaper to rent than London Transport-owned tunnels. However, one of the buggies required for the chase scenes was too large to fit through the access doors so an alternative had to be found for that scene.

The script also called for scenes set on the roof of the Company

Megropolis on Pluto, and the production team had assumed that they could use for this any high building in London. However, the script also specified that no other buildings were to be visible, and in London this was impossible. Roberts had almost resigned himself to using CSO to get around the problem, when one of the production team came to the rescue, as Roberts explained: 'My production assistant brought a copy of *The Architectural Review* into the office, with illustrations of the new Imperial Tobacco factory in Bristol. Not a very high roof, but the size of two football pitches. Enormous.' When they scouted the location, they found an unexpected bonus which resolved the problem of getting the large buggy into the Cambden Deep tunnels: the cigarette factory had a three-hundred-foot-long underground tunnel which ran between two halves of the facility.

Underworld has been mentioned previously as having been sorely in need of a decent cave location, but overspending on other sets for the story meant that it had to resort to the less than satisfactory medium of CSO. This left just *The Invasion of Time* which ended up with more location work than had been originally planned.

The story was already well behind schedule, due to an original script by David Weir, concerning a race of cat-people living on Gallifrey, not working out and a substitute script having to be written by producer Graham Williams and script editor Anthony Read. Then one of a series of wildcat strikes hit *Doctor Who*, causing the loss of some studio time. The only solution was for much of the material to be recorded on location, using OB cameras, rather than in studio. Luckily a partially disused hospital in Redhill was found by the production assistant Colin Dudley which provided the mixture of required settings, from rooms and corridors for the TARDIS interiors to a boiler room for the control centre of Gallifrey's transduction barriers. There was even a convenient quarry nearby for the filming of the sequences on outer Gallifrey.

This location did not, however, satisfy the requirement for the TARDIS to have a swimming pool, and so the pool at the British Oxygen Headquarters was used, together with the changing rooms. Stuntman Stuart Fell, who was playing one of the Sontarans, remembered the locations in an interview for *Doctor Who Magazine* in 1989: 'We used two contrasting locations: a cold, damp, disused mental hospital in Reigate, and a luxury swimming pool in Hammersmith. I suggested leaping over the corner of the pool, jumping onto a chair, which collapsed, and then doing a roll.'

AT-A-GLANCE SEASON FIFTEEN LOCATIONS

Image of the Fendahl   Stargroves, East End, Nr Newbury, Hants

The Sun Makers   Imperial Tobacco Factory, Bristol, Avon; Cambden Deep Tunnels, Camden

The Invasion of Time   St Anne's Hospital, Redhill, A23 Surrey; Bletchingley, Surrey; Laporte Industries Sandpit, Redhill, Surrey; British Oxygen HQ, Hammersmith Broadway, London

Season Sixteen

The Pirate Planet was the first story of the sixteenth season to require locations and production assistant Michael Owen Morris found all that he needed, including a power station, fields and meadows and caves, in Gwent, South Wales. The power station was used as the engine room of the space-hopping planet Zanak, while the fields and meadows were used for scenes where the Mentiads advance on the Captain's bridge, the entrance to which was a disused railway tunnel. The Abercrave Caves at Dan-yr-Ogof became mineshafts deep inside Zanak, the large Cathedral Cavern being used for most scenes.

For the following story, *The Stones of Blood*, a rather unusual requirement had to be met. Rather than a location to act as some alien planet, or to give the impression that it was somewhere other than where it really was, the story called for a circle of standing stones which was to be used in the story as precisely that – a circle of standing stones.

The circle used was the Rollright Stones which can be found just off the main A34 road in Oxfordshire. The circle in real life is small and insignificant-looking, and, as visual effects designer Mat Irvine explained to the fanzine *Temporal Limiter* in 1983, it had to be augmented: 'The stone circle we used was a real one and as a stone circle fairly boring. We wanted to make it more interesting, so we added a trinithon [two standing stones with a third stone lying across them] in the middle and things. In a lull during shooting a party of schoolkids came round and we let them through. They were going round counting the stones and counting our dummy ones as well as the real ones. It wasn't until one of the teachers went up and touched one of them that they realised it was a polystyrene one.'

The Stones of Blood's director Darrol Blake also recalled working on the show for *Doctor Who Magazine*: 'I remember we had K-9 running on ploughed fields and various other places. Dear old Mat Irvine said it couldn't be done, so we put planks down and we shot the field through some grass and weeds which masked the planks the tin dog was on. We got him travelling quite fast to rescue Romana which took quite a bit of ingenuity.'

One of the most impressive castles in the south of England, Leeds Castle in Kent, was used as the main location for *The Androids of Tara*. Paul Lavers, who played Farrah, remembered the storming of the castle in an interview for the fanzine *Web Planet*: 'It was about two o'clock in the morning, a night shoot with lots of lights. Just before we were about to start, Michael Hayes [the director] came over with a bottle of whisky to give us all a shot because it was quite cold by then, and coming across the car park to the castle he [Simon Lack, who played Zadek] slipped and this bottle of whisky smashed all over the place. Then Michael came up to us and said, "Listen, I know you've got to storm the castle, but could you do it quietly because there are people inside sleeping."'

The final location used in the sixteenth season was for *The Power of Kroll* and this time the crew travelled up to Suffolk to a section of flat marshland around Iken. One of the requirements was for the horizon to be flat and low to facilitate the appearance of the giant Kroll creature in the sky above, and the marshes provided such an environment. Effects designer Tony Harding, interviewed for the fanzine *Fendahl*, remembered the location: 'We were working in a tidal marsh alongside the Moultings in Suffolk. You can imagine the problems this presented. At the beginning of a sequence we would be on dry land, and at the end up to our necks in water. Because of this there were great problems with continuity, and it just so happened that we chose the few days of the year when the whole area was affected by spring tides. The tide came up twenty or thirty feet further than it normally would have done.' Mary Tamm, who played Romana, also remembered the mud when interviewed for *Doctor Who Magazine*: 'Tom and I got totally stuck in the mud, we just couldn't move until we were rescued. We were miles from anywhere and it was so bleak. There was absolutely nothing to do between takes because if you wandered off you'd probably have been swallowed up!'

Terry Walsh, who played the green-skinned Swampie Mensch in

the story, also recalled the location work for *Doctor Who Magazine*: 'We were running around in the marshes, and had to wear green waterproof make-up which had been specially ordered from Germany. At the end of the first day's filming they told us that they had forgotten to order the special stuff needed to get the make-up off. They sent us down to an American airbase to shower, and we arrived looking like a group of jolly green giants. There were all these black American airmen playing baseball, shouting out, "Hey, now you know how we feel!" We got in the showers, and it still wouldn't come off. We were using brushes and still nothing happened. We ended up back at the hotel at two o'clock in the morning stark naked in the kitchen, with a group of very embarrassed make-up girls trying to get it off with Ajax. The hotel bedsheets remained green for weeks!'

AT-A-GLANCE SEASON SIXTEEN LOCATIONS

The Pirate Planet	Berkley Power Station, Gloucestershire; Treorchy, A4061 Mid-Glamorgan, Wales; Abercrave Caves, Dan-yr-Ogof, Brecon Beacons, Powys, Wales; Blaneavon, A4043 Gwent, Wales; Nantyglo, B4248 Gwent, Wales
The Stones of Blood	Rollright Stones, A34 Oxfordshire; Reed Cottage, Little Compton, Oxfordshire; Little Rollright Quarry, Oxfordshire
The Androids of Tara	Leeds Castle, Nr Maidstone, A20 Kent
The Power of Kroll	River Alde, Suffolk; boat landing at the Maltings, Snape, Suffolk; The Wetlands, River Alde, Suffolk; Iken Cliff, Suffolk.

Season Seventeen

The first time the fourth Doctor visited Skaro, he found himself in Reigate Quarry, and for his next visit in *Destiny of the Daleks*, yet another quarry was used, this time Winspit Quarry near Swanage. The fanzine *Oracle* covered the location filming of this story in 1979 through an interview with visual-effects designer Peter Logan. Logan had to build a model which matched the location for the scenes where the Movellan spacecraft landed and then burrowed into the earth. Between the choosing of the location and the taking of the background photograph for matching with the model work, a heavy rainstorm had created an artificial lake just alongside the place where the spaceship was supposed to land. The main problem with the model lake was not the difficulty caused by water's refusal to miniaturise well, but its tendency to seep through sand. Since the lake was always as still as a millpond and muddy because of the sand, there was no difficulty in making the model look like the real thing. In any event, in many of the model shots the lake was partially obscured by a strategically placed bank of sand.

The feature went on to reveal that when the TARDIS was buried under rubble at the start of the story, it wasn't the weight of the rocks that was the problem, as they were made of polystyrene, rather it was that a half-mile walk around the cliff was necessary to get to a position above the TARDIS in order to drop the rocks. Two or three journeys were necessary for each retake as there were so many polystyrene rocks to be dropped.

Destiny of the Daleks was also the first *Doctor Who* adventure to make use of a Steadicam. This is a lightweight single-operator video camera, finely counter-balanced, giving its operator precise control over the image being recorded. It also allows for smooth tracking shots to be taken over a bumpy terrain. Previously, camera tracks had to be laid on the ground, and even then the smoothness of the shot depended on the care of those pushing the camera-dolly along the tracks. With a Steadicam, all these problems are removed, and fast, smooth camerawork is the result.

The next story, *City of Death*, took *Doctor Who* overseas for the first time ever, and the only way that Graham Williams managed it was to keep the costs involved down to a minimum as he explained to *Doctor Who Magazine*: 'No sooner had we settled on Paris than I decided to cost out the script. I felt that we could actually go to Paris at no extra cost as long as we were clever about it. I gave John Nathan-Turner, then my production unit manager, the list of the cast that I intended taking over and the time we'd be there, and he returned me a costing that was to within about fifteen pounds of what we'd have spent going to Ealing Studios to shoot it.' The reason that this worked out was that at Ealing there would have been the costs of designing and building the sets, buying in the props and other hire charges, whereas by taking a minimum of crew – just a film cameraman, a sound man, the director and producer – over to Paris the costs were minimised on the location. This was why K-9 was written out of this story as taking him out to Paris would have involved more people in the form of operators and visual-effects technicians.

Lalla Ward, interviewed in the fanzine *Eye of Horus*, remembered filming in Paris: 'Tom was a bit annoyed that the French were more interested in me and my schoolgirl outfit than him and his long scarf. Of course, *Doctor Who* isn't shown over there so the French didn't take too much notice of us. I remember on one location we were to film at the top of the Eiffel Tower, but we couldn't as it was so misty and there was four inches of snow on the ground. We couldn't see a thing!'

As it turned out, this was the last location work seen on screen from the seventeenth season, as both *Nightmare on Eden* and *The Horns of Nimon* were studio-bound stories (although *The Horns of Nimon* was originally planned to include some location work), and the season's final story, *Shada* ,was not completed due to another strike and was therefore never transmitted.

The location filming for *Shada* was done in and around the streets of Cambridge and Grantchester. Footage was also shot of the Doctor punting on the River Cam. Assistant K-9 operator Stephen Cambden spoke to *Private Who* fanzine about this sequence: 'Tom Baker, very much a land-lubber at heart, managed to move the punt in every conceivable direction except the one indicated by the director! He spun it, pitched it and even jammed the pole into the river bed while Lalla Ward, a nervous passenger, prayed for deliverance. On the one occasion Tom did steer the punt in for a perfect landing, the cameras were not rolling!'

AT-A-GLANCE SEASON SEVENTEEN LOCATIONS

Destiny of the Daleks	Winspit Quarry, Swanage, Dorset; Binnegar Heath, Wareham, Dorset
City of Death	Art Gallery, boulevard St Germain; Cafe Notre Dame, rue St Jaques; rue de Vielle du Temple; Eiffel Tower; Louvre; boulevard St Germain; rue St Juilen le Pauvre; rue St Jaques; boulevard St Michel

Shada   Emmanuel College, St Andrews Street,
                                 Cambridge; The Backs, River Cam,
                                 Cambridge; Botolph Lane, Cambridge;
                                 Trinity Lane, Cambridge; Garret Hostel
                                 Bridge and Lane, Cambridge; Portugal
                                 Place and Portugal Street, Cambridge;
                                 King's Parade, Cambridge; St Edward's
                                 Passage, Cambridge; Blackmoor Head's
                                 Yard, Cambridge; High Street and
                                 Grantchester Meadows, Grantchester

Season Eighteen

Tom Baker's final season reverted to all-British locations. After
Brighton beach for *The Leisure Hive*, the next location was Black Park
near Iver. This was used for two of the stories, *Full Circle* and *State of
Decay*. *Full Circle* featured a lake in the park, as well as some of the
forest surrounding it, and director Peter Grimwade told *Doctor Who
Magazine* about the alterations the crew had to make to the location:
'The huge coloured lights taken on location, which made Alzarius
seem as though it had a strange sun, were not conceived at an early
stage. That came along when the cameraman suggested lighting the
foreground as we were setting up the forest scenes. It worked especially well after the designer, Janet Budden, had made the set look
even more exotic by dabbing powder paint all over the foliage and
trees. It kicked back off the lights and gave a very garish feel to the
setting. The only problem was the stuff got everywhere and we were
continually having to clear it up because the park was National Trust
property.'
    State of Decay concentrated on the forest areas in Black Park. Due
to the park's location close to Bray House, the former home of Hammer
films in the sixties and early seventies, it was also used in many of their
horror films. For *Doctor Who* to have filmed sections of its vampire
story there seems somehow fitting.
    Logopolis, the final story of the eighteenth season and Tom Baker's
final story as the Doctor, made use of a number of locations in central
London, and also a lay-by and fields alongside the A40 in Buckingham-
shire. The production team had originally wanted to use one of the few
remaining police telephone boxes still in existence, located along the

Barnet bypass, but the box was vandalised in between their taking of reference photos and arriving to film and so a prop was used instead. Shortly after this the genuine box was dismantled and removed altogether.

AT-A-GLANCE SEASON EIGHTEEN LOCATIONS

The Leisure Hive	Brighton beach, Brighton, West Sussex
Full Circle	Black Park, Nr Iver, B470 Buckinghamshire
State of Decay	Black Park, Nr Iver, B470 Buckinghamshire
Logopolis	Henley-on-Thames, Oxon; A40 lay-by, Barnet bypass, Nr Denham, Buckinghamshire; Cadogan Pier, River Thames, London; Albert Bridge, River Thames, London

The era of the fourth Doctor had seen technology advance by leaps and bounds, with better, lighter cameras, and ever more realistic effects being achieved through digital technology. Although the budget had not increased to the extent that regular overseas filming was possible, through careful use of resources the production teams were able to make the most of what was available in Britain.

The filming of *City of Death* in Paris proved that locations could be found further afield as long as the schedules were carefully prepared, and this paved the way for several more trips abroad in following years. Some lessons were also learnt: K-9 was never successfully used on location, despite having his wheels modified for the eighteenth season, and his appearances were therefore limited mainly to studio-bound stories.

Other stories looked as though they had used locations, but had in fact all been made in studios. *Planet of Evil*, *The Creature from the Pit* and *The Nightmare on Eden* all featured realistic forests which had been artificially created. Even *Horror of Fang Rock*'s effective light-house interior was a set, created by designer Paul Allen up at the BBC's Pebble Mill studios in Birmingham.

As technology progressed and *Doctor Who* used what was available, so the quality of the finished product improved. *Doctor Who* at the end of the seventies was very different from what had been produced a decade before, and the use of location work more than ever augmented the final product as the integration of film, OB recording and studio recording became virtually flawless.

9: Selling the Doctor

Television programmes, perhaps more than any other form of entertainment, have a habit of creeping up on you unawares, and before you know it, catchphrases, mannerisms and images have insinuated their way into popular culture.

Television is the biggest and most popular form of mass entertainment, and a whole industry exists to try to capture and market something memorable, something which will make one particular product or person stand out from all the others. As often as not, it is the unlikely that succeeds and some products hyped up through expensive campaigns fall at the first fence.

When discussing *Doctor Who*'s impact on popular culture it is impossible not to mention the Daleks, the first great marketing success of the programme. Like other cultural icons of the same period, such as Superman, Batman, Tony Hancock, the Beatles and International Rescue's Thunderbirds, the Daleks were not planned to be a rip-roaring money-spinning success. On the contrary, the metal monsters from Skaro had been created by an author who agreed to write the story in the first place only because he was strapped for cash at the time; and their look came about through a logical progression on the part of the designer thinking about how best to achieve the effect required on screen. The final element was the voices, and these came about as simply a desire to get away from a human voice. Three disparate elements – the character, the look, and the voice – but together they captured the imaginations of a generation of children.

If the Daleks were *Doctor Who*'s first commercial success, then its second was the fourth Doctor. This is not to say that the previous three Doctors had been unpopular, but none of them had captured the imagination of the viewing public to the extent that the fourth Doctor did.

While the first three Doctors all had strong characters, and enjoyed a variety of entertaining and memorable adventures, their impact – at least as far as commercial prospects were concerned – was lessened by the far greater impact made by the Daleks. In 1965 and 1966, the Daleks ruled both the television and the toyshops. The other elements which made up the television series in which they appeared were relegated to the background – the Doctor, the TARDIS and the many other creatures he met were not given a look in. The manufacturers saw that the Daleks were popular, and if they couldn't have Daleks then they weren't interested.

One consequence of this was that when the Dalek boom tailed off in late 1966, those responsible for exploiting them commercially moved into other areas. *Doctor Who* had been mined, had been successful for them, but now they wanted another major success, and the Daleks and the Doctor were perceived to be rather old hat. This resulted in a lack of media coverage, made worse by the fact that the second Doctor, Patrick Troughton, rarely gave interviews to the press and kept personal appearances to an absolute minimum. With little backup from the BBC, it was better from the manufacturers' point of view to let *Doctor Who* lie and to try elsewhere.

When Jon Pertwee took on the role of the Doctor, all the elements required to make a successful impact on the media appeared to be there. Pertwee had the look: a frilly shirt, velvet jacket and swirling cloak. He had the gimmicks: a sonic screwdriver and his old Edwardian roadster Bessie. It wasn't that the actor was shy and retiring. Far from it: Jon Pertwee was a true showman and threw his all into promoting the programme and the Doctor. While he was playing the Doctor there was interest in the show, but despite the fact that Pertwee stayed in the part for over four years, the popular memory of his era focuses not only on the Doctor himself but also on the other elements which made the early seventies so successful in *Doctor Who* terms: primarily the Master, the Brigadier and the concept of UNIT.

When Tom Baker arrived, it coincided with the phasing out of UNIT and the re-establishment of the Doctor as an enigmatic traveller in time and space. The focus of the programme returned to its central character. The new Doctor was more instantly recognisable than he had been before, and his memorable costume combined with Tom Baker's eccentric portrayal helped to fix the character in the viewers' minds. The third Doctor had perhaps become somewhat predictable and staid, played seriously and with conviction by Pertwee, but Baker's fourth Doctor was an unpredictable maverick. You could never quite be sure how he would react in a situation or what he would do next. At times the character seemed packed so full of suppressed energy that he would explode at the merest provocation, and at other times he could be so mellow that nothing could perturb him.

Each of the actors who has played the Doctor over the years has brought a little of himself to the part – Pertwee's love of gadgetry being a good example. With Tom Baker's Doctor, there was more than just a little of the actor on show. Baker's unpredictable nature, his tendency toward self-contemplation, his immediate and tangible charisma all overspilled into the fourth Doctor. Tom Baker was a larger-than-life character himself, and that quality reinforced the part he played, creating a truly memorable Doctor.

Media

Tom Baker was a godsend to the media, and his characterisation of the Doctor resulted in more coverage – including pastiches – than any other.

There had been the occasional pastiche based on *Doctor Who* before Tom Baker came along. For example, newspaper cartoons had appeared in the sixties, a sketch ending with an appearance of a Dalek had been featured on *Crackerjack* and even pop star Cliff Richard had included a spoof of the series in one of his BBC variety shows in the early seventies. However, the real proliferation of *Doctor Who* parodies on TV started with Tom Baker's immensely visual Doctor. There were a number of parodies during his tenure and many others followed, so that a *Doctor Who*-inspired sketch could be found on the TV shows of most popular comedians.

One of the earliest parodies was presented by *Crackerjack* towards the end of 1975, when Don MacLean played the fourth Doctor, Peter

Glaze portrayed the Brigadier and Jacqueline Clarke played Sarah. Set in the control room of the TARDIS, which had landed atop the Post Office Tower, it featured the Doctor knitting his scarf throughout.

Another celebrated example was the 1979 *Doctor Eyes* item featured in an edition of the LWT sketch show *End of Part One*, written by Andrew Marshall and David Renwick. In this, actor Fred Harris, wearing an exaggerated version of Tom Baker's costume – complete with huge, bulging 'eyeballs' fixed over his own eyes – romped across a tacky alien landscape, accompanied by a female companion, Gloria, played by Sue Holderness and based on Mary Tamm's Romana. Gloria was periodically prodded with a stick from out-of-shot to make her scream on cue and was preoccupied with when in the script she was supposed to scream or sprain her ankle. The Doctor was forced to regenerate (the new version played by Tony Aitken) because his previous incarnation was getting far too expensive. The regeneration was triggered when a Dalek-like monster shot him through his contract. The skit was set on the planet Chromakey 5 and also featured the Doctor's computerised companion, 'Plastic-thing-that's-meant-to-look-like-a-dog'.

Other pastiches around this time were seen on *Emu's Broadcasting Company* and Spike Milligan's *Q6* – a classic 'Pakistani Dalek' sketch. Another example from TV, although this could hardly be classed as a bona fide pastiche, are the series of tongue-in-cheek futuristic commercials that Tom Baker and Lalla Ward made in 1979 for Prime Computers in Australia, wearing their original *Doctor Who* costumes – something they would never have been allowed to do in Britain!

Another *Doctor Who* parody of the period appeared in *Mad* magazine, which regularly features accurately caricatured parodies of topical films and TV shows, well drawn but usually with somewhat leaden text. Interestingly enough, although *Mad* originates in America, this was at a time when *Doctor Who* was almost entirely unknown in the States, only a few of the Jon Pertwee stories having been shown on PBS stations. Presumably, then, the *Doctor Ooh* feature that appeared in Issue 161 was for the British edition only. The five-page *Doctor Ooh* spoof, written by Geoff Rowley and heavily based on *The Ark in Space*, had characters similar to the fourth Doctor, Sarah Jane and Harry arriving in a remote, deserted spaceship where, as the Doctor puts it, 'a handful of the chosen few are hovering in suspended animation'.

The strip illustrations by Steve Parkhouse are well observed, although they obviously owe much to stock photos of the regular cast and the sets used in *The Ark in Space*. What wit there is relies heavily on the well-known limitations of the show's budget – "Doctor! There's a plastic bag full of ping-pong balls crawling towards you!" – and the by then established characteristics of the regular cast (renamed Dr Ooh, Squarer and Hairy).

Squarer spends the entire strip snivelling and having her clothes removed, rather like Carol Cleveland in the *Scott of the Sahara* sketch from *Monty Python's Flying Circus*. Hairy is bold, forthright – and transformed, frame by frame, from naval surgeon into full-blown, Robert Newton-style buccaneer. The bulk of the humour, though, relies on Tom Baker's scarf, which proves to be his undoing, and incidental appearances by everything from Cybermen to Peter Cushing. Devices that work well are Squarer being eventually reduced to a sniffle emanating from a Kleenex box, appearances by the first three Doctors and a Dalek using its eyestick as a watering can!

Elsewhere in the mass-market press journalists were finding tags for the Doctor: 'the curly-haired Harpo Marx with his wide-eyed projection of the Doctor', reported one newspaper in 1975; 'intellectual, eyeball-rolling', said another in 1977.

All through his time as the Doctor, and even once he had left, the press headlined their features about Tom Baker with puns and word-play such as 'Who's next as 007?', 'Doc's dilemma', 'Who goes hairless', and 'Yo, ho Who!'. All these examples and more appeared after Tom had hung up the Doctor's hat and scarf.

Tom loved to promote the show, and he was interviewed many times on television, including on *Nationwide* and *Pebble Mill at One*, discussing his past and his approach to the Doctor. The coverage was certainly helped in the latter part of the seventies by the start of Saturday morning kids' TV shows, with Noel Edmonds's *The Multi-Coloured Swap Shop* featuring many *Doctor Who* celebrities over the years. Other notable appearances by Baker included his presenting of *Disney Time* in August 1975. He did this in character as the Doctor, not as Tom Baker, and at the end of the show left saying that he had to get up to Scotland in time to help the Brigadier – a direct link into *Terror of the Zygons*. There was a specially recorded trailer for the seventeenth season in which the Doctor is awakened from sleep to hear a warning from the continuity announcer that he will be up against the Daleks again. After the announcer tells him to forget the warning, the Doctor returns to the TARDIS, placing a 'do not disturb' sign on the door. Another appearance was on Johnny Morris's *Animal Magic* where the Doctor spoke about some of the animals and creatures he had met on his travels. This sequence was recorded on the forest set from *The Creature from the Pit* during the filming of that story at Ealing Film Studios, and the Doctor is wearing the portable stocks placed on him by Lady Adrasta.

At this time *Doctor Who* had an especially large adult following and the press interest reflected this, returning again and again to the subject of the Doctor's – and Tom Baker's – sex life. The press seemed to delight in asking Tom about his private life, and Tom delighted in revealing very little to them, with the result that what little they did know (his failed marriage to Anna Wheatcroft, his romance with Lalla Ward) was pounced upon eagerly.

Further proof of Tom's incredible popularity came when he started writing a regular column in a weekly newspaper, the *Reveille*. The column ran for nine months, from March to November 1975, and was written in a chatty, friendly style, with a very broad range of subject matter. There were stories about Tom's fight against chicken bones which kept getting thrown into his front garden; faces in tree trunks; sponsorship of mountain rescue dogs; people with their heads stuck in pots; a visit to the zoo; Peter Pan; not talking to strangers; a dream in which Tom tap-dances in a London museum; and many more:

'Last week, dressed as an Egyptian mummy, I bumped into 36 schoolchildren. We were filming in Berkshire. They seemed very intrigued, then nervous, then vastly amused. We finally had a picture taken. The next day, in regular costume, I went to the school. The children were delighted. They all looked so well and cheerful. During the conversation, which was mostly about monsters, the excitement grew and the children teased each other and boasted of fantasy exploits. One lad, all of five, said he liked nettle and snake soup. During a lull, I heard a six-year-old singing: "Whistle while you work, Hitler bought a shirt . . ." "What's Hitler?" I asked him. "Oh, he was a German, nasty too," he replied. I wondered what programme he watched on television. Could it have been *Colditz*?' (6 June 1975)

'Trees have faces. You didn't know that? But you can find them if you just bother to look. Tree faces aren't like human ones – stuck at the top end and at the front. Sometimes they are halfway up, hidden under a branch. Often they are clown-like with big noses or funny staring eyes. So next time you go for a stroll in the park or through the woods, keep your eyes open and you should spot a few faces looking at you.' (27 June 1975)

'At rehearsal last week, the director asked me if I could do a double loop with my yo-yo. I said: "Of course, watch this." When I swung my yo-yo back it came and hit me between the eyes. Everybody was very amused – except me.' (7 November 1975)

The latter is one of a number of occasional anecdotes which were included about the making of *Doctor Who*, although these were usually very bland – tending to concern encounters with children or animals while away filming on location.

Other notable press coverage was generated when the production office decided to get rid of K-9. A 'Save K-9' campaign was even waged through the pages of the *Sun*. This was the first of new producer John Nathan-Turner's many ploys for getting additional press coverage for the programme, and it worked a treat. The *Sun* had readers writing in with protest letters, and ran a follow-up article featuring some of those who wrote in. There was even one girl who had written to the Queen on the subject, but the article does not reveal the reply.

The Press followed the fourth Doctor right up until the end of his era, and when Tom finally hung up the scarf and left, John Nathan-Turner, always keen to maximise publicity, arranged for Tom to 'let slip' that the next Doctor Who might not be played by an actor, but an actress instead. This masterstroke ensured banner headlines the following day as Tom was hounded by the press and TV for interviews. After all, he had played the Doctor for close on seven years, the longest of all the Doctors to date.

Companions

Not only Tom Baker was subject to the tender attentions of the press; so also were the actors and actresses who portrayed his companions. During the tenure of the fourth Doctor the press developed an obsession with the Doctor's travelling companions. No one had ever made a secret of the fact that this mysterious man travelled with a succession of pretty young girls, but neither had anything much been made of it.

Throughout the sixties, the press had reported when companions joined and left, but this had always been done in a serious, largely factual style. Even in the early seventies, not much fuss was made when Liz Shaw joined and left, and even Katy Manning was treated with some respect until her decision to reveal all in a set of nude photographs for a men's magazine called *Girl Illustrated*, the cover of which featured Katy with a Dalek.

All this was to change because, as the standards of the British press fell lower and lower, so the tabloids' reporting became less and less news and more and more sensationalism. When the 'good girl next door' Sarah Jane Smith decided to leave the Doctor, and his new travelling companion was announced to be a half-naked savage girl played by the attractive Louise Jameson, the reporters pounced on the story eagerly.

'Dr. Who's tough new Lady' screamed one headline, accompanied by a press-call photograph of Leela on the set of *The Face of Evil*, brandishing a knife in a very aggressive pose. 'A cave girl with a killer touch' was the description given, and when Tom Baker was asked what he thought of his new assistant he apparently said: 'You know the Doctor. He doesn't have a sex life.' One can only surmise that the question actually asked was rather different from that which appeared in print. As usual it was *The Sun* which made the most of the situation, asking on its TV pages: 'Is sex about to rear its irrepressible head in that most adult of children's shows, Dr Who? I'm getting worried about the doctor's attitude to his new assistant, Leela (Louise Jameson). It does not fit the pattern.' The writer goes on to describe the first three Doctors' attitudes to their assistants and ends up: 'But the present Doctor, Tom Baker, is definitely on the dishy side. And while he was purely avuncular towards silly Sarah, he seems to see Leela in a different light. I'm sure I detect the stirrings of something sexual. Perhaps he is turned on by the wash-leather the strange little creature wears on her bum. But this being a children's show, there won't be any hanky panky, I presume. So will it be Dr and Mrs Who?'

After Leela, the next companion to join the Doctor was Romana, played in her first incarnation by Mary Tamm. The press were in their stride by now, and the standard headlines, 'Who's next' and 'Who's in Luck', all appeared. This time the papers had even somehow got hold of several modelling shots of Ms Tamm, one with her hair blowing in the breeze, another with her hair pinned up, wearing classy clothes, holding classic modelling poses. These photographs were featured alongside stories which claimed that glamour was boarding the TARDIS, and that as well as being glamorous, Romana was – gasp – intelligent. Obviously a concept which the papers found hard to take, as the introduction of Romana generated a lot of coverage.

Lalla Ward, taking over the role of Romana, was the next companion. This time the *Daily Express* saw fit to give a large centre-page spread to a round-up of all of the Doctor's 'sexy assistants', describing Lalla Ward as the latest 'teatime sex symbol' and encouraging readers to draw their own conclusion as to whether being Doctor Who's assistant was a passport to stardom or a one-way hop to obscurity. At the time this article appeared (1979), only Jean Marsh had gone on to greater things, and since then only Louise Jameson, possibly the most stereotyped of all the female assistants in the press, has continued to carve out a high-profile acting career for herself through numerous parts in popular series.

Of course Lalla Ward went on to hit the headlines again when she and Tom Baker announced plans to marry in 1980, apparently confirming to all the newspapers that their suspicions had been correct all along and that there was hanky-panky in the TARDIS. The marriage lasted only sixteen months, and the break-up was again the subject of much press coverage.

Pretty much the same level of coverage occurred when Sarah Sutton and Janet Fielding were announced as joining the TARDIS crew towards the end of Tom Baker's tenure. In Fielding's case, the situation was similar to that in Mary Tamm's, in that the papers got hold of some glamorous photographs and ran those, presumably in preference to the BBC-supplied photographs.

During the seven years in which Tom Baker played the Doctor, the role of the assistant had been redefined by the popular press from being a simple acting job to that of some sexy bimbette cavorting through time with the eligible and desirable Doctor. Certainly in the eyes of the press, *Doctor Who* was no longer an educational tea-time series for children and adults alike, but a light-hearted space series, aimed firmly at kids, but with a pretty girl on board to keep the dads interested.

Overseas

Doctor Who had been sold outside Great Britain ever since it started in

1963, but at the time Tom Baker took over, all that American viewers had seen were a range of thirteen Pertwee stories from *Doctor Who and the Silurians* to *The Time Monster*. These were not particularly well received despite a fair amount of trade advertising, and it wasn't until 1977 that the BBC decided to sell, through its overseas agent Time Life, a new package of Tom Baker stories to America. This amounted to 98 episodes featuring the fourth Doctor, perceived by the BBC as being marketable as his image was more eccentric than Pertwee's and the American market tended to favour eccentrics. In February 1978 there was a press call to announce that the package of episodes was available to America. Photos were taken showing the Doctor and a variety of alien monsters supposedly queuing for visas outside the American Embassy in London.

What the American audience were faced with when *Doctor Who* Tom Baker-style first hit their screens was a very doctored and Americanised version. For a start all the episodes had a voiceover introduction by veteran actor Howard da Silva, which often blotted out dialogue to tell the viewers what they already knew or to give away vital plot twists before they were revealed in the story.

Other changes included the addition of a montage of clips from the forthcoming serial at the start of each part one, and a 'next episode' trailer at the end of all bar the final episode of a story – again with narration from da Silva. As the running time had to be around half an hour (including three commercial breaks and all the montages listed above) the actual episodes themselves were also trimmed down to ensure that they didn't overrun.

To give an example of the style of introductory voiceover, the opening episode of *Robot* was accompanied by Mr da Silva saying: 'Doctor Who's face is transformed as his friends watch – instant plastic surgery. But the change goes more than skin deep. The Time Lord, on the brink of death, is inducing a complete physical metamorphosis . . . Recently returned from a distant planet where he was exposed to deadly radioactivity, Doctor Who enters into his fourth incarnation, thus saving his own life. But his new personality is still erratic and in transition, so the Brigadier has no alternative but to place him in the hands of a mere Earth doctor.'

Another example which shows how innaccurate the voiceovers could be is from *Revenge of the Cybermen*, where 'The Cyberscheme unfolds as a plot to take over the galaxy, but the metal men can succeed only if they regain control of their home planet in order to blow it up. Its core is of pure gold, alluring to human kind but fatal to Cybermen.'

Doctor Who was seen in this form via the Public Broadcast Stations (PBS) in America for many years, and despite the detrimental impact on the stories, it quickly became a cult favourite thanks in part to almost continuous transmission of the stories. Eventually Lionheart distributed *Doctor Who* in its correct form, and also as movie-length compilations. Fan groups sprang up all over the country and Tom Baker was hailed by science-fiction writer Harlan Ellison, in his introduction to a range of *Doctor Who* novels published by Pinnacle in 1979 and 1980, as: 'The one and only, the incomparable, the bemusing and bewildering Doctor Who, the humanistic defender of Good and Truth whose exploits put to shame those of Kimball Kinnison, Captain Future and pantywaist nerds like Han Solo and Luke Skywalker. My hero! Doctor Who!'

Tom Baker made his first appearance at a fan convention in America in 1979 when the cancellation of *Shada* meant that both he and Graham Williams were free to attend. The event did extraordinarily well and even after he had finished playing the Doctor on television, Baker was in great demand to attend further American conventions. Because of the importance of American sales to the BBC, producer John Nathan-Turner encouraged this attention and even arranged whole planeloads of guests to travel out to attend events. Regrettably fan conventions in this country often lost out to their American counterparts, as the British organisers simply did not have the cash to compete with the fees offered by the Americans. While *Doctor Who* fandom was at its peak, British fans could forget about any reunion of Doctors in this country – come every anniversary, all the actors were in America; and Troughton and Baker, as well as some of the companions, were not keen to attend British events anyway.

Meanwhile in Australia, where *Doctor Who* had been screened since 1965 by the Australian Broadcasting Commission (ABC), Tom Baker's debut season coincided with a decision by the ABC to drop the show as the ratings were poor. Australian fans didn't think much of this and lobbied the ABC to continue with the show. Luckily they were granted their wish, and they also got a fan organisation, the Australasian *Doctor Who* Fan Club, which was originally created as a means to get the programme back on the air.

Since then, *Doctor Who* has rarely been off the air down under.

There is a policy in both America and Australia to keep repeating the shows that they have, so even after Tom Baker had moved on to other things, his shows were still being regularly aired.

One of the problems with which *Doctor Who* has had to contend abroad is that of stricter rules governing what can be shown at particular times of the day. In Australia, adventures like *The Deadly Assassin* and *The Brain of Morbius* were rated as being for an adult audience and unsuitable for transmission in a 6 p.m. timeslot, while others were considerably edited to remove any material which the Australian general public might supposedly have found offensive – for example two sequences from *The Talons of Weng-Chiang*, one in part three when the giant rat appears to bite Leela and the other in part four when the rat appears to bite Chang, were cut.

Just across the water in New Zealand, viewers had been enjoying *Doctor Who* since 1964, and when Baker came along, the show was aired almost all year round, giving the New Zealanders repeat after repeat of the Doctor's exploits. Indeed, the only place where *Doctor Who* was not repeated wholesale was Britain, where the norm was for a repeat during the summer break of just one or two stories from the most recently transmitted season.

Fandom

The BBC had for many years acknowledged that *Doctor Who* had a fan following. The first fan club had been set up by one such fan in 1965 as the William (*Doctor Who*) Hartnell Fan Club. This survived, following a change of name and several changes of organisers, into the seventies, but then folded.

The BBC continued to cater to the wide-ranging interest in the series with numerous competitions, normally of the 'draw a monster' type, with first prize being a trip to the BBC to see *Doctor Who* being made. There seemed to be many of these competitions, with visits made to the sets of *The Masque of Mandragora*, *The Deadly Assassin*, *The Face of Evil* and *The Stones of Blood* amongst others. Fans too were invited along to watch the proceedings (usually from the studio gallery, but occasionally from the studio floor), and news of forthcoming stories became much easier to obtain when some fans started working for the BBC, and therefore had almost unrestricted access to the observation galleries and other areas of the production process, depending on where in the Corporation they were employed. Some even worked on *Doctor Who* itself. When John Nathan-Turner arrived as producer in 1980, he was concerned about this fan 'grape-vine' and started taking steps to withhold information, leading to his closing the public viewing galleries and stepping up studio security, as well as logging in and out all the copies of the scripts each day when particularly newsworthy stories were being recorded. The recordings of *Logopolis* were the first for which the galleries were closed in an attempt to exclude the fans and to keep secret the circumstances of the Doctor's regeneration.

1976 saw the establishment of probably the most effective, and certainly the best run, *Doctor Who* fan group in Britain. The *Doctor Who* Appreciation Society began life as a group at Westfield College in London, but the organisers soon realised that there was much wider interest and so opened their doors to the rest of the country.

From mid-1976 the Society provided a monthly newsletter (*Celestial Toyroom*) and a magazine (*TARDIS*, which had actually been instigated earlier and was adopted as the Society's publication from issue 7) as well as pooling the respective resources of a number of fans to provide various departments such as Reference, Art, Fiction and Photographic.

Those who ran the DWAS were given information about the stories in production, which was relayed to the members via the newsletter. They were also supported in other ways by the BBC, who generally helped with any photographs, interviews and information the group wanted. When producer Graham Williams commented that they ought to check into clearing the copyrights on what they were doing, they did so and were able to negotiate a deal with the BBC for the reproduction and sale of photos to the Society members. When K-9 was announced as joining the TARDIS crew, Williams was careful to maintain the secret, and would not allow photographs or information out. However ,the Society managed to obtain a photograph and arranged for some artwork to be used on the cover of *TARDIS* to coincide with the transmission of *The Invisible Enemy*. Williams never asked how the Society came by the information, but this incident helped to show the production team that the Society could be trusted to keep secrets. The DWAS was also asked to provide assistance with putting together the first-ever *Doctor Who* documentary in 1977, a *Lively Arts* production presented by

Melvyn Bragg and called *Whose Doctor Who*.

The DWAS also organised the world's first *Doctor Who* convention, held on 6 August 1977, and it has followed this up with numerous events – almost one a year – ever since.

The original organisers of DWAS decided, almost unanimously, to throw in the towel at the end of 1979, and it was left to a handful of other fans, who had joined the Society and helped out with the organisation in one way or another, to pick up the pieces and restructure the fan club for the eighties. The fact that the DWAS has survived and is still going strong is down to the hard work and dedication of all the people who have helped in its organisation and running over the years.

The DWAS was not the only British fan group operating, but it was by far the biggest. Perhaps next in line, certainly as far as enthusiasm went, were the Friends of Tom Baker, or FOTB for short.

The FOTB was formed in 1976 as a focus for fans of, naturally enough, Tom Baker, and they published a bi-monthly newsletter containing a multi-part interview with Tom, reports of the recording of *The Hand of Fear* and *The Face of Evil*, news, reviews, items on Tom's other roles, transcripts of TV interviews with Tom and really anything and everything to do with Tom, including some FOTB members' breathless accounts of fleeting meetings with their idol.

There was also some poetry, and even Tom's horoscope appeared, painstakingly worked out by one of the group's members. It is quite apparent looking back at the newsletter that the FOTB's predominantly female membership were besotted with Tom Baker as a person, and the mix of material tended to reflect this.

It was not only Tom Baker who attracted fans; Elisabeth Sladen, who played Sarah Jane Smith, also had her own fan club, the Elisabeth Sladen Friendship League (ESFL). This was launched in October 1976 and it too produced a newsletter very similar to the FOTB one but lacking the personal 'trembly-kneed' descriptions of encounters with the members' heroine. Perhaps one disappointing thing for the ESFL was that in their first issue, they had to announce that Sarah Jane Smith was leaving *Doctor Who*. This did not daunt them too much and the newsletter continued regardless. It certainly looks today as though the ESFL was run more out of sheer enthusiasm than anything else, and much of the news and comment contained within the newsletters is of a superficial, rather than informative, nature.

Merchandise

Doctor Who in the late seventies and beyond has been intrinsically linked with the fourth Doctor. Ask anyone in the street what the Doctor looked like, and you will most likely receive a description of the fourth Doctor: curly hair, big eyes, wide smile, long scarf. Over fifteen years later, the media in all their forms still portray the Doctor as someone with curly hair and a long scarf. That image typified what the Time Lord was, and has proved unshakeable even in the face of the three Doctors who have followed.

Even before the twelfth season started there was interest from the merchandisers. It takes anything from six months to several years to get a new product off the ground, and as there were several Tom Baker-related items on sale late in 1974, early 1975, one can only surmise that the interest had been there almost as soon as Jon Pertwee hung up his cloak.

These early items included a set of photographic jigsaws, the photographs taken during location recording for *Robot*, a series of painting by numbers kits featuring the fourth Doctor and also some pencil sharpeners.

As the seventies progressed, more and more merchandise was produced by eager manufacturers to tie into the programme, and into its star. The Daleks had been supplanted by the Doctor, and although there were a few Dalek items available, the vast majority used other aspects of the series as well.

In terms of merchandise, the products released in the years 1975 through to 1981 were a bit of a mixed bag. The *Doctor Who* novelisations published by Target books (originally an imprint of Universal-Tandem, then of Wyndham Publications, then of W. H. Allen and now of Virgin Publishing Ltd) still formed the backbone, and with the adventures of the fourth Doctor being novelised, starting with *Robot* in 1975, Tom Baker undertook a great many countrywide signing tours, promoting both the books and the programme. As well as shops, these tours took in schools and hospitals.

In addition to the novelisations, there were a great many other books published. World Distributors continued with their *Doctor Who* Annual, as well as producing *Terry Nation's Dalek Annual* for four years. In 1976 Target released an updated version of Terrance Dicks and Malcolm Hulke's *The Making of Doctor Who*, and explored other avenues with a series of titles under the *Doctor Who Discovers* . . . banner in 1977. They released a second *Doctor Who Monster Book* (1977), two *Junior Doctor Who* books (1980), a *Doctor Who Quiz Book* (1981) and *The Doctor Who Programme Guide* (1981). From other publishers came *Doctor Who and the Daleks Omnibus* (Artus 1976), two Dalek activity books (Children's Leisure Products 1978), *A Day With A TV Producer* (Wayland 1980) which looked at the making of *The Leisure Hive* in the company of producer John Nathan-Turner, and four titles for young children featuring K-9 (Sparrow 1980).

Aside from the books, many other items were produced. These included a Fourth Doctor Scarf (Today Promotions 1976), *Doctor Who* underpants (BHS 1981), Milk Chocolate Bars (Nestlé 1975), Candy Favourites (Goodies 1979), two poster magazines (Legend 1975 and Harpdown 1976), numerous free promotions – including two with Weetabix breakfast cereal (free stand-up cardboard figures), and one with Ty-phoo tea (a set of twelve cards to collect, plus a poster and hardbacked annual-type book). There were several records, including a new *Doctor Who* adventure, *The Pescatons* (1976), a *Doctor Who Sound Effects* album (1978), *Genesis of the Daleks* LP (1979) plus several versions of the theme music, one of which – *Doctor Who* by Mankind – even got into the pop charts in 1978. There was bubble bath (Water Margin 1976), colour-in posters (Salter 1978), Greeting Cards (DAP 1979), a fourth Doctor costume and mask (Berwicks 1976), transfers (Letraset 1976), jigsaws (Whitman 1977/78, World Distributors 1979), bagatelle (Playtime 1978), TARDIS Tin (1980), Viewmaster slides for the story *Full Circle* (GAF 1980), two board games – *Doctor Who* and *War of the Daleks* (both Strawberry Fayre 1975) – a talking Dalek (Palitoy 1975), a range of action-man like figures of the Doctor, Leela, the Giant Robot, a Cyberman, a Dalek, the TARDIS (all in 1976) and K-9 (in 1978).

This burgeoning of interest in both the programme and its star continued into the eighties, providing a media boost to the show, something it had been looking for since the trailing off of the Daleks' popularity in the sixties.

Ratings

Part of the success of any television programme depends on when it is transmitted, and the subsequent ratings it receives. It is always dangerous to draw conclusions from ratings alone, as there are many different reasons why they can fluctuate: the weather, the time of year, what was on the other channels at the same time, and even whether the other channels were on strike (as ITV was for a time in the late seventies).

In the case of the fourth Doctor's era, stories from the first three seasons consistently received over ten million viewers. As the years went by the ratings remained high, although dropping slightly, until the eighteenth season when a dramatic drop was seen.

The two top-rated stories were *City of Death* and *Destiny of the Daleks*, both of which were transmitted during the ITV strike between August and October 1979, and the stories at the bottom of the pile, *Meglos* and *The Leisure Hive*, were up against ITV's offering of a glitzy new space series from America, *Buck Rogers in the 25th Century*. Season eighteen was also relegated to a 5:20 time slot, earlier than the more successful stories of the thirteenth and fourteenth seasons which tended to start transmission at around 5:45 for the thirteenth season and after six o'clock for the fourteenth.

Relative to other TV programmes at the time, *Doctor Who*'s popularity leaped about a great deal. The highest placed episode was part two of *The Ark in Space* which came in fifth in the weekly chart, with parts two, three and four of *The Deadly Assassin* next at positions 11, 12 and 12 respectively. The lowest placed was part two of *Full Circle* which was almost at the bottom of the barrel at position 170, with part three of *State of Decay* at 145 and part two of *Meglos* at 139.

Again, it is very difficult to draw firm conclusions from ratings, but it certainly appears that during his seven-season run as the Doctor, Tom Baker saw *Doctor Who* fall from being one of the top-rated programmes, with over 12 million viewers, to one struggling near the bottom of the pile with around 5 million. This appears to have been the result of an amalgam of poor scheduling on the part of the BBC, an entertaining American import series showing on ITV at the same time, and perhaps even a public beginning to tire of Tom Baker as the Doctor.

TOP TEN RATED TOM BAKER STORIES
(Average viewing figures per episode in millions)

1	*City of Death*	14.5
2	*Destiny of the Daleks*	13.5
3	*The Robots of Death*	12.7
4	*The Deadly Assassin*	12.2
5	*The Android Invasion*	11.68
6	*The Face of Evil*	11.2
7	*The Ark in Space*	11.1
8	*The Hand of Fear*	10.95
9	*The Seeds of Doom*	10.9
10	*The Sontaran Experiment*	10.75

BOTTOM TEN RATED TOM BAKER STORIES
(Average viewing figures per episode in millions)

41	*Meglos*	4.65
40	*The Leisure Hive*	5.1
39	*State of Decay*	5.2
38	*Full Circle*	5.25
37	*The Keeper of Traken*	6.25
36	*Logopolis*	6.7
35	*Warriors' Gate*	7.5
34	*Terror of the Zygons*	7.5
33	*Image of the Fendahl*	7.8
32	*The Invisible Enemy*	7.9

Afterword

All good things must come to an end and in the autumn of 1980 the announcement was made that Tom Baker would shortly be leaving *Doctor Who*. Baker has often asserted in interviews that it was entirely his own decision to give up the role, but it might be more accurate to say that his departure was by mutual agreement with the series' producer, John Nathan-Turner. Having only recently been appointed to that job, Nathan-Turner was keen to make his mark. He felt that the time was ripe for the introduction of a new Doctor and he relished the idea of casting his own leading man. When Baker spoke of resigning he therefore saw no reason to disagree, still less to try to dissuade him from such a course, and at the end of *Doctor Who*'s eighteenth season the Time Lord underwent his latest regeneration.

During season eighteen the seeds were sown for the new era which was to follow. Romana and K-9 were both written out, while three new companions – Adric, Nyssa and Tegan – were introduced to take their place; and all the regulars, including the Doctor himself, were given heavily designed, uniform-like costumes which went unchanged from one story to the next. The scripts became more scientific in content, reflecting the interests of new script editor Christopher H. Bidmead, and there was a noticeable change in their basic approach to storytelling, with less emphasis being placed on detailed, straightforward plotting and more on concepts, style and imagery.

This shift of emphasis was also reflected in the production values, the whole season having a glossy, highly stylised look about it as John Nathan-Turner strove to make the most of the relatively small budget at his disposal. An attempt was also made to bring the series up to date: a new star-field title sequence and a more trendy theme tune arrangement were commissioned and Dudley Simpson's relatively conventional incidental music, for so long a staple ingredient of the programme, was dispensed with in favour of fully electronic scores provided by the BBC Radiophonic Workshop. All these developments would be carried forward to and expanded upon in the fifth Doctor's era.

Another pointer to the future was the way Nathan-Turner handled the press when releasing the news of Tom Baker's impending departure. He deliberately led journalists to believe that the next Doctor might be a woman, even though this was completely untrue, since he knew that such a controversial idea would be bound to generate maximum publicity for the announcement – as indeed it did. This was the first time that *Doctor Who* had been associated with a publicity stunt of this sort, but it would not be the last.

Although new lead actor Peter Davison was seen briefly in the regeneration sequence which ended the final episode of *Logopolis*, viewers had to wait another nine months for him to make his full debut appearance in *Castrovalva*. Until then, they could only guess at what the fifth Doctor would be like and what his era of the programme would hold in store. In the meantime, the only new *Doctor Who*-related programme to be seen on British TV was the 50-minute pilot episode, *A Girl's Best Friend*, for a proposed new spin-off series called *K-9 and Company*, featuring Elisabeth Sladen as former companion Sarah Jane Smith and John Leeson as the voice of the programme's real star, robot dog K-9. Transmitted on 28 December 1981, this enjoyable English village witchcraft tale was well received by viewers and gained very respectable ratings, but despite this the BBC chose not to pursue the idea of making a full series.

As well as this pilot show, John Nathan-Turner managed to persuade the BBC that the time was ripe not only for the traditional repeats of *Doctor Who* in the summer break, but also for a proper retrospective of the programme so far. Therefore British viewers were treated, first of all to repeats of *Full Circle* and *The Keeper of Traken* on BBC1 during August, and then to a season of repeats on BBC2, entitled *The*

Five Faces of Doctor Who and commencing on 2 November 1981 with *100,000 BC* and continuing with *The Krotons*, *Carnival of Monsters*, *The Three Doctors* and finally *Logopolis*. Following this recap of the Doctor's past, there was just one month to go before the debut proper of the fifth Doctor.

Just as the popularity of the first three Doctors had been largely eclipsed by that of Tom Baker, so Baker's successors in the role were to find that his was a very hard act to follow. So ideally suited had he been to the part of the Doctor that it seemed he could almost have been born to play it; and so great an impact had he made on the public consciousness during his uprecedented tenure that his performance was now widely regarded as the definitive one. Indeed, so inextricably had Baker become linked with the Doctor in viewers' and casting directors' minds that it would be many years after his departure from the series before he could again find regular work in TV; and, for many people, *Doctor Who* itself would never be quite the same again.

Production Credits

TITLE	AUTHOR	DIRECTOR	COSTUME	MAKE-UP	VISUAL EFFECTS	MUSIC	DESIGNER
			SEASON TWELVE				
		Producer - Barry Letts, Script Editor - Robert Holmes					
Robot	Terrance Dicks	Christopher Barry	James Acheson	Judy Clay	Clifford Cully	Dudley Simpson	Ian Rawnsley
			Producer - Philip Hinchcliffe				
The Ark in Space	Robert Holmes *John Lucarotti	Rodney Bennett	Barbara Kidd	Sylvia James	John Friedlander Tony Oxley	Dudley Simpson	Roger Murray-Leach
The Sontaran Experiment	Bob Baker Dave Martin	Rodney Bennett	Barbara Kidd	Sylvia James	John Friedlander Tony Oxley	Dudley Simpson	Roger Murray-Leach
Genesis of the Daleks	Terry Nation	David Maloney	Barbara Kidd	Sylvia James	Peter Day	Dudley Simpson	David Spode
Revenge of the Cybermen	Gerry Davis	Michael E. Briant	Prue Handley	Cecile Hay-Arthur	James Ward	Carey Blyton Peter Howell	Roger Murray-Leach
			SEASON THIRTEEN				
Terror of the Zygons	Robert Banks Stewart	Douglas Camfield	James Acheson	Sylvia James	John Horton John Friedlander	Geoffrey Burgon	Nigel Curzon
Planet of Evil	Louis Marks	David Maloney	Andrew Rose	Jenny Shircore	Dave Havard	Dudley Simpson	Roger Murray-Leach
Pyramids of Mars	Stephen Harris (*Lewis Griefer Robert Holmes)	Paddy Russell	Barbara Kidd	Jean Steward	Ian Scoones John Friedlander	Dudley Simpson	Christine Ruscoe
The Android Invasion	Terry Nation	Barry Letts	Barbara Lane	Sylvia Thornton	Len Hutton John Friedlander	Dudley Simpson	Philip Lindley
The Brain of Morbius	Robin Bland (*Terrance Dicks Robert Holmes)	Christopher Barry	L. Rowland Warne	Jean McMillan	John Horton	Dudley Simpson	Barry Newbery
The Seeds of Doom	Robert Banks Stewart	Douglas Camfield	Barbara Lane	Ann Briggs	Richard Conway	Geoffrey Burgon	Jeremy Bear (1-2) Roger Murray-Leach

TITLE	AUTHOR	DIRECTOR	COSTUME	MAKE-UP	VISUAL EFFECTS	MUSIC	DESIGNER
				SEASON FOURTEEN			
The Masque of Mandragora	Louis Marks	Rodney Bennett	James Acheson	Jan Harrison	Ian Scoones	Dudley Simpson	Barry Newbery
The Hand of Fear	Bob Baker Dave Martin	Lennie Mayne	Barbara Lane	Judy Neame	Colin Mapson	Dudley Simpson	Christine Ruscoe
The Deadly Assassin	Robert Holmes	David Maloney	James Acheson Joan Ellacott	Jean Williams	Len Hutton Peter Day	Dudley Simpson	Roger Murray-Leach
The Face of Evil	Chris Boucher	Pennant Roberts	John Bloomfield	Ann Ailes	Mat Irvine	Dudley Simpson	Austin Ruddy
The Robots of Death	Chris Boucher	Michael E. Briant Peter Grimwade	Elizabeth Waller	Ann Briggs	Richard Conway	Dudley Simpson	Kenneth Sharp
The Talons of Weng-Chiang	Robert Holmes *Robert Banks Stewart	David Maloney	John Bloomfield	Heather Stewart	Michealjohn Harris	Dudley Simpson	Roger Murray-Leach
				SEASON FIFTEEN Producer - Graham Williams			
Horror of Fang Rock	Terrance Dicks	Paddy Russell	Joyce Hawkins	Jackie Hodgson	Peter Pegrum	Dudley Simpson	Paul Allen
The Invisible Enemy	Bob Baker Dave Martin	Derrick Goodwin	Raymond Hughes	Maureen Winslade	Tony Harding Ian Scoones	Dudley Simpson	Barry Newbery
Image of the Fendahl	Chris Boucher	George Spenton-Foster	Amy Roberts	Pauline Cox	Colin Mapson	Dudley Simpson	Anna Ridley
The Sun Makers	Robert Holmes	Pennant Roberts	Christine Rawlins	Janice Gould	Peter Day Peter Logan	Dudley Simpson	Tony Snoaden
				Script Editor - Anthony Read			
Underworld	Bob Baker Dave Martin	Norman Stewart	Rupert Jarvis	Cecile Hay-Arthur	Richard Conway	Dudley Simpson	Dick Coles

TITLE	AUTHOR	DIRECTOR	COSTUME	MAKE-UP	VISUAL EFFECTS	MUSIC	DESIGNER
The Invasion of Time	David Agnew (Graham Williams Anthony Read)	Gerald Blake	Dee Kelly	Maureen Winslade	Colin Mapson Richard Conway	Dudley Simpson	Barbara Gosnold
SEASON SIXTEEN (Key to Time)							
The Ribos Operation	Robert Holmes	George Spenton-Foster	June Hudson	Christine Walmsley-Cotham	Dave Havard	Dudley Simpson	Ken Ledsham
The Pirate Planet	Douglas Adams	Pennant Roberts	L. Rowland Warne	Janice Gould	Colin Mapson	Dudley Simpson	Jon Pusey
The Stones of Blood	David Fisher	Darrol Blake	Rupert Jarvis	Ann Briggs	Mat Irvine	Dudley Simpson	John Stout
The Androids of Tara	David Fisher	Michael Hayes	Doreen James	Jill Hagger	Len Hutton	Dudley Simpson	Valerie Warrender
The Power of Kroll	Robert Holmes	Norman Stewart	Colin Lavers	Kezia Dewinne	Tony Harding	Dudley Simpson	Don Giles
The Armageddon Factor	Bob Baker Dave Martin	Michael Hayes	Michael Burdle	Ann Briggs	John Horton Steve Lucas Jim Francis	Dudley Simpson	Richard McManan-Smith
SEASON SEVENTEEN **Script Editor - Douglas Adams**							
Destiny of the Daleks	Terry Nation	Ken Grieve	June Hudson	Cecile Hay-Arthur	Peter Logan	Dudley Simpson	Ken Ledsham
City of Death	David Agnew (David Fisher Douglas Adams Graham Williams)	Michael Hayes	Doreen James	Jean Steward	Ian Scoones	Dudley Simpson	Richard McManan-Smith
The Creature From the Pit	David Fisher	Christopher Barry	June Hudson	Gillian Thomas	Mat Irvine	Dudley Simpson	Valerie Warrender
Nightmare of Eden	Bob Baker	Alan Bromly Graham Williams	Rupert Jarvis	Joan Stribling	Colin Mapson	Dudley Simpson	Roger Cann

TITLE	AUTHOR	DIRECTOR	COSTUME	MAKE-UP	VISUAL EFFECTS	MUSIC	DESIGNER
The Horns of Nimon	Anthony Read	Kenny McBain	June Hudson	Christine Walmsley-Cotham	Peter Pegrum	Dudley Simpson	Graeme Story

SEASON EIGHTEEN

Executive Producer - Barry Letts, Producer - John Nathan-Turner, Script Editor - Christopher H. Bidmead

TITLE	AUTHOR	DIRECTOR	COSTUME	MAKE-UP	VISUAL EFFECTS	MUSIC	DESIGNER
The Leisure Hive	David Fisher	Lovett Bickford	June Hudson	Dorka Nieradzik	Andrew Lazell	Peter Howell	Tom Yardley-Jones
Meglos	Andrew McCulloch John Flanagan	Terence Dudley	June Hudson	Cecile Hay-Arthur	Steven Drewett	Paddy Kingsland(1) Peter Howell(2-4)	Philip Lindley
Full Circle	Andrew Smith	Peter Grimwade	Amy Roberts	Frances Needham	John Brace	Paddy Kingsland	Janet Budden
State of Decay	Terrance Dicks	Peter Moffatt	Amy Roberts	Norma Hill	Tony Harding	Paddy Kingsland	Christine Ruscoe
Warriors' Gate	Steve Gallagher	Paul Joyce Graeme Harper	June Hudson	Pauline Cox	Mat Irvine	Peter Howell	Graeme Story
The Keeper of Traken	Johnny Byrne	John Black	Amy Roberts	Norma Hill	Peter Logan	Roger Limb	Tony Burrough
Logopolis	Christopher H. Bidmead	Peter Grimwade	June Hudson	Dorka Nieradzik	John Horton	Paddy Kingsland	Malcolm Thornton

NOTES:

* Indicates the original writer of a script where another person has performed an extensive rewrite.

Names in brackets indicate that these people actually did the work.

It must be presumed throughout that the respective script editors had input into all the scripts to a greater or lesser degree.